Federalism, Bureaucracy, and Party Politics
in Western Germany

Federalism, Bureaucracy, and Party Politics in Western Germany

The Role of the Bundesrat

By

EDWARD L. PINNEY

Chapel Hill

THE UNIVERSITY OF NORTH CAROLINA PRESS

PRINTED BY SEEMAN PRINTERY, DURHAM, N. C.

THIS BOOK WAS DIGITALLY PRINTED.

For
T. O. O.

Preface

The re-emergence of an independent and powerful, if truncated, German state since 1945 has been the occasion for a burgeoning literature dealing with German political development. This writing was varied in tone but has generally put emphasis on phases of German politics whose ultimate significance must depend upon the incorporation into Germany of values and practices that are characteristic of the rest of the West. Thus a heavy share of the published writings dealing with the Federal Republic has been concerned with political parties and party leadership, local government and local political participation, interest group activity and the growth of a parliamentary tradition. This book focuses on an agency that is traditional and indigenous to Germany and that is probably the only major political institution in the Federal Republic whose main characteristics are pre-republican. One other recent work on this subject, Karlheinz Neunreither, *Der Bundesrat Zwischen Politik und Verwaltung (1959)*, covers much of the same ground, mainly from the perspective of examining the Bundesrat's relationship to the other constitutional organs of the Federation and to the party system. Neunreither furthermore gives considerable attention to the possibilities of changing the composition and structure of the Bundesrat.

The ultimate concern of this study is democracy in Germany. More specifically, the concern is with the West German Bundesrat and with the problems of party politics, federalism, bureaucracy and conservatism as these are manifested in the "upper house" of the West German Parliament, and to the extent that they reflect native political values and tendencies. This book is intended for an audience to include not only specialists in German political affairs, but hopefully also social science analysts with a broader span of interests and persons generally interested in European political developments.

I wish to acknowledge my indebtedness to the Ford Foundation for a grant under its program for assisting American university presses in the publication of works in the humanities and the social sciences. I am also indebted to the Graduate Council on Research of the Louisiana State University for a grant during the summers of 1960 and 1961 that enabled me to complete the final draft of the manuscript.

Several persons read the manuscript in whole or in part and offered criticisms whose helpfulness it would be hard to exaggerate. Especially to Charles B. Robson and to Andrew M. Scott am I indebted for a thorough and critical reading of an earlier version. Rene de Visme Williamson and Robert S. Friedman read parts of the work and were the source of many constructive suggestions. The Director of the Bundesrat, Dr. Alfred Pfitzer, and his staff were hospitable and cooperative in making available to me necessary documents and printed matters. Dr. Eugen Rapp, formerly of the Bundesrat Secretariat staff, was a particularly valuable and willing counsel and helped me to avoid many technical errors. I wish finally to thank my wife, Winston, who was the most uncompromising and, in many ways, the most discerning critic of all. To all of them I am grateful. Errors of interpretation and fact can of course be attributed exclusively to me.

Baton Rouge, Louisiana
November, 1962

Contents

Tables

Federalism, Bureaucracy, and Party Politics
in Western Germany

CHAPTER I

Introduction

The cause of federalism in Germany has an ambiguous heritage. Experiences under the Bismarckian Empire and the Weimar Republic have left a residue of doubt as to the efficacy of a federal order for achieving in Germany a parliamentary republic founded on democratic principles. The determination of the Allied Military Governors to preside over the reconstruction of a federal republic after 1945 made the whole issue a sensitive point in the relations between Military Government and German political leadership. It was natural therefore, when the Basic Law (*Grundgesetz für die Bundesrepublik Deutschland*) was being formed at Bonn in 1948-1949 in accordance with Allied directives, that the most controversial provisions should be those dealing with the Bundesrat as the primary carrier of the federal principle and the main protector of the federal order.

The aim of this study is to examine the role of the Bundesrat in legislative policy-formulation in the German Federal Republic. The major effort falls on the description of three major persistent characteristics and on testing the apparent durability of each. These concern, first, the peculiar function of the Bundesrat as the protector of peculiar Land interests as these interests are understood by the Land Cabinets; second, the internal effects of active participation in Bundesrat deliberations by civil servants from the Land governments; and third, the applicability to the present Bundesrat of the traditional axiom that second chambers as "upper houses" represent conservative interests that do not find adequate expression in the more democratic lower houses.

The method chosen for verifying each apparent characteristic is the advancement and testing of three major hypotheses by means of data derived from the examination of several legislative case-histories. In every case measures are selected which had a distinct bearing upon the stated interests of a particular Land or Land interests generally, measures which should logically excite professional administrators' interests in administrative subtleties, or measures which raised issues on which articulate social groupings in Germany had taken a rather clear stand. Since the emphasis of the overall study falls on the Bundesrat's role in respect to these three primordial characteristics, each corresponding hypothesis is given separate treatment in some detail and either verified or rejected. For performance of the testing function Bundesrat action in the following policy questions has been more or less exhaustively accounted for: rearmament legislation, specifically the *Freiwilligengesetz* and to a lesser extent the *Soldatengesetz* and the *Personalgutachterausschussgesetz;* refugee legislation, specifically a series of *Umsiedlungsgesetze* providing for the re-settlement of German refugees from three refugee-crowded Länder to the other Länder of the Federation; and the Codetermination Laws, especially the *Mitbestimmungsgesetz*, the *Betriebsverfassungsgesetz*, and to a lesser extent subsequent changes in the original *Mitbestimmungsgesetz* in its application to holding and joint-stock companies.

Within any of these broad fields of legislation each specific measure raised slightly different issues reflecting

variations of the same problem. By considering more than
one measure in each field a more typical set of actions by
the Bundesrat was observed in each instance. In this way
the possibility was reduced of prejudicing the Bundesrat's
actual position by generalizing on the basis of small sub-
issues that do not fully traverse the range of the bigger
issue. It is always possible of course for the selection of
data to force this or that conclusion, but it would appear
doubtful in this instance that other legislative data derived
by the same method and addressed to the same questions
would return significantly different findings. Furthermore
the limits of inquiry are extended at times to social issues
outside the ambit of the three policy areas mentioned in
order to amplify positively or negatively a major hypothesis. The derivation of conclusions from case data in
the form of legislative histories seems to justify describing
the study as proceeding from the case study method.
The presentation of material is informal and non-quanti-
tative, the categories drawn are relatively crude, and
the conclusions therefore are highly impressionistic.

The important dimensions of history and procedure
are given fairly detailed consideration. The strategic
location of the Bundesrat in the Federal Parliament as the
second chamber makes desirable a brief survey of popular
ideas and accepted notions about second legislative
chambers in western political cultures and a short
historical narrative describing the tradition of the Federal
Council in Germany. Similarly a rather detailed presentation of legislative procedure is necessary, mostly pertaining
to the Bundesrat. In this case the danger of introducing an
excess of obscure legalisms and technicalities is the price
of placing the substantive parts of the study in their
appropriate situational contexts.

Additionally, special consideration is given to the factor
of national party leadership. This fourth element, though

not entered as a testable hypothesis, comes into the picture with the need for determining to what extent the Land governments are fixed in their Bundesrat actions by party considerations at the federal, rather than the Land level. The element of national party controls, rather like the restraint of correct legislative procedure, partially describes the limits of independent Land actions and so is part of the basic equipment of membership in the Bundesrat. That Land government attitudes in the Bundesrat are often determined by national party considerations is accepted as a fact, not a fact internalized in the Bundesrat but imposed from without.

First Major Hypothesis: Federalism

In a federal system such as the German, which might best be described as "functional,"[1] a legislative body can act most effectively to protect that system when it participates directly in the operations of government. Certainly this was the assumption of the partisan groups assembled in the Parliamentary Council at Bonn in 1948-49, and they took up positions accordingly, depending on the intensity of their ideological commitment to the federal principle.[2] It was no surprise that the heaviest portion of the debates of the Council should be devoted to the form, composition, and legal powers of the Bundesrat. The Bundesrat was to occupy the key position for keeping the federal equilibrium, and for protecting the rights of

1. A succinct description of German federalism since 1871 is in Arnold Brecht, *Federalism and Regionalism in Germany* (New York, 1945), esp. pp. 47-73. See also Olle Nyman, *Der Westdeutsche Föderalismus* (Stockholm, 1960), and Hans Ehard, *Freiheit und Föderalismus* (München, 1948).

2. See the monograph *Parteien in der Bundesrepublik: Studien zur Entwicklung der Parteien bis zur Bundestagswahl 1953 (Schriften des Instituts fur Politische Wissenschaft, Bd. 6)*, Mit Beitragen von Max Gustav Lange et al (Stuttgart, 1955), esp. pp. 117-25, 228-36, 304-8. See also the highly illuminating study by John Ford Golay, *The Founding of the Federal Republic of Germany* (Chicago, 1958), ch. 2.

the Länder by resisting intrusions by the Federal Government into functional areas consigned to the Land governments.

This first hypothesis affirms that the Bundesrat does in fact act to preserve governmental integrity at the Land level and thus consciously promotes federalism in western Germany. To avoid presuming on the peculiar nature of German federalism, the federalism hypothesis is reduced to two separate dimensions, each of which is geared to register official Bundesrat resistance to apparent encroachments upon a Land's or Länder affairs. The first is the extent to which members of the Bundesrat take positions clearly defensive of Land interests generally, as well as the "visibility" of arguments pitched to defend the general rights of the Länder in legislative matters. The second dimension concerns the actions of individual Länder in matters which affect them all in different ways and which are likely to provoke diverse, or even conflicting, responses. While the resistance of all Land governments might be expected to be uniformly aroused by a Federal Government measure that appears to pre-empt a field of administration typically reserved for Land execution, another measure can be expected to cause sharply conflicting reactions if it stands to benefit only one or a small group of Länder at the expense of the others. The second alternative was anticipated with certain refugee laws, especially those measures which required some Länder to accept resettlement of refugees from a limited number of Länder which were over-crowded with refugees.

Second Major Hypothesis: Bureaucracy

A striking and traditional peculiarity of German federalism has been that administrative officials of the member states exercise an important legislative function through participation in the staff work of committees of the Federal Council. Although this practice has varied somewhat in the different constitutional arrangements Germany has had since 1871,[3] it has remained constant that regular members of the Land delegations to the Bundesrat are also members of their respective Land governments. Because members of the Bundesrat are responsible under the Bonn regime to their respective governments, and because they are closely attuned to the administrative needs of their particular public policy fields, one might reasonably expect that they should be sensitive to enforcement aspects of federal laws, which are for the most part administered by the Land governments.

The second hypothesis states that the official energies of Bundesrat members are largely directed to administrative problems, and that the Bundesrat is an instrument through which the administrative pressures and points of view of the professional bureaucracy are brought to bear in the legislative field on policy-making in general. This hypothesis, together with the first, is closely bound up with legislative procedure in the Bundesrat in a manner which is described in detail. For example, since the career civil servants from the Land governments who staff the Bundesrat committees take up most of the allotted time in the "preliminary-stage" consideration of bills introduced by the Federal Government, this passage provides an in-built mechanism for bringing the bureaucrat's point of view into play. The connection between bureaucratic tendencies and Bundesrat procedure seems to justify giving somewhat more attention to this particular stage in a bill's progress through the German Parliament.

3. K. C. Wheare, *Federal Government* (New York, 1947), pp. 25-26, 29, 30.

Third Major Hypothesis: Conservatism

Bearing an integral relationship to the first two characteristics of the Bundesrat is a third hypothesis: that the Bundesrat is an instrumentality through which certain interests not effectively represented in the Bundestag seek (and often are able to obtain) modifications in legislative bills favorable to them. A cursory glance at second chamber attitudes on crucial social issues in the past in Germany indicated this to be likely, and further indicated such interests to be distinctly conservative. Part of the tradition of second chambers as "upper houses" in western political systems, at least those that spring from feudal pasts, has been that they exist to protect, by the artful ways of class engineering, the entrenched privileges of a particular class. To avoid over-intellectualizing the problem, no effort is made to define the term "conservatism" rigidly, so that it means absolutely this or absolutely that. By "conservatism" is meant simply a disinclination to accept radical departures from the status quo, and an inclination to be defensive of existing arrangements. Recognizing that stormy debates sometimes rage about the utility of the concept,[4] prudence suggests keeping to a definition that is not radically operational, but sufficiently so to permit drawing conclusions and contrasts.

The idea of conservatism, as defined, presents nevertheless some difficulties when applied to German circumstances. The curious twists and turns of German ideological currents and the demise of German liberalism make it difficult to explicate German ideological distinctions in terms of the British or American liberal-conserva-

4. See for example Herbert McCloskey, "Conservatism and Personality," *American Political Science Review,* LII (March, 1958), 27-45; and Willmoore Kendall, "Comments on McCloskey's 'Conservatism and Personality,'" *American Political Science Review,* LII (June, 1958), 506-10.

tive traditions. Partisan feeling and social issues being what they are in post-war Germany, the major ideological divisions have been between sympathy with and opposition to the doctrines of socialism, however attenuated these doctrines may be. While this might not be particularly appropriate to any conservatism in the Bundesrat, it is fair to regard an anti-socialist viewpoint as conservative. Admittedly the issue is seriously confused by the fact that the small Free Democratic Party, self-proclaimed standard bearer of German liberalism, persists as the most vigorous opponent of socialist dogmas.

Of several currents which appear to be directing attitudinal traffic in the Bundesrat one is singled out as especially revealing. This one stems from the nature of the composition of Bundesrat membership and is directly bound up with both of the first two hypotheses. The conservative idea relative to the Bundesrat is traced to identification of that body as being primarily concerned with the acceptable and convenient administrability of federal laws, most of which are executed by the Land governments. One cannot assume of course that simple identification of the Bundesrat as less "policy-oriented" than "administration-oriented" automatically leads that body into doctrinal conservatism. Rather the idea suggests only that the Bundesrat is encouraged to play a conservative role (as defined above) in legislative policy-formulation by virtue of its institutionalized expertise and skills. The question then would become academic whether or not the Bundesrat assumes a peculiar role in defense of a particular social class.

These three trial postulates provide orientation for the study. No effort is made at comprehensive analysis of the Bundesrat, except insofar as this result might be achieved from close examination of the propositions. Still each hypothesis contributes to a general empirical description of the "federative organ" in the West German Parliament. Together with description of procedural peculiarities and discussion of national party controls, they should offer a reasonably complete survey of the role of the Bundesrat in legislation in the German Federal Republic.

CHAPTER II

The Legendry of Second Chambers

A. GENERAL UTILITY

The development of theoretical propositions about the value and functions of a second chamber as a legislative body has been closely tied to arguments about federalism versus unitarism, and to a host of democratic assumptions relating to this issue. Similarly, though to a lesser extent, the question of the form of the executive attaches to these views, and utility concepts are always conditioned by the factor of executive accountability to the legislature when that relationship exists. What, for example, could be mustered in the camp of democratic theory to support the idea of executive responsibility to two legislative houses in a non-federal system?

In the literature dealing with legislatures the functional utility of second chambers generally is accepted as self-evident in federal systems since the federal principle can be formally written into such a body.[1] A

1. K. C. Wheare, in *Federal Government* (New York, 1947), p. 11, uses the term "federal principle" to mean "the method of dividing powers so that the general and regional governments are each, within a sphere, coordinate and independent." Without prejudice to Professor Wheare's definition, the terms "coordinate" and "independent" are not notably applicable to the German variety of federalism. Throughout this chapter federalism will be construed to mean a political system that is consciously structured to accommodate to the territorial sub-units a degree of authority in the legislation of the larger polity, while at the same time permitting those same sub-units independent authority in certain matters.

federal second chamber, of course, can be something more than a duplicate of the popularly-elected house. This appears to be so even if both houses are elected in the same manner. Certainly from a formalistic point of view the purpose of the United States and Australian Senates is to represent the constituent states in the Union, although they are directly elected in both cases. One writer on the subject says the federal principle in the United States was only made secure when the Seventeenth Amendment eliminated the partial control of the state legislatures over the national Congress.[2] In any event the coincidence of a formal federal structure and a second chamber to represent at least nominally the territorial sub-units, is without exception. Some non-federal systems incorporate second chambers which serve to some extent the same purpose, although that is not typically the major role of such a body. The Italian Senate, for example, bears some of the marks of an organ to secure representation of her "Regions."[3]

The explicit incorporation of the federal principle into a second chamber by no means necessarily describes what is most important or characteristic of that body. Even in federal systems, excluding altogether second chambers in unitary states, the "upper house" cannot always be demonstrated to be more endowed with a "federal conscience" than the other house. The United States Senate, often recognized as more influential generally than the House of Representatives, can hardly be characterized as less nationalistic than the other house. Excepting the equality of representation in the Senate from every state, the federal principle might more fruitfully be looked for elsewhere. This was probably so even

2. *Ibid.*, p. 3.
3. See Arnold J. Zurcher, "The Government and Politics of Italy," in James T. Shotwell (ed.), *Governments of Continental Europe* (New York, 1952), pp. 279-81.

before the adoption of the Seventeenth Amendment. There is evidence that selection of U. S. Senators prior to 1913 was less the result of purely state considerations than of national ones. Sir John A. R. Marriott observed that the American Senate had drawn to itself so much attention and filled so large a space in the political life of the United States that elections to the state legislatures were made largely, if not primarily, with a view to the election of U. S. Senators.[4] Thus Senators were directly elected by the people "once removed." This must not obscure the fact, however, that orginally the American Senate was a counterpoise to the principle of popular representation. The Senate came into being as the guarantor of the rights of small states, and it clearly reflected the centrifugal tendencies which constituted the main impediment to national union. It is little wonder that equal representation in the Senate is the most rigid and most unalterable part of the Constitution.

Despite the fact that second chambers are almost always distinguished by function from the lower houses,[5] in a federal system they can find justification by reference to popular images of representation; that is, they provide representation to States, Cantons, Länder, or Provinces in the national legislature. Whether or not they actually serve to protect these distinct interests in a competitive sense is more difficult to establish. A further notion enjoying wide currency in connection with the utility of a second chamber is the idea of a restraint on popular impulses. Very likely the second chamber would have won a big following even aside from federalism. The spirit of a curb is always evident, suggesting that the purpose of a second chamber should be essentially conservative,

4. John A. R. Marriott, *Second Chambers: An Inductive Study in Political Science* (Oxford, 1927), p. 66.

5. The Ständesrat of Switzerland is the only major exception. There are no legislative power differences between it and the National Council.

at least at the outset. This anti-popular idea carries with it certain assumptions, and it takes more than one form. Most often it assumes the form of extra deliberation, the assumption being that added deliberation and solemnity strengthen a measure's prospects for being obeyed. Should a given drift of policy be felt undesirable, then at least the additional deliberation can break the speed of the resolution.

In the United States the Senate was not solely the creature of federalism, and its most enthusiastic defenders justified it on other grounds as well. Alexander Hamilton, who was openly suspicious of a non-hereditary second chamber and, in fact, of democracy generally, said a second house must be "a permanent barrier against every pernicious innovation . . ." and one which would stand "opposed to the amazing violence and turbulence of the democratic spirit."[6] While Hamilton's monarchist views were not usually shared by his fellow Constitution-makers at Philadelphia, there was some consensus on the desirability of hedging about the legislature. Madison, for example, spoke of "firmness seasonably to interpose against impetuous councils"; McHenry of Maryland even urged building "adequate barriers against democracy."[7] Hamilton furthermore pointed up the overriding necessity of a more solemn and experienced second chamber by adducing "the propensity of all single and numerous assemblies to yield to the impulse of sudden and violent passions, and to be seduced by factious leaders into intemperate and pernicious resolutions."[8]

It should not escape notice that this concern for mature deliberation sprang not from the intrinsic merits of such deliberation but from a need felt by those

6. *The Federalist,* No. LXII.
7. Max Farrand, *Records of the Federal Convention,* I (New Haven, 1911), 27.
8. *The Federalist,* No. LXII.

holding power and possessions to defend them from the advances of impetuous majorities. In the eighteenth century the Founding Fathers sought to institute a second chamber partially to deepen the legitimacy of property by surrounding it with protective encumbrances. Herman Finer has observed, "Revolution is not the only movement of the human spirit to produce barricades; conservatism has produced more." He continues, "Although the downfall of social monopolies in the twentieth century might tend to weaken this protectiveness, the spontaneous desire for unhurried deliberation will probably not lose its need for institutional embodiment."[9] The starting point for this idea was the English House of Lords which rested, then as now, on anything but democratic functional utility. Lacking a defense on the utilitarian grounds of federal systems, the traditional claim most often advanced for the Lords is that they deliver the people from their own elected representatives by revising, or even rejecting, bills until there is no longer any doubt that serious reconsideration warrants their passage. This is essentially the same argument as that advanced by the Hamiltonians, the need for a "chamber of reflections."

A convenient classification of second chambers is the dual one for contemporary legislatures offered by Lord Campion.[10] There are "strong" (co-ordinate) second chambers and "useful" (limited) ones. The purpose of a "strong" chamber is to stand up to the popularly-elected house for any of several reasons, whereas the design of a "useful" house is to maintain some degree of control over the form of legislation within the limits of restricted powers. Probably the best example of the first type is the United States Senate, often acclaimed the world's most

9. Herman Finer, *Theory and Practice of Modern Government* (New York, 1949), p. 402.
10. Lord Campion, "Second Chambers in Theory and Practice," in Sydney Bailey (ed.), *The House of Lords* (New York, 1954), pp. 23-25.

powerful second chamber.[11] Of the second there are many examples, such as France (Fourth Republic), the Netherlands, and more especially Great Britain.

The House of Lords offers the only instance wherein the institution as a fact preceded in time the second chamber issue as a democratic controversy. In all other major countries constitution-makers in the 18th and 19th centuries made up their minds about the desirability and purpose of such a chamber and proceeded to build on that basis. The British problem, short of abolition, was how to make the best of an accomplished fact. But even in Britain a calculated effort was made to salvage something of the representative idea on behalf of the Lords, in spite of the aristocratic and hereditary composition of that body. It is a tribute to the staying power of the House of Lords that it was not eliminated outright after 1832, during the years that marked the high point of Benthamite radicalism. Once it was removed from the center of power in the early 20th century, the utilitarian argument for the House of Lords shifted. The search has never ceased for rational—but not anti-democratic—uses for an "upper house" in Britain.

Perhaps the most important (one might even say most typical, despite the absence of agreement among members of the Commission) suggestions have been those of the Bryce Report. According to the Report issued by a Royal Commission of Inquiry under the chairmanship of Lord Bryce, a second chamber in Britain should be constructed and empowered to do the following things:[12]

11. This is the view of Marriott, *Second Chambers*, p. 64. See also the view of H. B. Lees-Smith, *Second Chambers in Theory and Practice* (London, 1923), p. 154: "The [American] Senate is now the only example in the world of a Second Chamber that is incontestably more powerful than the first." See also Donald R. Matthews, *United States Senators and Their World* (Chapel Hill, 1960), pp. 5-6.

12. Conference on the Reform of the Second Chamber. Letter from

(1) to examine and revise bills coming from the lower house, a particularly helpful function in this age since the popularly-elected house must act under special rules of debate;

(2) to initiate non-controversial bills, which can have an easier passage through Commons if first put into a well-considered shape. In this respect the expert and practiced participation of the Lords can be of undisputed assistance;

(3) to interpose enough delay, and no more, to permit adequate expression of the opinion of the nation on the matter;

(4) to hold full and free discussion of important questions such as foreign policy at moments when the other house may be too occupied to find sufficient time for them. This could be all the more "useful" since the life of the Government is not dependent on it.

Evidently the representative argument, such as was mustered by the Duke of Wellington a hundred years earlier in defense of the House of Lords, was displaced by one emphasizing the "usefulness" of a second chamber possessing powers subordinate to those of the popular house. The new defense also reflects Bagehot's prophetic views not so much in his defense of the Peerage "in its dignified capacity," as in its "revising and suspending" power, which consists of "temporary rejectors and palpable alterers."[13] But then this notion is applicable to second chambers only when they fall into the weak and "useful" category.

Theoretical supports for a "strong" second legislative chamber in a non-federal state are not so easily come by. In such a case the supporting argument must almost necessarily be to pose an impediment to surging popular momentum, and the Third French Republic offers a good example. The Senate, although distinguished from the

---

Viscount Bryce to the Prime Minister, April, 1918, Cd. 9038, Appendix VII to Bailey, *The House of Lords*.

13. Walter Bagehot, *The English Constitution* (rev. ed.; New York, 1890), p. 168.

Chamber of Deputies in several ways, was sufficiently strong to warrant description of the French National Assembly as a "legislative dualism" and made government impossible without the Senate's approval. In the succession of French regimes after 1789 a remarkable coincidence always existed between a strong second chamber and dominant monarchist or conservative sentiment. The idea of an "upper house" in France therefore has traditionally carried with it the spirit of a chamber of reflections.[14] On the other hand, when the tides of democratic sentiment have run strong the second chamber is visibly weakened or disappears altogether. While the Rousseauan spirit of revolutionary France was dominant all obstructions to speedy formation of the popular will were swept away, and the glib aphorism of the Abbé Siéyès was accepted dogma.[15] With the Restoration the French second chamber was established once more as a restrictive force in legislation, and such it has remained. One can have no fair argument with Lidderdale's insistence that the Senate's role in the Third Republic was most emphatically in the spirit of a denial, a negative check—*ni réaction ni révolution*—on the democratic inclinations of the Chamber of Deputies. This was perhaps the secret of the Senate's influence, that it catered to the social *immobilisme* of the French electorate.[16] Ideological currents and partisan composition of the Senate and Chamber were substantially different, encouraging the hardening of suspicions and deepening the difficulties of reconciliation. No one could have been surprised, therefore, when the French Constituent

14. See D. W. S. Lidderdale, *The Parliament of France* (London, 1951), *passim*.

15. "If the second chamber agrees with the first, it is superfluous; if it disagrees, then it is obnoxious." See Lidderdale, *The Parliament of France*, chap. 1.

16. See the comment roughly to this effect in Philip Williams, *Politics in Post-War France* (London, 1954), pp. 267–86.

Assembly of 1945-1946, under the heavy influence of the Left parties, sought with some success to strip the second chamber of its strength.

Perhaps one other way exists for examining the merits of second chambers in non-federal political systems. The great nineteenth century libertarian John Stuart Mill, while acknowledging that the idea of a second chamber has typically distinguished "the partisans of limited from those of uncontrolled democracy," placed little credence on the second chamber as a thing "to prevent precipitancy." Mill did consider it of some moment, however, to ponder "the evil effect produced on the mind of any holder of power, whether an individual or an assembly, by the consciousness of having only themselves to consult."[17] But the great reformer could never be wholly sympathetic with the English House of Lords as a "good" second chamber, for it represented only one social class. That class, like others, should seek its political fortunes through election—by proportional representation!—to the popular branch of Parliament. A more perfect chamber should spring from a different purpose:[18]

The deficiencies of a democratic assembly which represents the general public are the deficiencies of the public itself— want of special training and knowledge. The appropriate corrective is to associate with it a body of which special training and knowledge should be the characteristics. If one House represents popular feeling, the other should represent personal merit, tested and guaranteed by actual public service and fortified by practical experience. If one is the People's Chamber, the other should be the Chamber of Statesmen—a council composed of all living public men who passed through any important political office or employment. Such a Chamber would be fitted for much more than to be merely

17. John Stuart Mill, *Considerations on Representative Government* (New York, 1875), pp. 250-51.
   18. *Ibid.*, p. 255.

a moderating body. It would not be exclusively a check, but also an impelling force.

The idea of the House of Lords as an impelling force was one from which many arguments have subsequently been gleaned, especially those advancing the need for expertness in legislation. Walter Bagehot reasoned along similar lines but was less persuaded of the superior excellence of deliberations among the Peers. Bagehot was prompt to acknowledge the inestimable value of leisure in studying legislative bills, not to mention the merits of a class-based chamber to offset "the idolatry of office and money natural to the Anglo-Saxon."[19] The Bagehot-Mill arguments encompass the whole range of utility supports for a second chamber in a unitary state. The question of conservatism or "constructive negativism" is integrally related to both of course, but the appropriateness of the connection will depend on whether the house is "strong" or simply "useful."

Perhaps Dr. Thomas Dehler of the West German Free Democratic Party makes a blend of the two ideas of expertness and parliamentary foot-dragging when he raised his voice in the Parliamentary Council for a "mixed" second chamber for western Germany. Cautioning against the "Jacobinical notions" of the twentieth century, Dehler said:[20]

Here is a solution that I enthusiastically support in which a real second chamber is created enjoying legislative parity with the lower house of Parliament, and in which the second chamber can act as a counter-weight to undesirable tendencies toward an over-active parliamentarism. We deem it necessary to build checks against a major sickness of our time, against the hypertrophy of legislation, against the mistaken belief

19. Bagehot, *The English Constitution,* p. 181.
20. Speech by Thomas Dehler in the Plenum of the Parliamentary debates. *Stenographische Berichte über die Plenarsitzungen,* October 21, 1948.

that everything in life can be regulated, that by regulation one can accomplish any miracle.

Dehler's statement of course reflects the conservative, anti-particularistic bias of the minority Free Democrats, but it also speaks on behalf of a native German suspicion of parliamentary processes that lack the conditioning force of expertise.

THE SECOND CHAMBER IN GENERAL LEGISLATIVE EXPERIENCE SINCE 1871

From the outset in 1871, in which year Germany ceased to be merely a geographical expression, the second parliamentary chamber was designed to represent the monarchist and particularist states in the Imperial Union. Originally styled the Bundesrat, it has managed to withstand in three successive constitutional phases unitarist tendencies to compromise its importance as a force in German government. In this respect it superficially resembles the other federal second chambers, such as the United States Senate. Still the similarity here does not stem from an effort to defend the political autonomy or political "states' rights" of the Land governments. Rather the Bundesrat design was to accept (with some notable exceptions, e.g., Bavaria) the necessity, or even desire, for centralized political controls while maintaining a forward position in supervising their exercise.

Another feature by no means characteristic of the American Senate has been the ebb and flow in the power of the German "upper house." Whereas the existing arrangements at Bonn demonstrate a strengthening of the Bundesrat over the Reichsrat of the Weimar Republic, the present chamber cannot be fairly characterized as comparable to the Imperial Bundesrat in power. In any case the point is stretched a bit far to make much of the likeness in the German and American "upper houses," especially in view of the basic differences between the two federalisms and because of two wholly diverse understandings in those countries of the proper relationship between the governing officials and the governed. The tap roots of the German *Rechtsstaat* were nurtured in a political mystique far removed from the empirical origins of individual American responsibilities and rights. Perhaps Erich Fromm's "authoritarian ethic" gives correct emphasis to the sociological underpinnings of German political culture, while pointing out the non-transferability of concepts from one cultural setting to another when these cultures fail to share the same ethical premises.[21]

Within these limitations the German second chamber, at least until 1949, has been like the English House of Lords and the French Senate and (in the Fourth Republic) the Council of the Republic in that it was usually found in defense of the existing order and traditional conservative elements.[22] Certainly the Imperial Bundesrat and Reichsrat of the Weimar Republic were conservative, both being manned by Land Ministers and civil servants from the upper service levels who were normally loyal to principles of monarchy and to themselves as a conservative, powerful and status-dominated administrative class. This was conservatism on the one

21. In authoritarian ethics, because individual man is believed not to have the capacity to know what is good or bad, an authority states what is good and lays down laws and norms of conduct. Erich Fromm, *Man For Himself: An Inquiry into the Psychology of Ethics* (New York, 1947), pp. 8-14.

22. Any recognizable conservatism in the present Bundesrat appears to rest on somewhat more precarious grounds. Owing to the shifting sands of central party controls and their effects on Bundesrat attitudes, the Bundesrat has lately lost some of its former flavor of non-partisanship. In this way the Bundesrat's conservatism could be integrally related to the general picture of partisan attitudes in the Diet, and therefore markedly different from that of the earlier regimes. This of course would be so only if the Bundesrat can be seen to be conservative at all.

hand of loyalty to the Emperor and hostility to demand for reform; and conservatism on the other hand of a permanently assembled body whose professional homogeneity and *esprit de corps* converged on a general attitude of skepticism toward abrupt and radical reform measures. Furthermore, because the German Liberal Movement embraced the nationalist cause against the reactionary particularism of the German states and their feudal remnants as obstructing liberal reforms, liberal thought in Germany has had little esteem for federalism or for such patently federal organs as the Bundesrat and the Reichsrat.

When Bismarck summoned the "German Parliament" in 1871, he fulfilled the dream of the Revolution of 1848, except that the effective agent of national unification was Prussian power, not liberalism. By enlisting the support of the German princes for the Reich and by improvising a federal structure which moved effective power to the center without unnecessarily disrupting the apparatus in the states, virtual control of Reich affairs passed into Prussian hands. A fairly wide range of legislative powers was vested in the Reich which together with imperial prerogatives in foreign and military affairs gave Prussian leadership effective tools for consolidating its control over the whole of Germany. But it was not Bismarck's intention that the new Parliament should have much authority. So he devised a constitutional structure that was described by the Prussian Crown Prince as "an artfully manufactured chaos."[23] Under the Imperial Constitution most political authority rested not with the popularly elected Reichstag, but with the Bundesrat, the federal council of princes. Bundesrat approval was required for all Reich legislation,

23. Richard K. Ullman and Sir Stephen King-Hall, *German Parliaments: A Study of the Development of Representative Institutions in Germany* (New York, 1954), p. 67.

and it could initiate measures and decide what legislation was to be considered by the Reichstag. In addition to its clear legislative supremacy the Bundesrat shared an executive function in that it supervised the whole administration of Reich laws. In its administrative function it issued all administrative ordinances necessary for enforcement of imperial laws, and could eliminate deficiencies of state execution of those laws by simple decree.

The Bundesrat was not a House of Lords, such as the Prussian upper house, nor a Chamber of States, such as the proposed second chamber of 1848. It was presented by Bismarck as the direct successor to the Confederate Diet of the old North German Confederation—an assembly of envoys from state governments (now 25) who had no representative rights as voters in a legislative body. In practice Prussia dominated the Bundesrat, although having only 17 of 58 votes, and the Prussian Prime Minister, who was also Imperial Chancellor, was *ex officio* chairman of the Bundesrat and cast Prussia's 17 votes as her Foreign Minister. Since 14 votes could forestall constitutional changes and since powerful Prussia effectively controlled the votes of several weaker states she surrounded, there was little likelihood that Bismarck's "Orchestra of the Reich" would be seriously disturbed.

Neither the Chancellor nor any of his subordinate Cabinet members (State Secretaries) was responsible directly or indirectly to the Reichstag. Reinforced by constitutionally guaranteed Prussian control of the Bundesrat, a close community of interests developed in the form of strong anti-democratic bonds between the Bundesrat and the Kaiser's appointed government. Essentially it was not so much that Prussia was federated with the other German states as rather the reverse. Of course the imposition of Prussian efficiency and authoritarianism on the German Reich after 1871 is not a fact attributable to Bismarck's Constitution or to the composition of the Bundesrat. Still the development of the first German "upper house" under Hohenzollern auspices as basically "conservative" was to have important consequences later.

As centripetal tendencies and popular national consciousness gained momentum in Germany, the role of the Bundesrat began to shift in emphasis. Even under Bismarck, who fell into the habit of by-passing the Bundesrat in his dealings with the south German states, the Bundesrat bore the early stamp of a chamber of bureaucrats seeking particularistic concessions, mostly of an administrative nature, for their state governments. This development was partly due to the rising importance and assertiveness of the Reichstag as the natural forum chosen by universal suffrage, but it was mostly accounted for by the peculiar nature of federalism under the Empire.

Federalism in Germany has been aptly described as "functional" or "horizontal," as opposed to the American version as "authoritative" or "vertical."[24] When power was given to the United States Government in a field, for example, it was normally given full governmental authority to include the power of administration as well as legislation. Hence the distribution of power was "vertical," and the same government controlled every phase of action along the legislative-administrative continuum. This was not the case in Germany. While the Imperial Constitution gave impressive legislative powers to the Berlin Government the administrative and judicial functions were generally left to the states.[25]

24. Arnold Brecht, *Federalism and Regionalism in Germany: The Division of Prussia*, (London, 1945), pp. 3-13; but see also Wheare, *Federal Government*, pp. 29ff. Wheare denies that the German Empire qualified as a "federal" system; see also Olle Nyman, *Der Westdeutsche Föderalismus* (Stockholm, 1960).

25. Other than the Reichsbank, the only federal field agencies under

On the other hand only in critical fields involving cultural differences among the states were the states permitted any legislative autonomy. These were always confined to religion, local government and education. Thus the federal division in Germany was effected by a formal dichotomy between policy-making and execution. When the question arose in Germany of increasing the power of the Federation, a German immediately thought in terms of multiplying the number of federal administrative agencies or of decreasing the powers of the Bundesrat. It was this legislation-administration dualism that gave the Bundesrat its most distinguishing quality as a second chamber—the decided emphasis in its composition on career professionals and state government officials whose bureaucratic attitudes had been generations in the making.

It would be difficult, if not impossible, to measure the extent to which the Bundesrat's role in legislation under the Empire was shaped by bureaucratic fixations. The views of Max Weber on bureaucracy suggests that such officials as these, who always have strong feelings of attachment and loyalty to the monarchy and who naturally gravitate toward conservative stability, will necessarily share an authoritarian outlook.[26] For one thing, despite the modest efforts of some of the German states to broaden the training of higher administrative people, after about 1850 they remained heavily concentrated in law and the

the Empire were in the postal service and the navy. Although this was subsequently altered under the Weimar system, and an "administrative federalism" developed with the expansion of federal administrative services to duplicate those at the Land level, the principle essentially remained in effect. See Brecht, *Federalism and Regionalism*, pp. 47-70; also Frederick Blachly and Miriam Oatman, *The Government and Administration of Germany* (Baltimore, 1928), chaps. IX, XVI, XIX.

26. Hans Gerth and C. Wright Mills, *From Max Weber: Essays in Sociology* (New York, 1958), pp. 234-35; also J. P. Mayer, *Max Weber and German Politics* (London, 1955), pp. 82-92.

administrative sciences.[27] But this was not necessarily what was most important about the Bundesrat as bureaucracy. According to Weber, analysis of any modern institutional order starts with the fact that a system of rational-legal authority can only operate by the imposition of sanctions with relative efficiency, creating seriously frustrating limits on many human interests which are themselves generated by the strains inherent within the particular structure. The major cause of these strains is "the segregation of roles, and of the corresponding authority to use influence over others . . . , which is inherent in the functionally limited sphere of office."[28]

The "segregation of roles" in German bureaucracy began early and grew out of the complex and highly rationalized state apparatus in Brandenburg-Prussia which in turn had its origins in the seventeenth century.[29] Accustomed for two hundred years to an authoritarian system, German civil servants in the Empire looked upwards for their orders and passed them on with reliable and undemocratic vigor. Interestingly, for Weber the decisive connecting link between Kaiser and administration was the regularized network of relationships under constitutionalism, "which binds the bureaucracy and the ruler into a community of interests against the desires of party chiefs for power in the parliamentary bodies."[30] It was a mutually rewarding authoritarian arrangement, although sometimes an uncomfortable one for the monarch because his own internal success was dependent

27. Finer, *Theory and Practice of Modern Government,* pp. 794-96. For the background to this development see the excellent recent study on the emergence of bureaucratic absolutism in Germany by Hans Rosenberg, *Bureaucracy, Aristocracy and Autocracy* (Cambridge, Mass., 1958), esp. pp. 202-28.
28. Max Weber, *The Theory of Social and Economic Organization,* trans. A. M. Henderson and Talcott Persons (New York, 1947), p. 68.
29. Rosenberg, *Bureaucracy, Aristocracy and Autocracy, passim.*
30. Gerth and Mills, *From Max Weber,* pp. 234-36.

upon his bureaucrats. For, according to Weber, under the rule of expert knowledge, which is part of the regularized equipment characteristic of constitutionalism, "the authoritarian controls of the Kaiser can attain steadiness only by a continuous communication with the bureaucratic chiefs." This interaction must be planned and directed by the heads (or head) of the bureaucracy to stabilize their own tenure and to further their own advantages. If, therefore, the ruler is ultimately unable to muster support in the popular assembly, the Constitution renders him powerless against the bureaucracy. This would follow because of "the indispensability of expert knowledge and the impersonal and functional routinization of administration which constitutionalism requires."[31]

While Weber might deplore the theoretical ineptitudes and inflexibilities of an overweening bureaucracy, and while he might plead for the "overdue parliamentarization of the Bundesrat,"[32] he recognized that these were not simply products of an unending process in the political degradation of man, but that they reflected an almost instinctive devotion of his fellow countrymen to a *Politik des Unpolitischen.* He further recognized that the Bundesrat represented, despite its pronounced anti-democratic leanings, the successful image of a generation's efforts to de-politicize the Empire. Since the truly political functions were not really very important, most of the valuable work could be done by the concerted efforts of experts who had been specifically recruited into the system. What in this view could be more suitable to German "needs" than the Bundesrat?

The passing of the Imperial constitutional edifice came at the high tide of German unitarism, so that the power balance was tilted sharply toward the center legally as

31. *Ibid.*, p. 237.
32. Mayer, *Max Weber and German Politics*, p. 73.

well as politically. Under the Weimar Constitution of 1919, although all the major participant parties wanted a successor to the old Bundesrat, there was little sympathy for a chamber of states (now called, for the first time, Länder). Consequently the newly created Reichsrat was to be a body representing the Länder for federal purposes, and not an organization of states joined to promote state particularism. In contrast with its predecessor the Reichsrat was markedly inferior to the popularly-elected Reichstag. Now the political centers of gravity were the Reichstag and the Reich Cabinet. In fact the Constitution explicitly stated, "Reich laws shall be enacted by the Reichstag."[33] Despite its clear displacement as the most important legislative force, however, the tradition of a federal council was sufficiently strong to give it a permanent, if weakened, status as the federal organ for representing the governments of the states. A report of the Main Committee of the Constituent Assembly at Weimar said:[34]

The committee has accepted the constitution of the Reichsrat to maintain the organic connection of the Reich with the individual states, and thus it has expressed the sense of historical evolution and the living necessities of the Federation. This Reichsrat is, however, not intended to be either a first or a second chamber, or a parliament or a house of states, but a body to represent the German states in the legislation and administration of the Reich.

A great deal of legal argument has been heard about whether the Reichsrat was an essentially federal or Land organ. Politically of course, by virtue of its composition, it remained loyal to the Land Governments; but this was

33. The Constitution of the German Reich of August 11, 1919, Article 68.
34. Konrad Haussmann, Second Reading, Weimar Constitutional Assembly, July 2, 1919. Quoted in Gerhard Anschütz, *Die Verfassung des Deutschen Reichs*, (12th ed.; Berlin, 1930), p. 42.

in a manner scarcely designed to obstruct the advancing wedge of Reich legislation. Probably a characteristic contemporary view was that of Heinrich Oppenheimer, who wrote in reference to this "dualistic" institution:[35]

It is in this very dualism that the main value of the institution lies. For in Germany where local sentiment is still strong and quite able to hold its own in competition with national feeling, an organ is indispensable in which the national will and national wants can be harmonized with the particular aims and aspirations of the states, and where, if the conflict of interests proves too strong for that, a compromise at least may be arranged acceptable to both.

This dualism seems not to have counted for very much in practice. Now the Reich Government was responsible to the Reichstag and by constitutional provision indirectly controlled the Reichsrat. The centralized republic gave almost unlimited legislative power to the Reichstag, and with its *Kompetenz-Kompetenz* it could effectively pre-empt every important field for Reich legislation. With the legislative competence of the Länder strictly curtailed, the constitutional role of the Council shifted from that of chief law-maker to that of an administrative overseer. One cannot fairly state, however, that the Reichsrat was unimportant in legislation. In fact it came to exercise an unanticipated and strategic function in the enactment of Reich policy. The fact remains that it was most important as an organization of Land ministerial officials.

As had been the case under the Empire the composition of the Reichsrat reflected the disparity in population, except that this time Prussia was forced to accept a weaker position numerically. Article 61 said:

Each Land has at least one vote in the Reich Council. In the case of larger Länder there shall be one vote for every

35. Heinrich Oppenheimer, *The Constitution of the German Republic* (London, 1923), p. 110.

700,000 inhabitants. A surplus of at least 350,000 inhabitants shall be reckoned equivalent to 700,000. No Land may be represented by more than two-fifths of the total number of votes.

The purpose of this distribution plan devised by Hugo Preuss and the supporting partisans of the Weimar coalition, was to effect a balance among the "contrasting magnitudes" of the German Länder by fixing some constitutional impediments to Prussian hegemony.[36] Thus Prussia received 26 of a total of 66 Reichsrat seats, and half of these 26 went to her 13 provinces as "independent" entities. These 13 "free" votes were more imaginary than real, however, and although Prussian members of the Reichsrat could never be certain of a uniform vote from all her provinces, dissenting votes were relatively rare.[37] Besides Prussia, Bavaria received 11 votes, Saxony 7, Württemberg 4, Baden 3, Thuringia Hesse and Hamburg 2 each, and 1 for each of the remaining ten Länder. The comparative voting strength of all successive German states in the Federal Council is shown in Table I. The diminution of Prussian strength could not be brought about solely through reduced representation in the Reichsrat, however, and by comprising two-thirds of the bulk of the entire Reich, Prussia continued until 1933 to exercise a major influence.

Despite the expressed intention of the Main Committee to deny to the Reichsrat the status of a second chamber, developments in the Reichstag projected the Council into the role of a surprisingly effective legislative

36. The term is used by Brecht, *Federalism and Regionalism,* chap. II. The need for territorial readjustment and elimination of Prussia is the dominant theme of this small study. See especially Chapters II, III, VIII, IX and X.

37. K. H. Schoppmeier, *Der Einfluss Preussens auf die Gesetzgebung des Reiches* (Berlin, 1929), pp. 90-91. Bloc voting by Länder was not explicitly required as had been the case under the Empire, but the natural responsibilities of Reichsrat members made this the rule.

TABLE I

VOTING POWER OF THE GERMAN STATES IN THE
UPPER HOUSES, 1871-1933[a]

	Confederate Diet, 1815-1866—39 member states	Federal Council 1871-1918 25 states	Reichsrat 1919-1933 18 member states
Austria	4	no longer member state	
Prussia	4	17	13
Bavaria	4	6	11
Württemberg	4	4	4
Saxony	4	4	7
Hanover	4	incorporated into Prussia	
Baden	3	3	3
Hesse (Grand Duchy)	3	3	2
Hesse (Electorate)	3	incorporated into Prussia	
Holstein (Duchy)	3	incorporated into Prussia	
Luxembourg	3	no longer member state	
Brunswick	2	2	1
Mecklenburg-Schwerin	2	2	1
Nassau	2	incorporated into Prussia	
Thuringia	created after 1919		2
Hamburg	1	1	2
Number of other states with one vote each	23	16	8
Votes of Prussian provinces	—	—	13
TOTALS	69	58	66

[a] Compiled from Richard K. Ullmann and Sir Stephen King-Hall, *German Parliaments* (New York 1954), Appendix D, pp. 147-148.

body. The most important legislative powers of the Reichsrat were its consideration of all Government bills before their introduction into the Reichstag and, more important still, its right of a suspensive veto over all non-financial legislation.

The requirement of introducing Government measures first into the Reichsrat is found in Article 69. Although the Reich Government could get around this provision in one or more ways, it generally declined to do so. Prudence dictated that the Government maintain smooth relations with Land representatives in the Reichsrat, since most Reich laws even as late as 1939 would be executed by the Länder. If policy uniformity and continuity were to be preserved a calculated effort had to be made to avoid alienating the executors. The amount of bustle in the Government caused by Reichsrat objections and recommendations has led Finer to observe: "There is no doubt that this power of the Reichsrat was compelling and . . . that it gave the states as states the opportunity to resist encroachments on their freedom. . . ."[38]

As party life in Weimar Germany developed (or failed to develop), the crucial phase of the Reichsrat's role in legislation was its right of a suspensive veto. Article 74 says:

> The Reich Council is entitled to raise an objection to laws passed by the Reichstag. The objection must be submitted to the Reich Government within two weeks following the final vote in the Reichstag and sustained by reasons at the latest within two further weeks. When such objection has been raised, the law is again submitted to the Reichstag for redecision. If by this means no agreement is reached between the Reichstag and the Reich Council, the President may, within three months, order that a referendum be taken on the matter in dispute. If the President does not exercise this right, the law is considered not to have been passed. If the Reichstag has passed the law in spite of the objection by the Reich Council by a two-thirds majority, then the President must either proclaim the same within three months in the form approved by the Reichstag or order a referendum to be taken.

With the range of competent Reich legislation covering virtually all public policy fields either exclusively or concurrently, and since any given Reich Government at Berlin rested on a narrow parliamentary majority (or even a minority), the right of the Reichsrat to challenge a bill became a substantial one. One can easily understand that the Government should try to avoid the necessity of having to muster a two-thirds majority in the Reichstag

38. Finer, *Theory and Practice of Modern Government*, p. 204.

in order to overrule an objection, prospects for which could never have been very good after 1920. Certainly neither the Government nor the Reichstag enjoyed contemplating a popular referendum. Consequently a tendency developed for both Government and Reichstag to treat favorably the view of the Reichsrat whenever possible, and for the subsequent strengthening of the Reichsrat in this regard.[39]

All these considerations are in addition to the Reichsrat's authority as a powerful decision-making organ in Reich administration, in which respect it would compare favorably with the formerly dominant Bundesrat. Furthermore, whereas recognition is usually given to the continuity of composition in the Council from Empire to Weimar, it also would seem that even in the legislative sphere the break with Imperial traditions was less abrupt than first glance would indicate. The most impressive similarity between these two organs nevertheless was in their mutual domination by administrative experts from the Land Ministries. This had not been the purpose of the Weimar scheme which originally was to bring to the Reichsrat people who were directly responsible to their Land Parliaments. This fact was to earn the Weimar Reichsrat some later derision from German leaders in 1948/1949 who sought to erect safeguards against the recurrence of an assembly of civil servants.[40]

The language of the Reich Constitution had been sufficiently vague to permit a variance of opinion as to who was authorized to represent the Land governments in the

39. See, for example, Herbert Kraus, *The Crisis of German Democracy: A Study of the Spirit of the Constitution of Weimar* (Princeton, 1932), p. 125.

40. The Socialist attack in the Parliamentary Council against bureaucratic control of a second chamber was led by Carlo Schmid and Walter Menzel. Plenum of the Parliamentary debates. *Stenographische Berichte,* September 10, 1948, pp. 29ff.

Reich Council.[41] In fact all Länder resorted early to the practice of sending their permanent officials as Land representatives, usually civil servants of the highest rank *(Beamten des höheren Dienstes)*. It was debatable whether such persons would consistently act according to the democratic intentions of the Constitution. On the other hand it was impractical to expect Land Ministers to absent themselves regularly from their Land duties to attend frequent Reichsrat sessions. So the hopes of Preuss, Weber, and Naumann that the popularization of the Land governments would result in a popularly responsible (i.e., responsible to Land legislatures) second chamber were thwarted.

Article 63 also specified that each Land might send as many representatives as it had votes, this being the usual practice. With the lone exception of Prussia (and the true cause of federalism was to be served by splitting up Prussian votes), a uniform pattern of voting among a Land's delegation was observed. No forceful reason existed for requiring Land Ministers always to be present at the Reichsrat. Their governments' votes after all had been cast in bloc, and a fair amount of time spent in that chamber had been directed to "routine matters of administration and tedious concern." It was only when the most important matters were being discussed that a Land's elected leaders would appear in the Reichsrat. Furthermore, having proved a handy repository in which to vest many other administrative duties, the Reichsrat was important in passing on in German political experience the major role of expertise in legislative affairs. At first endowed with only nominal powers its permanent sessions gave it the admired flavor of stability and soundness in contrast to the hectic ups-and-downs of changing

41. Article 63 said simply: "The Länder shall be represented on the Reich Council by members of their governments."

party formations. Together with the remoteness of a possible two-thirds vote in the Reichstag against it and with the administrative powers of the Länder in the foreground, the Reichsrat had to be recognized as a political force of no mean significance.

Since only the most highly qualified career people were appointed to serve in the Reichsrat and since they often had direct association with administrators in the Reich body of officials, it is little wonder than an *esprit d'administratif* should characterize the deliberations of such a body much as it had those of the old Bundesrat. Neither should there be any doubt that it fitted well into the form already tried for a German second chamber, despite its pronounced dissimilarity with almost all other federal second chambers. The tradition of a federative council active in German legislative affairs had the advantage of social momentum long before the construction of the Bonn system, and through it the Länder could participate directly in legislation. It had the further merit of giving direct supervision over administraton of laws to persons who were directly involved with putting them into effect. When therefore, German leaders assembled at Bonn in 1948 to build a new system on the ashes of the old, the influence of a "council-type" second chamber was quite strong. Partisans of a "pure" Bundesrat, that is, of a second chamber composed solely of Land government representatives, could point with considerable justification to its earlier successful application to Germany in the interests of federalism.

The major determinants forcing the issue in 1948-49 were markedly different, however, from those in 1871 and 1919. They reflected to a large extent the policies of other countries and were inextricably bound up with global questions. When the three western Allied Occupation Powers announced that the licensed political parties in Germany would be permitted to convene a constituent assembly to draw up a constitution for a restored republic, the only agreement about the form of Government was that a federal form had to be adopted.[42] At the time the Bonn *Grundgesetz* was being framed, the German leaders were under official Allied influence, as well as their own personal inclinations, to avoid an overly centralized regime. Generally the unitary tendencies of Weimar, having prepared the way for the monolithic Nazi state, were morally discredited.[43] There was some early evidence of Allied tendencies to intervene in order to effect a centralist bias, on the one hand, or a de-centralist one on the other, depending on the presumed contingency of national interest at stake.

Despite early inability among the Allied Powers to agree on the specific details of power distribution in the new Germany, engaging sometimes in "pernicious abstractions" that reflected the particular sentiments of an occupying power,[44] the Germans were nevertheless given

42. The text of the London Six-Power Agreement Protocol is in the United States Department of State Publication 3556, *Germany, 1947-1949, the Story in Documents,* European and British Commonwealth Series 9 (1950), pp. 76-80.

43. In February, 1934, Hitler had summarily dissolved the Reichsrat, and it never met thereafter. Federalism under Hitler became a highly academic matter, with the Länder reduced to administrative districts under close direction of party *Gauleiter.* See Franz Neumann, *Behemoth: The Structure and Practice of National Socialism* (London, 1942), especially "The Synchronization of Political Life," pp. 51-56; also Brecht, *Federalism and Regionalism,* pp. 120-32.

44. The term was used by American Secretary of State Marshall following the unsuccessful London Conference of Foreign Ministers in December, 1947, and in a similar context. It was interestingly the Americans who were most insistent, however, about application of the federalism idea, and American suspicions relating to the quite different German species of power distribution were never quite eliminated. See, for example, the statement by John Foster Dulles in The New York Times of January 18, 1947; he urged that Americans be entrusted with the guidance of the federal question because "we have, more than any other people, experience in using the formula, and in developing its manifold possibilities." See also Lucius Clay, *Decision in Germany*

wide latitude and shaped their Basic Law according to party attitudes and German traditions. Probably the most important thing affecting the disposition of post-war German federalism was the disappearance of Prussia as a dominant political force operating on the fringes of democracy. The abolition of Prussia by Allied Control Council Law No. 46 in 1946 was hardened into geographical reality with the territorial readjustments that were effected under Allied Military Government. The eleven Länder in the western zones which sent delegates to the Parliamentary Council at Bonn were "states" only in the loosest sense. Most of them consisted of omnibus territorial appendages, and only Bavaria and the Hansa cities could claim status as historic German states. Despite this strong element of artificiality the necessity of a federal structure was accepted by all the major parties and supported in varying degrees at least in principle. This fact, compounded with issuance of the Allied *Aide-Memoire* of November, 1948,[45] outlining Allied expectations concerning the new German Government, focused attention on the powers and composition of the second chamber of the legislature and on the distribution of power between Federation and Länder. Since the latter proposition was felt by the Germans to turn on the former, the constitution of the Bundesrat was the center of controversy during Parliamentary Council debates.

Because party attitudes were crucial in determining the form of the new German "upper house,"[46] party

(Garden City, N. Y., 1950); also Harold Zink, *The United States in Germany, 1944-1945* (Princeton, 1957), chap. 3.

45. Text of the *Aide-Memoire on German Political Organization Presented by the Military Governors to the Council at Bonn* is in U. S. Department of State Publication 3556, *Germany, 1947-1949, the Story in Documents,* European and British Commonwealth Series 9, p. 278.

46. The Allied *Aide-Memoire* had stated explicitly that there would be "a bicameral legislative system in which one of the houses must represent the individual states and must have sufficient power to safeguard the interests of the states . . . . " *(ibid.).*

strengths and alignments at the Council were to prove decisive. The party breakdown, on the basis of elections to the Parliamentary Council by the newly constituted Landtage, produced twenty-seven delegates for the Social Democratic Party (SPD) and twenty-seven for the Christian Democratic/Christian Social Union (CDU/CSU); five for the Free Democratic Party (FDP); and two each for the German Party (DP), the Communist Party (KPD), and the Center Party (Z). Three proposals were made for the form of the new second chamber. Whereas the party groups drew on the experiences of many constitutions to support their arguments, their positions always accorded closely with anticipated party advantages. The most federalist of all parties, the CDU/CSU, supported a "pure" Bundesrat in the German tradition, to represent and be responsible to the Land governments. The Socialists, as advocates of centralized planning and control wanted a "senate-type" chamber elected by the Land legislatures on the basis of proportional representation. The third approach offered by the minority Free Democrats, was that of a "mixed" chamber combining the virtues of the other two.

In support of a Bundesrat the sanction of tradition could be invoked. Since the Land governments would be called upon to enforce the laws, they could perform this task more intelligently if they had participated personally in their passage and could thereby prevent the cropping up of misunderstandings between legislator and executive. Also the binding of Bundesrat members to instructions from their governments together with the varying partisan texture of those governments, would insure an "objective" outlook on legislative problems. These were essentially the arguments used by the Christian Democrats. The SPD on the other hand urged adoption of a chamber which would reflect popular influence, but which could at the same time enable the Länder to exert a positive influence in the republic. Generally the Socialist concept of federalism fell short of the Allied directive of November, and there was cause here for some friction. Carlo Schmid expressed the skepticism of his party when he said: "While federalism everywhere else in the world implies the unification of what was separated, with us it is apparently intended to separate what had already been united." And also:[47]

I doubt that the federalization of Germany would guarantee our neighbors their security. I do believe that a democratized Germany would provide this security. If we had had, in 1914, a government operating under parliamentary control, the peace would have been safer than it was under the federal system at the time. The federal Bundesrat did not impede the coming of the war, but a strong central Parliament would probably have done so.

The official position of the SPD was to favor a senate which might consider political problems from a higher, detached level, but one which would bear a closer resemblance to popular moods and could avoid the bureaucratic inflexibility of earlier Federal Councils. The third suggestion for a "mixed" body composed of members chosen by both the Land governments and legislatures was supported by the FDP. The reluctance of the Free Democrats to accept either of the other two plans reflected their ideological opposition to state particularism and their fears that as a minority party they would be submerged in the instructed delegations sent to a "pure" Bundesrat by Land governments controlled by the two largest parties.

Closely related to the question of the form of a Second Chamber was the matter of its power and the mode of

47. Plenum of the Parliamentary debates, *Stenographische Berichte*, September 8, 1948, p. 16.

Land representation in it. Here again party doctrine was dominant in directing the flow of debate. The most important concern for the CDU for example, was to achieve complete equality of power *(Gleichberechtigung)* in legislative matters for the Bundesrat. This was particularly noticeable among members of the CSU, Bavaria's CDU affiliate. Deputy Joseph Schwalber, a leading Bavarian federalist, urged that the mistake be avoided of slipping into the pitfalls of a unitary, authoritarian state. He said, in this connection:[48]

The individual states will be the supporting props for the new political structure. States can only be preserved according to historical experience and by the forces which they create. Our new German state must be built on the Länder as essential states, not on unprotected agencies of administration. The new German state must be a real *Bundesstaat*, whose members have their own state personalities, as is the case in the United States. Each constituent state must be able to lead an independent existence of its own as a state, and in a way to permit the free development of its own people. It was the autonomous vigor of the separate Länder that gave the old Reich its greatest strength.

In the interest of unity with its Bavarian affiliate, the CDU found it necessary to make its strongest stand for *Gleichberechtigung* and then trust to its national strength to give it secure representation in a second chamber by any method of election.

The Socialists made their strongest bid for maintenance of the Bundestag as the dominant force in legislation, while seeking to make the second chamber as broadly representative as possible. As events actually worked out they were prepared to sacrifice the senate-principle if there were some assurance that the "Council" was to be put in a decidedly inferior position to that of the "Diet." In fact, when it had appeared that Robert Lehr,

48. Plenum, *Stenographische Berichte*, September 9, 1948, p. 36.

vice-chairman of the CDU *Fraktion*,[49] had convinced members of his group that a compromise with the FDP was feasible over a "mixed" chamber possessed with *Gleichberechtigung*, the Socialist abandoned the *Senatsbegriff* and found a strange ally in Bavarian particularism. When Hans Ehard, Minister-President of Bavaria, came to Bonn as requested by Lehr to join the negotiations, the result was not to strengthen the chances of *Gleichberechtigung*. Ehard struck a bargain with the SPD out of which came a Bundesrat representing the Land governments. The compromise between the FDP and CDU never took place. The Bundesrat developed from an agreement between the most centralist and most federalist parties in Germany, the SPD and the CSU. With the threatened possibility of a mixed chamber involving a confusion of responsibilities distasteful to Bavarians, and with *Gleichberechtigung* anathema to the Socialists, these two interests found common cause in a pure Bundesrat with powers fashioned after those of the old Reichsrat. The old institution of "instructed Land blocs" was reestablished as had been the case tacitly under Weimar and had been written into the Constitution of the Imperial Bundesrat.

Whether this retreat into the traditional Bismarckian form was well-timed and appropriate for the new problems of Germany is open to question. Theodor Heuss expressed the disappointment of those seeking reform when he said:[50]

49. Arnold Heidenheimer reports that Lehr, and for that matter most of the members of the CDU group, were "informally sympathetic" with the idea of a variant of the senate principle. ("Federalism and the Party System," *The American Political Science Review*, LII [September, 1958], 811-12.)

50. Statement by Dr. Heuss during the closing days of the Parliamentary Council; quoted in John Ford Golay, *The Founding of the Federal Republic of Germany* (Chicago, 1958), p. 50.

These two latter day 'Bismarcks' have forgotten one thing, however—that Bismarck's edifice, as the essential feature of its federalism, had Prussia in the background. Without Prussia, that whole historical structure cannot be understood. And now in place of this Bismarckian federalism, something else has emerged. . . . Now we face the very great possibility of getting a federalism of bureaucracies and, with it, the trouble of having uniform conditions of life for the whole community upset.

With these major issues out of the way most of the other problems relating to the Bundesrat were resolved rather easily. Of immediate interest is the closeness with which Socialist and CDU positions toward representation in the Bundesrat accorded with their fortunes in the 1947 elections. Each group sought a scheme of representation which would guarantee it a majority in the Council. The Socialists, for example, now became the big defenders of equal representation because it would give them, on the basis of earlier election results, control of Land governments having a majority of votes in the Bundesrat.

Ultimately the small Länder, though by no means the recipients of equal representation, secured a voting strength which gave them a much weightier vote than had been the case under the Weimar regime. Every Land was to receive at least three votes, Länder with more than two million inhabitants would have four, and Länder with more than six million inhabitants would have five. Until the consolidation of the three Länder of the Southwest into Baden-Württemberg in 1952,[51] this arrangement left the CDU with a slight edge in a total of forty-three votes.

The balance between the two largest parties in the Bundesrat, that is, the ratio of votes controlled by Land governments which were in turn controlled by one of the

51. For a critical discussion of the issues relating to the referenda held in those Länder see Chester B. Lewis and Robert D. King, "The Southwest State," HICOG, *Information Bulletin* (February, 1952).

two large parties, was to be decisive in several instances. One such occasion involved the ratification of the EDC Treaties. Partisan difficulties developed over the Treaties while Chancellor Adenauer was in the United States in April, 1953. At the time the Treaties came before the Bundesrat the CDU was certain of only eighteen votes in favor, with the fifteen votes of the Socialist-controlled Länder definitely opposed (Lower Saxony, Hesse, Bremen, and Hamburg).[52] The remaining five votes of Baden-Württemberg were in doubt, depending on which way Minister-President Reinhold Maier would vote. Although Maier was a Free Democrat and therefore under some compulsion to fall in with his party's partnership in the Bonn coalition, he ruled in Baden-Württemberg by means of a tenuous coalition with the Social Democrats. The SPD at Stuttgart made it clear to him they would defeat his government if he voted in favor of the Treaties. Obviously feeling the limelight a bit uncomfortable, Maier at first decided not to decide. Then, in May, as President of the Bundesrat he cast his Land's five votes in favor of only two phases of the Treaties, letting the rest of it by-pass the Bundesrat. In this way Maier managed to satisfy both contestants although the episode was to cost him his office, and he was defeated a few months later. Evidently the partisan composition of the Bundesrat could be vitally important. It is also clear that the result of the original Bundesrat decisions at the Parliamentary Council does not clearly indicate either a detached or an objective preoccupation with Land problems. This matter is discussed more fully in a later chapter.

52. It was by no means clear that Bundesrat approval was required for all provisions of the EDC Treaties, and this question was later the occasion for a great deal of bewildering argument. See the excellent discussion of the whole question in Karl Loewenstein, "The Bonn Constitution and the European Defense Community Treaties, a Study in Judicial Frustration," *Yale Law Journal*, LXIV (May, 1955), 805-39.

Rounding out the issues bearing on the new Bundesrat were those dealing with what persons might be assigned by their Länder to the Bundesrat, and with the specific problem of the Bundesrat's power over federal legislation. In both these cases the groundwork had already been laid and the area of subsequent disagreement was more limited than had earlier been the case. It was already established, for example, in the matter of Bundesrat membership that only members of Land governments might be eligible for appointment. If eligible, Land Cabinet members could be named either "regular members" of the Bundesrat (*ordentliche Mitglieder*) or "deputy members" (*stellvertretende Mitglieder*). Concerning the legislative powers of the Bundesrat the issue of *Gleichberechtigung* had been settled, and it remained only to be determined what cases would require Bundesrat consent and which ones would not.

A major principle that had been urged by the SPD was that the Parliament (both houses) should be in close contact with the people, and that the appointment of civil servants to the Bundesrat would violate this principle. The Socialists had been severely critical of the tendency of the Reichsrat to open its doors to Land bureaucrats and to reduce itself to a narrow and inflexible body. Once agreement was reached that each Land's votes would be cast in bloc, it was further agreed that one responsible Minister might act for his Land and do the voting. As the concept of membership has developed in practice since 1949, the language and sense of Article 51 have been that only such persons having seats and votes in their respective Land Cabinets are eligible for membership in the Bundesrat as *ordentliche Mitglieder*. This has prompted Friedrich Giese to describe the Bundesrat as "a board of governments."[53] Most recently the member-

53. "Der Bundesrat ist ein Regierungskollegium, kein Abgeordnet-

ship Article has been understood to include Land Ministers and Minister-Presidents and, in the case of Hamburg and Bremen, *Bürgermeister* and *Senatoren*. The only exceptions are in the Bavarian and Baden-Württemberg Constitutions. In the former, State Secretaries might also be members; and in the latter, State Secretaries and State Councillors.[54] Particularly noteworthy is the fact that a strict reading of the term "membership" in the Bundesrat does not extend to its committees. Other persons (i.e., permanent civil servants from the Länder) might be commissioned *(Beauftragte)* to serve on the committees. This is a significant exception, especially in view of the importance of the committee deliberations on Bundesrat decisions.

On the matter of Bundesrat legislative strength the SPD had only been reconciled to the idea of a Bundesrat-type second chamber in the first place with the absolute proviso that in ordinary legislation it should have only a suspensive veto *(ein überwindbares Veto)*. In the Socialist view it would be sufficient for the Bundestag to muster an absolute majority of all members to overrule a Bundesrat objection. The CDU had wanted to require a three-fourths vote of all Bundestag members. The compromise version accorded closely with the position of the FDP: if the Bundesrat objection was adopted by a majority of its votes then a corresponding majority in the Bundestag was sufficient; and if the Bundesrat rejected a measure by two-thirds of its votes, then the Bundestag needed a two-thirds vote to overrule the protest. In the latter case at least a majority of the members of the

---

engremium; ihn bilden die Landesregierungen, nicht die Landtage." Friedrich Giese, *Grundgesetz für die Bundesrepublik Deutschland* (Frankfurt a/M, 1955), p. 91.

54. See the comment by Hans Schäfer, *Der Bundesrat* (Köln, 1955), p. 34. Schäfer says these exceptions are valid only when these functionaries enjoy the right to vote within their governments.

Bundestag was necessary.[55] The greater weight of the Bundesrat in legislation, however, lay not in its qualified *Vetorecht* but in the absolute requirement of its concurrence to a certain type of law: *Zustimmungsgesetze,* or laws which particularly affect Land interests in one way or another. These are discussed in the examination of procedural details of the following chapter.

55. Basic Law, Article 77, para. 4.

CHAPTER III

Bundesrat Folkways: Organization and Procedure

An initial examination of the German Parliament reveals that the Bundesrat exists as a federative organ, as opposed to the unitary reflection of the popularly representative Bundestag.[1] In the language of the Basic Law, "The Länder participate through the Bundesrat in the legislation and administration of the Federation."[2] Through the artful balancing of these two legislative chambers the republic of western Germany achieves at least formally the character of a *Bundesstaat*.

The periodic re-emergence of the Second Chamber's strength in Germany, as outlined in Chapter II, correlates more or less directly with the fortunes of federalism in that country. And nowadays one can speak of a genuine Second German Chamber, which within the shifting confines of its competence exercises joint control over federal

1. Land representation in the Bundesrat now is as follows:

Baden-Württemberg	5 votes
Bavaria	5
Bremen	3
Hamburg	3
Hesse	4
Lower Saxony	5
Northrhine-Westphalia	5
Rhineland-Palatinate	4
Schleswig-Holstein	4
Saarland	3
(Berlin Has 4 Non-Voting Seats.)	————
TOTAL:	41 votes

2. Basic Law, Article 50.

legislation. This is so despite the relative obscurity of the Bundesrat as a federal legislative agent; obscure, that is, from popular understanding in Germany. A sample of public opinion in 1956 indicated that 86 per cent of the respondents either had no idea of what the Bundesrat was or had vague or false impressions of it.[3] But even this was an improvement over earlier years. In 1950, for example, the same question drew a correct response from only 8 per cent. Perhaps this is just as well for members of the Bundesrat, for of respondents asked for their personal reactions to the Bundestag in 1950, 56 per cent responded unfavorably or were undecided.[4]

Probably a big part of the explanation for popular ignorance about the Bundesrat lies in the esoteric nature of its discussions and its exacting, business-like, and sometimes tedious debates. A glance at the Bundesrat Hall during a meeting of the Plenum would reveal a strong contrast to the vigorous partisan debates and limelight tactics of the *Parteifraktionen* in the Bundestag. Even the seating arrangement in the Bundesrat assembly hall is geared to the strict routine of business, with the Land representatives seated directly behind the senior delegates of the Länder, and with the Länder arranged alphabetically from left to right facing the permanent functionaries of the Chamber (i.e., the Presidium, committee secretaries, etc.).

But at least one other reason exists for the lack of public attention to Bundesrat activity. Though continously in session, the Bundesrat has been holding its plenary meetings more and more infrequently. This growing apparent inattention to federal legislation by the Bundesrat was explained by a Bundesrat official as

3. *Jahrbuch der öffentlichen Meinung,* 1956, edited by Elisabeth Noelle and Erich Reyer Neumann (Allensbach am Bodensee, 1957), p. 278.
4. *Ibid.,* 1949-1955, 1956 ed., p. 278.

primarily the result of an absolute decrease in the number of bills, regulations, etc., brought in by the Federal Government and the Bundestag; and secondarily as a result of streamlining the preparation and handling of bills so that a greater number can be discussed per session. Furthermore, close examination of reports of Bundesrat meetings indicates that at least as much time has been devoted to individual bills in the years after 1954 as before, even though the number of meetings diminished steadily after 1950. Consequently there is only feeble support for the conclusion that the Bundesrat has most recently shown a failing interest in federal legislation.[5]

The figures in Table II do permit the reasonable inference, however, that growing changes and readjust-

TABLE II

AN INDEX OF BUNDESRAT LEGISLATIVE
ACTIVITY, 1950-1960.[a]

	1949	1950	1951	1952	1953	1954	1955	1956	1957	1958	1959[b]
No. of meetings											
Plenary	10	34	33	23	19	17	17	18	17	14	8
Committee	30	206	237	213	155	134	145	174	142	121	72

[a] Compiled from *Statistik: Aus der Arbeit des Bundesrates* (Bonn, 1957); and *10 Jahre Bundesrat* Bonn, 1959).
[b] The figures for 1959 include meetings only up to July 10.

ments within the Bundesrat have made it possible for Land governments and their Bundesrat members to make strong representations in federal legislative processing without having to do so specifically in the plenum phase of the enactment process. Thus there has been a distinct

5. *10 Jahre Bundesrat* (Bonn, 1959), pp. 190-91. Arnold J. Heidenheimer infers from available statistics that after about 1953 the Bundesrat began paying less attention to its prerogatives in the decision-making process through legislation. See Arnold Heidenheimer, "Federalism and the Party System: the Case of West Germany," *The American Political Science Review*, LII (September, 1958), 824-25.

falling off of the practice of initiating legislative bills by the Bundesrat.

The official attitude of the Bundestag has always been that the Bundesrat is a permanent Länder "government conference" whose members are properly bound by the instructions of their respective governments. During the debates in the Bundestag over the Common Market proposals in 1957, for example, when the question came up whether the Bundesrat might send representatives to the Consultative Assembly (the Bundesrat had insisted on having 11 of 36 German seats), party leaders pointed out that the presence of 11 German representatives who were bound to instructions from their governments would violate the principle of popular election. And according to the Treaty the Consultative Assembly of the Economic Community was to consist of persons chosen by direct popular vote in their states. Speaking for the Bundestag viewpoint, Deputy Carlo Schmid reminded the Bundesrat that it was a purely federative organ and did not share in "national representation."[6]

The Articles of the Basic Law descriptive of the Bundesrat are Numbers 50-53, but their prescriptions and allowances are amplified in the Standing Orders of the Bundesrat *(Geschäftsordnung des Bundesrates)* which were approved and put into effect on July 31, 1953. The Bundesrat forms its conclusions and resolutions by at least a majority, in some cases a "special" (two-thirds) majority being necessary.[7] Normally the Bundesrat holds public meetings, but it is authorized to meet secretly. Its President is elected annually, and the practice has been followed of rotating the Presidency from Land to Land. Although it is rarely necessary, the Bundesrat President is empowered to maintain order and to eject from the

6. *Frankfurter Allgemeine Zeitung* (FAZ), July 20, 1957.
7. Basic Law, Article 52, para. 3.

meeting any person causing a disturbance. Every Land and all committees have the privilege of hearing expert advice from qualified sources, although too frequent exercise of this privilege is explicitly discouraged in the Standing Orders.[8]

Members of the Federal Government have the right to share in the deliberations of the Bundesrat and its committees, and on demand of the Bundesrat this becomes an obligation. Generally the Bundesrat is to be kept abreast of the direction of affairs by the Federal Government. In practice this has devolved primarily upon the office of the Federal Minister for Bundesrat Affairs. As will be seen below, the smooth flow of communications between the Federal Government and the Bundesrat and their mutual cooperation in legislative matters have been made necessary in the development of legislative responsibilities. This is especially true when the Government must rely on the cooperation of Land Ministries to enforce its policies, this being usually the case. Thus the Federal Government to a fair extent has followed the permissible practice of assigning deputized persons *(Beauftragte)*, usually civil servants from interested federal ministries, to participate in the deliberations of Bundesrat committees.[9]

The Basic Law makes a distinction between "exclusive" legislation *(ausschliesslich)*, for which only the Federal Parliament is competent, and "concurrent" legislation, for which both the Federation and the Land Parliaments are competent. Of exclusive legislative concern for the Federation are such problems as foreign affairs, citizenship, monetary matters and coinage, international travel, tariffs, border protection, highways, post-and

8. *Geschäftsordnung des Bundesrates (GeschO)*, Article 8.

9. See the comment by Theodor Eschenburg, *Staat und Gesellschaft in Deutschland* (Stuttgart, 1956), pp. 714-15; also Hans Schäfer, *Der Bundesrat* (Köln, 1955), pp. 48-50, 56.

airmail service, rights of federal civil servants, federal statistics, and others.[10] There is a much longer list of "concurrent" legislation, for which the Federation has priority by being itself able to determine when it will take advantage of its concurrent right in these matters.

In these concurrent areas, the Länder have the right to legislate only when and as far as the Federation does not use its legislative power and declines to pre-empt the field. The Federation can exercise this right when:[11]

(1) a matter cannot be effectively dealt with by Land legislation, or

(2) dealing with a matter by Land law might prejudice the interests of other Länder, or

(3) the maintenance of legal or economic unity, especially concerning uniform living conditions, requires it.

In this way federal supremacy in legislation is given constitutional sanction in the manner of the Weimar Republic, and the new Parliament is given an "inside track" to legislative areas which it ostensibly shares with the Länder. It was incidentally this division of legislative powers between Bonn and eleven Land capitals that caused the most serious rift at the Parliamentary Council between the Allied Military Governors and German party leaders, especially the SPD. This was especially true of the American and French Military Governors. In a memorandum of March 2, 1949, the Council was urged to make explicitly clear that the Federation would be entitled to exercise its "concurrent" powers only when it was "clearly impossible for a single Land to enact effective legislation. . . . ."[12]

10. Basic Law, Articles 73 and 105.
11. *Ibid.*, Article 72.
12. Text of the Memorandum is in United States Department of State Publication Number 3556, *Germany, 1947-1949: the Story in Documents*, European and British Commonwealth Series 9 (1950). See also Lucius Clay, *Decision in Germany* (Garden City, N. Y., 1950), pp.

By closing ranks the Germans managed to hold their own against the Military Governors on this matter; and although relations were strained throughout March and April, the original Main Committee draft was written into the Basic Law. It was unacceptable to the Germans that the projected Constitutional Court should become the arbiter of the federal system, which would have been the outcome under the Military Government plan. Rather this function had to be reserved for the Bundestag and Bundesrat.[13]

Apart from the legislative dualism urged by the Military Governors, which the German federalists themselves viewed as not well-suited to their federal tradition, another type of dualism was created to strengthen the Land Governments in another respect. The Basic Law provides, although in no single Article is this provision elucidated in detail, that certain kinds of laws passed by the Bundestag must have the concurrence of the Bundesrat *(Zustimmungsgesetze)*. Other, simple federal laws *(einfache Bundesgesetze)* do not require Bundesrat consent and are subject only to a suspensory veto.

In this manner the federal power balance is entrusted to the Bundesrat, and it is here that the bulk of the

---

421-25. General Clay's opinion was that the Basic Law as it came out of the Main Committee "... not only provided far too much centralization of authority but also failed to clearly distinguish between the responsibilities to be retained by the individual states and the responsibilities to be assumed by the federal government." For a critical commentary on the idea that a government is truly federal only when the central authority is limited to certain delegated functions, see Carl J. Friedrich and Herbert J. Spiro, "The Constitution of the German Federal Republic," in E. H. Litchfield (ed.), *Governing Postwar Germany* (Ithaca, N. Y., 1953), pp. 126-27.

13. See the statement by Walter Strauss (CDU) quoted in John Ford Golay, *The Founding of the Federal Republic of Germany* (Chicago, 1958), p. 61; see also the more general statement by Kurt Schumacher in *Parteien in der Bundesrepublik, Studien zur Entwicklung der deutschen Parteien bis zur Bundestagswahl 1953* (Stuttgart, 1955), pp. 235-36.

Bundesrat's legislative power is concentrated. This right of absolute veto is particularly important and binding in matters relating to the physical structure of the Federal Republic, the rights and competence of the Länder in administration (that is, the administration of federal laws), and their rights in the finance and tax fields.

That the *Zustimmungsgesetze* are not itemized in any one place in the Basic Law partially accounts for their elasticity. It must also be acknowledged that under the circumstances the Germans probably did not want to attract too much attention to them after the March intervention, and the list provided a handy "grab-bag" from which compromises that had been upset might be restored. They can only be found by an examination of all 146 Articles of the Basic Law, and in their appropriate chapters. By the end of 1959 there were 17 such law-types requiring Bundesrat consent. They are:

Article 29, Para. 7: the procedure for making territorial changes by federal law in any way other than that described in paragraphs 1-6.

Article 79, Para. 2: changes in the Basic Law.

Article 84, Para. 1: federal laws which establish administrative procedures other than those provided by the Länder in administering federal laws as matters of their own concern.

Article 84, Para. 5: federal laws authorizing the Federal Government to issue individual instructions for particular cases, normally to the highest Land authorities, unless urgency requires otherwise.

Article 85, Para. 1: federal laws authorizing the Federal Government, instead of the Länder, to regulate the establishment of agencies for the administration of federal laws.

Article 87, Para. 3: federal laws establishing federal authorities at intermediate and lower levels in case of urgent need arising from new federal functions.

*Article 87 B, Para. 1: federal laws assigning non-military tasks to the administration of the Federal Defense Forces; similarly federal laws empowering the administration of the Federal Defense Forces to interfere with rights of third parties, exclusive of personnel.

*Article 87 B, Para. 2: federal laws concerning defense matters which stipulate that they shall be carried out by the federal administrative sub-structure; or federal laws administered by the Länder as agents of the Federation which stipulate that the rights of the Federal Government and of the highest federal authorities as derived from Article 85 shall be transferred to the highest federal authorities.

Article 105, Para. 3: federal laws relating to taxes the yield of which accrues, wholly or in part, to the Länder or local communities.

Article 106, Para. 4: federal laws relating to financial equalization between the Federation and the Länder.

Article 106, Para. 5: federal laws to issue grants of money to the Länder in compensation for additional burdens on the Länder resulting from extra expenditures or the withdrawal of revenues.

Article 107, Para. 1: federal laws determining the allocation of local receipts from specific taxes.

Article 107, Para. 2: federal laws establishing financial equalization among the Länder.

Article 108, Para. 3: federal laws concerning the organization of Land finance authorities which regulate the procedure to be used by them and the uniform training of the civil servants.

Article 120a: federal laws concerning the equalization of burdens which are to be executed partly by the Federation and partly by the Länder acting as agents of the Federation.

Article 134, Para. 4: federal laws regulating the details of transferring unredeemed Land property from the Federation back to the Länder.

Article 135, Para. 5: federal laws regulating the details of

* Added by Amendment on March 19, 1956.

agreements among the Länder in the settlement of unredeemed property.

It would probably not be overstating the case to remark that the strength of federalism in Germany hinges on these laws and through them on the effective protection of Land prerogatives by the Bundesrat.

COMMITTEES

As in most other parliamentary bodies of the West, the role of committees in the Bundesrat is a strategic one.[14] But in the Bundesrat the standing committees assume an added importance and weight by the virtual identity, as a rule, of committee recommendations with the formal decisions of the Bundesrat Plenum. Because of the traditionally acknowledged reliance of administrators on expert advice and because of the pressing factor of limited time in most cases, an unusually heavy emphasis is placed on committee deliberation and study. Also, since a matter under concern has already been taken up in exhaustive detail in committee, discussions in the Bundesrat plenary sessions are not likely to be either long or searching. This is a conscious feature of the Bundesrat.

The apparent importance of committees can hardly be deduced from an examination of the Basic Law, which mentions them only in two particulars (Articles 52 and 53). On the other hand, of thirty-two Articles in the Standing Orders of the Bundesrat, scarcely half a dozen fail to mention the standing committees in any connection. Sixteen of the thirty-two are exclusively confined to describing committee rules, composition and procedures. The actual privileged and influential role of the committees lies in their strategic status as "stage men" in

14. For the growth of legislative committees in Germany see Bruno Dechamps, *Macht und Arbeit der Ausschüsse: Der Wandel der Parlamentarischen Willensbildung* (Meisenheim-Glan, 1954).

a situation where the principal players, being Land Ministers or Minister-Presidents, are necessarily required to spend most of their time looking after local obligations.

As of 1960, there were thirteen regular standing committees in the Bundesrat and two special standing committees, one for questions of the European Common Market and the Free Trade Zone and one for Reparations (1959). Every Land is represented on each of these by one of its Bundesrat members or "someone else acting as an agent of its government."[15] The Land governments are required to select, for their "regular committee members," only their Bundesrat members and deputy members, both of whom must be members of their Land governments and therefore responsible to their respective *Landtage*. But they are permitted, and this has almost invariably been the case, to pick senior civil servants from the appropriate ministries as "deputy committee members." This practice of attaching field-experienced Land ministerial people to the appropriate Bundesrat committees has the obvious advantage that the esoteric knowledge of technical experts from Land bureaucracies can be made available for the vital work of the committees, while at the same time these ministerial representatives and department heads can profit from the committee discussions.

An additional result, whether advantageous or not for parliamentary life in western Germany, is that the committee voice is a highly skilled and authoritative one. Land conditions usually make it necessary for Bundesrat members to remain permanently in their Land capitals, attending the meetings of their assigned committees only irregularly. So authorized Land deputies who are permanently settled in Bonn as "deputy committee members" exercise a forceful and continuous influence on committee actions.

15. *GeschO*, Bundesrat, Article 15.

One is not particularly surprised, therefore, that virtually all decisions and resolutions of the Bundesrat are based on committee recommendations, and the voting can be expected to follow accordingly. Even a hasty examination of the stenographic reports of the Bundesrat illustrates the almost complete monopoly which the committees hold over Bundesrat resolutions. It is rare that the plenary body deviates from the specifications of its committees, even in the important matter of calling the *Vermittlungsausschuss,* a joint committee of two houses for settling differences between them.[16] This fact must not be understood to mean that Land votes are in any way bound to committee decisions. The Land representatives are bound only to votes made in their respective Land Cabinets, and the work in committee is of a preliminary nature. The question rather is how coercive, in fact, are the expert views of committee members on the decisions of their formal leaders in the Land cabinets? This question is taken up in some detail in a later chapter.

The routine aspects of committee procedure are described in Articles 15-23 of the Bundesrat's Standing Orders. It is important to recognize that each Land has only one vote, so that in committee the principle of Land equality is preserved literally. Frequently more than one person from a single Land will attend a committee meeting. The Standing Orders also permit attendance at committee meetings by Bundesrat members who are not members of that committee, as well as by other agents *(Beauftragte)* of the Land governments.[17]

Further specifications of the Standing Orders serve to expedite the work of committees for plenary con-

16. Hans Nawiasky, *Grundgedanken des Grundgesetzes für die Bundesrepublik Deutschland* (Stuttgart, 1951), pp. 56-57. Although this writer's analysis only accounts for the first year of Bundesrat procedure, subsequent practice did not materially change.
17. *GeschO,* Article 18.

venience, and to effect a timely termination of study so that actual decisions in the Land Cabinets will be possible and then made available for the plenary meeting. This is the purpose, for example, of Article 21, which requires the committees to have completed their debates by Thursday of the week preceding the next plenary meeting of the Bundesrat. On the following day (Friday) the Secretariat is obliged to make the results of these talks available to the office of the plenipotentiaries of the Länder in Bonn. Although the Standing Orders authorize the practice of common deliberations by more than one committee, not very extensive use is made of it. Rather one standing committee with specialized competence is given responsibility for a measure and makes its report singly, while occasionally concurrent talks are held on the measure by another interested committee. On the other hand committees frequently resort to the formation of sub-committees, especially when the measure is important and deserves specialized treatment.[18] Express provision for creation of sub-committees does not appear in the Standing Orders, but no objections have been raised against it.

A SKETCH OF LEGISLATIVE PROCEDURE

In order to understand fully the formal legislative role of the Bundesrat a rough description of the procedures followed in passing bills through the Bundesrat will be necessary. The Land chamber has a limited number of opportunities for channeling bills this way or that, and each opportunity tends to suggest varying degrees of legislative activism by the Bundesrat. These will be discussed under four major headings below.

18. This has been the habit, for instance, of finance and budget bills. See Schäfer, *Des Bundesrat,* p. 50; and Eschenburg, *Staat und Gesellschaft,* p. 630.

A potential source of confusion about Bundesrat procedure is the generally accepted terminology of "first passage" *(erster Durchgang)* and "second passage" *(zweiter Durchgang)*. Although in a strict parliamentary sense the Bundesrat acts but once on any measure, on some measures (measures introduced by the Federal Government) it is expected to take a modified form of action before the official passage of those measures through the Bundesrat. While not all persons accept the term "first passage" as quite accurate for this preliminary action,[19] it is often the occasion for a strong position by the Bundesrat vis-à-vis the Federal Government. Sometimes the desired effects have been secured before the measure is put before the Bundestag for the first time. Thus, as had been the practice with the Weimar Parliament, the Second Chamber is given the right of first examining all bills originating from the Government.[20]

Admittedly the term "first passage" is somewhat pretentious, suggesting that the Bundesrat has a doubly influential role in legislative matters. But that is perhaps not far wrong, and anyway the term is used by members of both Bundesrat and Bundestag and in most of the literature covering the subject. The idea of a prior consideration of certain bills is an old German legislative habit, and today as earlier it reflects for the most part the relationship of shared executive power existing between the Bundesrat and the Federal Government.

GESETZESINITIATIVE AND ERSTER DURCHGANG

The coupling of the Bundesrat's right to initiate laws with that of the Federal Government was not fortuitous. A major characteristic of German constitutions has been

19. Nawiasky, *Grundgedanken des Grundgesetzes*, pp. 118ff., finds the term misleading and prefers to speak instead of a "Vorstadium."
20. *Reichsverfassung* (Weimar), Article 69.

that the *Bund* and the Länder are made interdependent in the initiation of laws. The language of Article 76 of the Basic Law explicitly eliminates the direct introduction of bills into the Bundestag by either the Bundesrat or the Government:

2. Bills of the Federal Government shall be submitted first to the Bundesrat. The Bundesrat is entitled to state its position on these bills within three weeks.

3. Bills of the Bundesrat shall be submitted to the Bundestag by the Federal Government. In doing so the Federal Government must state its own views.

Thus the right to initiate legislation by the Federal Government on the one hand, and by the Bundesrat on the other, are inseparably linked. The three-week interval specified in Paragraph 2 for Bundesrat examination of Government bills is the period of the so-called "first passage." To the extent that the Bundesrat enjoys a legislative initiative it does so as an organ of the Federation, not as a college of Land government officials. The absence of clarity in this procedure, however, tends to make the whole matter somewhat obscure. Quite often Land proposals are introduced into the Bundesrat that raise the highly technical question whether they are to be understood as falling under the *Initiativrecht,* and therefore subject to Bundesrat initiation procedure. The practice has been to assign proposals of the Länder *(Vorschläge)* which have as their clear intention the use of the Bundesrat's *Gesetzesinitiativerecht* to standing committees as "subject-matter parliamentary bills" *(Vorlage)* and to decide later within the Bundesrat Plenum and on the basis of committee recommendations whether this makes use of the *Gesetzesinitiative.* This would appear to be an overworked proposition, except that the question has been raised repeatedly and raises important issues of procedure.

The same subtlety of differentiation holds true for proposals to change the Basic Law. Amendments to the Constitution require a favorable two-thirds vote in both houses of the West German Parliament.[21] On the other hand, unlike the earlier Weimar Reichsrat, only a simple majority is necessary for the Bundesrat to propose a change in the Basic Law. Presumably a proposal for constitutional change that passed the Bundesrat by a slender majority would not be likely, except under substantially altered circumstances, to win the necessary two-thirds margin when the Bundesrat voted conclusively on the matter. But this ignores the possibility that between the first and second passages an important realignment of interested parties could occur to affect the fortunes of the anticipated change.

René Allemann has suggested that the Bundestag could be easily induced to hold off on a proposed change that had left the Bundesrat with a narrow majority until changes at the Land government level had set the matter straight by bringing in the necessary number of friendly votes.[22] This is especially feasible since the composition of the Bundesrat, unlike that of the Bundestag, varies from time to time with changes in the Land governments. The staggering of Land elections from year to year, with the concomitant result of a more or less regular ministerial reshuffling in the Länder, is unlikely to yield a consistent front of political sympathies in the Bundesrat. The immediate result is at least a good possibility of reversals. Furthermore, a change in the position of individual Land governments, particularly Cabinets that had been wavering on the issue, could take place within the second passage itself. In all cases, decisive action by the Bundesrat

21. Basic Law, Article 79.
22. Fritz René Allemann, *Bonn ist nicht Weimar* (Köln, 1956), p. 359.

comes after the measure has been voted on in the Bundestag, and this fact encourages the Bundestag to exercise some latitude in timing its Bundesrat relations.

That proposals of the Bundesrat are delivered to the Bundestag by the Government indicates a genuine legal obligation here for the Federal Government, although this obligation is not spelled out in the Basic Law. Should the Government disagree with the substance of the proposal, then it might state its own views; but it cannot ignore its obligation to make the delivery. For the processing of Bundesrat *Vorlagen* by the Federal Government the Basic Law makes no clear statement about time limits. There seems to be consensus that the Government should "allow itself time" *(sich Zeit lassen)* to ponder the matter to its satisfaction.[23]

The purpose of Article 76 relating to Bundesrat *Vorlagen* can only be to give the Bundestag, for the first time that chamber is concerned with the measure, the Government's opinion along with the proposal itself. In some cases, if the Federal Government intends to propose a measure dealing with the same thing but varying from the Bundesrat plan, then it is appropriate for the Government to hold back the proposal of the Länder. Such was the case, for example, involving the Bundesrat's initial draft of a Bavarian proposal to change the Reinstatement Act of 1951, which had been passed on to the Federal Government by a vote of 34 to 9.[24] The measure was to extend the interval from three months to a year between the beginning effectiveness of the law and compliance with its terms by the Land governments. Ultimately the Bundesrat accepted in first passage another measure of the Federal Government changing the time interval to

23. Hans Kutscher, "Verfassungsrechtliche Fragen aus der Arbeit des Bundesrates," *Die öffentliches Verwaltung*, 1952, pp. 717-19.
24. Bundesrat *Sitzungsberichte*, 57. Sitz., May 25, 1951, p. 346.

six months, the Government having withheld the Bundesrat proposal until its own version had been completed in draft form.

In view of the general, if sometimes contrived, atmosphere of cooperation between the Federal Government and the Bundesrat, it has rarely been found necessary to issue a complaint in this regard. In one instance, however, the Bundesrat Judiciary Committee *(Rechtsausschuss)* in its 121st meeting of June 11, 1953, unanimously held the view that the Federal Government had not, after four months, fulfilled its obligation under Article 76 within a "reasonable" span of time.[25] At issue was the draft of a Federal Compensation Law which had been released by the Bundesrat on February 20, 1953.[26]

The three-week interval of first passage originates from a similar provision in the Weimar Constitution, although doubts developed in the 1920's about whether the Government could send bills to the *Reichstag* without the consent of the *Reichsrat*.[27] The possibility of a recurrence of doubts was obviated in the Basic Law with the simple requirement that in first passage there is to be a "formal position" *(Stellungnahme)* by the Bundesrat. To pick at this point just a bit, it is not in fact necessary for the Bundesrat to make a statement every time. Rather its *Stellungnahme* can be to decline to take a position. Otherwise there are three possible alternatives:

(1) It can concur with the Government proposal (that is, it raises no objection to Government proposals); (2) it

25. Report of the *Rechtsausschuss* in the Bundesrat *Sitzungsberichte, 110. Sitz.*, June 23, 1953, p. 285.

26. In this same connection, as Chancellor Adenauer said in a letter to the President of the Bundesrat of September 11, 1953, the Federal Government shared the view of the Bundesrat, whereby their legislative proposals had to be delivered within a reasonable span of time; and this might be understood to be one in which the Federal Government can normally be expected to take a competent position on the measure.

27. Article 69 stated: "The introduction of bills by the government of

can suggest changes in Government proposals, which if made are at least a likely indication of what the Bundesrat's attitude will be in second passage; and (3) it can disapprove the measure outright, which would serve to put the Government on notice of Bundesrat opposition.

Cases in which the Bundesrat makes suggestions in the way of proposed changes are quite frequent. Even within the three-week period the Bundesrat does not confine itself to a general examination. Often the Land representatives make some positive and specific suggestions for improvement here, clarity there; and they can be expected normally to make pointed complaints and to make their wishes known. This arises partly from the fact that Government bills are sent promptly to the appropriate standing committees for specialized and competent scrutiny, and that most of the allotted time is dedicated to committee work on the measure.

In this way the administrative experience of the Länder is brought into play, although it can be strongly argued that the more important consequence for parliamentary vitality in Germany is the development through this practice of a ministerial bureaucracy closely attuned to its own convenience in the formulation of laws. Occasionally instead of making one or several specific suggestions on a number of smaller matters relating to the bigger issue, the Bundesrat will collect all its impressions into the form of a new draft. Article 76 says nothing about the form and content of the Bundesrat's *Stellungnahme,* and there is no question that the Bundesrat, if it is thought desirable, may discard the existing draft to draw up a new one covering the same material. In that case the Federal

the Reich requires the consent of the Reich Council. If no agreement is reached between the Reich Government and the Reich Council, the Reich Government may introduce the bill notwithstanding, but must state the contrary opinion of the Reich Council."

Government is still obligated to deliver the new draft to the Bundestag with a representation of its own views. This was what happened, for example, during the controversy over the application of the Codetermination Laws to holding companies in the Ruhr. In this particular instance it was the Government draft which was passed into law ultimately, but the Bundesrat version was duly considered, and according to former Land Minister Karl Siemsen, most of the important suggestions for change were incorporated into the final arrangements.[28]

The *Stellungnahme* can furthermore be a recommendation to the Federal Government to issue a new draft-law, or to withdraw the present one and reintroduce it later after specific changes. In this case the Federal Government is under no legal constraint to comply. On the contrary, if the Federal Ministry deems that the action of the Bundesrat to prolong work on the measure is inconsistent with the design of the Basic Law, then it can persist by pushing its original version. The Government can do so of course only by representing the Bundesrat position before the Bundestag.

In this connection a rather lively exchange took place in 1952 between the Bundesrat and the Federal Finance Ministry. The Bundesrat received in first passage a Government draft of a law to control venereal disease by various licensing methods. The decision of the Bundesrat here was not to debate the merits of the measure, but simply to forward to the Federal Government the results of committee deliberations as well as all specific proposals of the Land Cabinets for a new draft-law. This was the first passage outcome, and this was the Bundesrat's *Stellungnahme*. In the 181st plenary meeting of the Bundesrat in March, 1952, the venerable Dr. Spiecker

28. See the statement by Siemsen (Northrhine-Westphalia) in Bundesrat *Sitzungsberichte, 161. Sitz.,* June 29, 1956, p. 239.

(Northrhine-Westphalia) responded heartily to anonymous charges made within the Federal Government about Bundesrat "obstructionism." Spiecker was referring to an article written in the *Bulletin* of the Government's Press and Information Department entitled "Finanzpolitische Mitteilungen des Bundesministeriums der Finanzen." He reminded the unnamed writer of the article that the position of the Bundesrat in this case was taken, as always, only after the most careful examination in the competent committee and in the Land Cabinets; and furthermore that it was done in the interest of the whole republic. Spiecker said the Bundesrat had to be cautious with Government measures, since it assumed joint responsibility for them when they left the Bundesrat for the Bundestag as "acceptable pending final adjustments."[29]

Instances have occurred in which the Bundesrat availed itself of this device to recommend reformulation of a draft, and in so doing touched off a storm of political controversy. When the Adenauer Government introduced its Volunteers Bill to the Bundesrat for first passage in May, 1955, the unanimous reaction of the Bundesrat was to send the bill back to the Chancellery as unsatisfactory and to request a new one.[30] Chancellor Adenauer's move was obviously designed to augment Germany's new defense commitment to general European security, and his bill therefore reflected his concern for haste. But unlike most matters of concern to the Land governments, this

29. This is a summary of Dr. Spiecker's much longer statement. Relative to the responsibility of the Bundesrat in First Passage bills and in acting on Government Rechtsverordnungen, Spiecker said: "Zustimmung des Bundesrates heisst doch, dass der Bundesrat ausdrücklich zum gesamten Inhalt einer Vorlage Ja sagen muss. Der Bundesrat muss mithin den gesamten Inhalt zustimmungsbedürftiger Verordnungen eingehend prüfen; denn durch sein Ja übernimmt der Bundesrat zusammen mit der Bundesregierung die Verantwortung für den ganzen Inhalt." *Ibid.*, p. 131.

30. *Ibid.*, *142. Sitz.*, June 10, 1955, pp. 134-141.

issue had enormous partisan and international implications. Arguments used for one purpose in the Bundesrat were picked up and used for quite another in the Bundestag to the advantage of the Opposition SPD. Ultimately the Federal Government accepted the Bundesrat's demands and formulated another, more circumspect, measure.

From this incident one might conclude that what the Bundesrat does in first passage can be of overriding concern to all involved, and it could also be the occasion for a major concession to the Länder for the Federal Government, especially if the Government is caught in a politically vulnerable spot. The Volunteers Bill was such an occasion. At the same time, however, the Bundesrat must take its position within the prescribed time limits, and the three-week period does not always afford the opportunity for close scrutiny. The first passage interval of Article 76 cannot be prolonged, and an overdue *Stellungnahme* does not require the Government to wait. Sometimes this rigid time allocation works such a hardship on the Land representatives that the Bundesrat is reduced to arriving at a preliminary *Stellungnahme* within the required time. Then later it would offer a more complete one. Then it becomes a "command of loyalty" for the Government to deliver this later one to the Bundestag.[31] Since this is only the merest formality, there is normally no reason for the Government to balk; and otherwise, Bundesrat members could only resort to their right to be heard in the Bundestag personally as guaranteed in the Basic Law. This last eventuality would seriously strain the tight routine of the members of that chamber.

Evidently the time element could be the source of

31. Thus the Bundesrat sent the Government only a "preliminary" statement, then a detailed one later, on the Reinstatement Act of 1951 and on the Special Codetermination Law for Coal, Iron and Steel. See Schäfer, *Der Bundesrat*, p. 71.

a good many headaches and long hours for Bundesrat members. In order to acquit themselves of first passage adequately and to make an effective representation before the Government when that is felt necessary, they have developed several techniques to apply appropriate administrative knowledge to individual problems with maximum speed. Probably the most important way by which the Bundesrat manages to stay abreast of the accumulation of Government bills is by giving the standing committees the bulk of the three weeks within which to consider them. This practice has to some extent required the cooperation of the Federal Government. Since the time interval begins with the actual appearance of the bill before the Bundesrat, and since the Bundesrat meets normally on Fridays, the Government usually sends its bills to the Bundesrat on Fridays. In this way most of the allotted time can be devoted to expert consultations.

Another means by which the stricture of time is accommodated is by the free and frequent participation of Land ministers in law-making plans of the Federal Ministries. The Bundesrat Secretariat reports that customarily the Federal Ministry for Bundesrat Affairs notifies the Land representatives of planning sessions, and that Land ministers are invited to attend.[32] But even here the routine is usually no more than a briefing by a Federal minister of the corresponding Land minister, who is then expected to inform the other Land ministers of what is being done. Additionally, it is evidently with the need for haste in mind that the Standing Orders require all standing committees to have completed their deliberations on Thursday of the week preceding the next plenary assembly of the Bundesrat.[33]

In connection with the Bundesrat's examination of

32. *Die Bundesrepublik*, 1956-1957 (Berlin, 1958), p. 205.
33. Article 21.

Government bills, the experience of the first legislative period (1949-1953) raised some doubt about the "unchangeability of the vote" (*Unverrückbarkeit des Votums*) after first passage. Although the decision of the Bundesrat in second passage is considered definitive, the question has come up whether the Federal Government could deliver to the "new" Bundestag, without renewed consideration by the Bundesrat, a bill on which the Bundesrat had already taken a *Stellungnahme*. The Adenauer Government hedged on this question somewhat, enabling the Bundesrat Judiciary Committee to clear up the matter. The position of the committee has been that, from the principle of "discontinuity of the Bundestag," the expiration of an electoral period necessarily gives the Bundesrat the right (Articles 50 and 76) to re-examine all Government measures on which the Bundesrat had ruled before their delivery to the "new" Bundestag.[34]

ZUSTIMMUNGSBEDÜRFTIGKEIT

Once the decision was made in the Parliamentary Council not to endow the Upper House with legislative powers equal to those of the popular chamber, it became of strategic importance when the Bundesrat veto was to be absolute and when only suspensory. So the distinction was made between *Zustimmungsgesetze,* which are subject to an absolute Bundesrat veto because they directly affect Land interests, and *einfache Bundesgesetze,* which are "simple federal laws" and are subject only to a suspensory veto. The *Zustimmungsgesetze* are sometimes called "federative," as opposed to "federal" laws; and through them the substantive (mostly administrative) rights of the Länder are protected by the Bundesrat against federal encroachment.

34. Bundesrat *Rechtsausschuss, 129. Sitz., Kurzprotokoll,* p. 26.

A close examination of legislative records indicates that this "restricted" power of the Bundesrat to control legislation has in fact proved to be quite extensive. Perhaps the most important explanation for this has been the necessity for its concurrence to laws enabling the Federal Government, instead of the Länder, to regulate the establishment and procedures of (Land) administrative agencies that will execute the federal laws as matters of their own concern.[35] The figures in Table III, showing

TABLE III
TYPES OF BILLS REACHING
SECOND PASSAGE STAGE[a]

	Government Bills	Bundestag Bills	Bundesrat Bills
Zustimmungsbedürftige Gesetze	385	174	13
Nicht Zustimmungsbedürftige Gesetze	395	110	7
TOTALS	780	284	20

[a] Compiled from *Handbuch des Bundesrates* (Teil II), (Darmstadt, 1958), 94-98.

the types of bills entering the Bundesrat between September 7, 1949, and March 28, 1958, indicate that more than half of the bills reaching the second passage stage are of the type requiring Bundesrat concurrence. Thus of a total of 1,084 bills considered in the Bundesrat in second passage, 572 of them, or 52.8 per cent, were bills requiring its consent for passage. Furthermore these figures do not suggest the heavy political weight that measures of this type carry individually. Excluding purely foreign questions, and there are many exceptions in that area,[36] virtually all phases of federal policy come within

35. Basic Law, Article 84, para. 1.
36. Laws concerning foreign affairs, treaties, etc., can also be *zustimmungsbedürftig*, depending on whether the treaties themselves or

the category of *Zustimmungsbedürftigkeit* at one time or another.

That the Federal Government has been the only organ to introduce a preponderance of laws not requiring Bundesrat concurrence is mostly accounted for by its primary concern for foreign and defense policies, much of which does not affect the Land governments directly. The Federal Government has also led in promoting legislation to cover fields that are generally removed from questions of Federal-Land relations. The overall picture of Bundesrat prerogatives in legislation is nevertheless impressive. This is particularly noteworthy in view of the fact that the Parliamentary Council appears to have expected the *Zustimmungsgesetze* to be the exception rather than the rule.[37]

The development since 1949 of attitudes in the Bundesrat toward Article 84, Para. 1, has been important in this regard. This Article states: "If the Länder execute federal laws as matters of their own concern, they provide for the establishment of authorities and the regulation of administrative procedures insofar as federal laws consented to by the Bundesrat do not otherwise provide." As more and more federal legislative measures sought to provide centrally directed administration by regulating the creation of new Land administrative agencies and by fixing administrative procedures to be followed by existing Land organizations, the Bundesrat came more into the picture as an equally determinate body in federal legislation.

---

the implementing legislation contains provisions falling under Art. 84, para. 1; Art. 105, para. 3, etc.

37. See the comment by John Ford Golay, *The Founding of the Federal Republic*, p. 110; also *Entstehungsgeschichte der Artikel des Grundgesetzes, in Aufträge der Abwicklungsstelle des Parlamentarischen Rates und des Bundesministers des Innern auf Grund der Verhandlungen des Parlamentarischen Rates, Neue Folge* (Tübingen, 1951), pp. 379-97.

Interpretation of this Article in the Basic Law has led in the recent past to serious divergencies of opinion between the Bundesrat on the one hand and the Federal Government, occasionally also the Bundestag, on the other. Arguments between the Government and the Bundesrat about Article 84 are generally reflections of a broader difference between their respective understandings of *Zustimmungsbedürftigkeit*. The stenographic reports of Bundesrat meetings abound with cases in which the Bundesrat resolutely decided that the bill under question was a *Zustimmungsgesetz,* and to which a Federal minister present (or often a federal civil servant obediently reflecting the views of his superiors) disagreed. These questions can only be decided in the last analysis by the Federal Constitutional Court at Karlsruhe.

One writer has suggested that Article 84 is "the great opening wedge" through which the Bundesrat has cultivated a role in legislation which in fact equals that of the Bundestag.[38] But other arguments, such as that by Harry Rohwer-Kahlmann, hold that the result has been quite the reverse. Rohwer-Kahlmann illustrates convincingly that it has been with the assistance of Article 84 that the Bundestag, normally with the blessings of the Federal Government, has vigorously pursued a series of measures whose purpose is to reduce substantially the constitutional rights of the Länder in contravention of the Basic Law. This idea rests on non-legal premises, suggesting that the national political parties have effected a high degree of uniformity among their Land components and have required them to concur in the Bundesrat with measures that lead toward a transformation of the Länder into "districts" for legislative purposes.[39]

38. Hans Schneider, "Die Zustimmung des Bundesrates zu Gesetzen," *Deutsche Verwaltung* (1953), p. 257.
39. Harry Rohwer-Kahlmann, *"Verfassungsrechtliche Schranken der*

This same controversy has another side, one that is more than faintly reminiscent of the legal hair-splitting characteristic of earlier German political thought. The question has been raised among German publicists whether the application of Article 84, para. 1 to federal laws gives the Bundesrat a right to veto the whole measure, or just those parts of it which involve either the establishment of new Land agencies (*Einrichtung der Behörden*) or the fixing of administrative procedures (*Verwaltungsverfahren*). Schneider, for example, insisted that the Bundesrat has only a suspensory veto over the material content of such laws, and that they are to be split into two parts in the abstract. But he had to acknowledge the difficulties in trying to make such a distinction effective when he said:[40] "Where the *zustimmungsbedürftigen* parts of a law stand in an inseparable connection with the other provisions, then the question of concurrence must be settled at the outset."

Actually the Federal Government has occasionally tried to make exactly this distinction by introducing different laws, one for the substance and one for the procedure, to cover the same problem. Despite this infrequent effort the Bundesrat has regularly taken advantage of Article 84 to apply its right of concurrence to the stuff of such laws. And in this way the expanse of Bundesrat coverage of the field of legislation has been greatly extended. The conclusion can be drawn from this that the Bundesrat has in fact gone a long way toward the achievement of *Gleichberechtigung,* and that in a very real sense the Bundesrat has been elevated to a status which it was denied in 1949.[41]

Zustimmungsgesetze (Artikel 84 abs. 1 GG)," *Archiv des öffentlichen Rechts,* Bd. 79, 208 ff.

40. Schneider, "Die Zustimmung des Bundesrates," p. 261.

41. This is the point of view of Bavarian Minister-President Hans Ehard in "Aufgabe und Bewährung des Deutschen Bundesrats,"

VERMITTLUNGSAUSSCHUSS AND EINSPRUCH

The Bundesrat may, within two weeks of the receipt of the adopted [by the Bundestag] bill, demand that a committee for joint consideration of bills, composed of members of the Bundestag and Bundesrat, be convened. The composition and the procedure of this committee are regulated by rules of procedure adopted by the Bundestag and requiring the consent of the Bundesrat. The members of the Bundesrat on this committee are not bound by instructions. If the consent of the Bundesrat is required for a law, the demand for convening this committee may also be made by the Bundestag or the Federal Government. Should the committee propose any amendment to the adopted bill, the Bundestag must again vote on the bill.[42]

With this simple and unequivocal language the Basic Law introduced a new technique into German political life—the technique of formal parliamentary compromise. The incorporation of a *Vermittlungsausschuss* (Joint Mediation Committee), symbolic of the calculated dualism in the legislative process, replaced the discredited mechanism of the referendum, which had existed during Weimar days as a last-ditch solution when a legislative deadlock occurred. Having no precedent anywhere in earlier German experience, the *Vermittlungsausschuss* bears a faint resemblance to the Conference Committee institution of the United States Congress. Like its American cousin, the competence of the Joint Committee is confined to working out conflicts over measures between the two legislative houses. But unlike the American example the German Committee must serve two chambers

Presseveröffentlichungen über den Bundesrat (Number 126), March 20, 1961, esp. pp. 29-37. See also Golay, *The Founding of the Federal Republic*, pp. 110-11; Jakob Kratzer, "Zustimmungsgesetze," *Archiv des öffentlichen Rechts*, vol. 77, 271; and Karlheinz Neunreither, "Politics and Bureaucracy in the West German Bundesrat," *American Political Science Review*, LIII (December, 1959), 718-19.

42. Basic Law, Article 77.

having totally different make-up, possessing ostensibly different if not conflicting interests, and not sharing quite equally in legislative power.

As stated above, any of the three formal participants in law-making can demand a meeting of the Committee under certain conditions. It would seem, however, that the Bundesrat has the advantage of access to the Committee under any circumstances, whereas the Federal Government and Bundestag may demand a meeting only when necessary Bundesrat concurrence has been denied. Since 1950 it has been accepted practice that the Bundesrat can call the Joint Committee to consider laws that require its consent as well as simple federal laws. Most observers agree, however, that the Bundesrat is only likely to call the Joint Mediation Committee on a *Zustimmungsgesetz* if it feels that its desires for change are likely of adoption. In fact it has been generally successful in this respect.[43] Of seventy cases during the first legislative period in which the Bundesrat demanded a meeting of the *Vermittlungsausschuss*, no less than sixty-five of them were to make specific changes, sometimes detailed but not trivial.[44] Obviously the purpose of this institution is either to obviate the necessity for the protest *(Einspruch)* procedure in Article 77 of the Basic Law, or to facilitate Bundesrat concurrence when that has been earlier denied in the record vote during second passage.

The size of the Joint Committee has always corresponded with the number of German Länder. Since 1957, therefore, with the incorporation of Saarland into the Federation, there have been eleven members and

43. Franz Wessel, "Der Vermittlungsausschuss nach Artikel 77 des Grundgesetzes," *Archiv des öffentlichen Rechts, Bd. 77*, 283 ff., also Kratzer, Zustimmungsgesetze," p. 276.

44. Bundesrat *Statistik: Aus der Arbeit des Bundesrates*, (Bonn, 1958); also Schäfer, *Der Bundesrat*, p. 77.

eleven deputy members from each chamber.[45] Ostensibly these persons are assembled to exercise independent powers of arbitration. As with standing committees in the Bundesrat, the development has been that each Land sends one member (and one deputy member); but this committee differs from regular standing Bundesrat committees in that as a rule only "regular members" of the Bundesrat are assigned.[46] As of October, 1960, the Bundestag's membership on the Committee consisted of six CDU/CSU Deputies, four Socialists and one Free Democrat, with a similar list of deputy members.

As an integral part of German legislative machinery the Joint Committee is commonly expected by both houses to conform to certain standards. In case a meeting is called by demand of the Federal Government (i.e., following the denial of concurrence by the Bundesrat to a *Zustimmungsgesetz)* the Committee must effectively resolve the outstanding conflicts in the desires of the two chambers. To this extent the Joint Committee members find themselves having to assume responsibility for authoritatively displacing the work of many committee meetings and plenary discussions and then having to put the matter up for renewed debate. Still the Committee is no "third house" in the sense that it can act on its own initiative or can exercise free judgment. Only in a formal way are the products of its agreements independent judgments. Rather they are proposals *(Vorschläge)* which must be re-submitted to both houses, and under anything but the most auspicious circumstances having to arrive at a common proposal could be an unpleasant task. Reporters from the Committee are chosen respectively from the Bundestag and Bundesrat. Owing to the requirements

45. *Geschäftsordnung des Vermittlungsausschusses* in *Handbuch des Bundesrates (Teil I),* 132-34.

46. This of course does not mean that civil servants are never in attendance.

of secrecy each reporter is required to make an oral representation to his parent chamber with only the most general references to debates within the Committee. Anticipation of the Committee's report can be the cause for concern among its members, and this fact seriously qualifies the presumed independence of the members in their task of mediation. They can be understood to act independently only after it is recognized that they must offer a solution which will be neither rejected nor will bring into question their standing in their respective chambers.

There has been some vaporous and speculative reasoning about the authority of the *Vermittlungsausschuss* to exert influence directly and indirectly upon the two houses of Parliament. Franz Wessel, for example, observes that the Joint Mediation Committee is no *Fachausschuss*, that its members are not specialist; and that hence, having no extraordinary expertise, its members must be expected to have a "general competence" to redirect the course of legislative action.[47] It was incumbent upon the Committee from its inception to create a mutual feeling of genuine confidence and trust among its members and to make of itself a suitable climatic force for the furtherance of the conciliatory spirit. Composition of the Committee, therefore, had to be as fixed as possible in order to avoid unnecessary and disruptive fluctuations in Committee membership. Thus Section 4 of the Committee's Standing Orders states that a member of the Committee or his deputy representative may be recalled, but that only four such changes are permissable for each member within a single legislative period. Serious doubts have been raised in the past as to

47. Wessel, "Der Vermittlungsausschuss nach Artikel 77," pp. 283-84; also Wolf von der Heide, "Der Vermittlungsausschuss, Praxis und Bewährung," *Die öffentliches Verwaltung*, 1953, p. 131.

the adequacy of this provision for preserving steady continuity in membership.[48] Whereas the Bundestag has only rarely made membership changes, frequent government changes in the Länder have resulted in a rather unstable list of Bundesrat members from year to year. Furthermore, as von der Heide points out, the temporary replacement of a regular member by his deputy requires only that the member fail to appear for a meeting.

The Standing Orders of the Bundestag now make changes somewhat more difficult for that house. Previously (before adoption on December 6, 1951, of the Standing Orders now in effect) the members of the *Vermittlungsausschuss* from the Bundestag were selected according to the d'Hondt system by the President of the Chamber. They are currently chosen directly by the house itself. It was anticipated from this that the Committee's continuity of attitude (*Stetigkeitsgesichtspunkt*) would be stronger than it had been earlier. The suggestion was frequently made that the Bundesrat as a matter of course adopt the policy that no more than one change be made within one legislative period.[49] According to the argument, the Committee would thus be sustained by both sides as a forceful and independently operating institution.

In addition to the factor of personnel variance in membership, the matter of the apparent independence of the Committee's members is another matter of dubious aspect. The simple affirmation of release from instructions cannot be understood to alter completely or even importantly a Bundesrat member's commitment to his chamber. Of course, the habit of holding these members absolutely bound to their Land government positions on particular measures would eliminate the practical utility of a compromise agency such as the *Vermittlungsaus-*

48. Von der Heide, "Der Vermittlungausschuss," p. 130
49. *Ibid.*

schuss. To give the Committee at least potential useful-ness for making real compromises, some degree of flexibility and latitude was necessary by all participants. Still it would be incorrect to assume that these members have acted as free agents unfettered by political controls. It requires some stretch of the imagination to expect a Bundestag Deputy to jeopardize his standing within his *Partei-Fraktion,* or a Bundesrat member to endanger his relationship with his Land government or Parliament by seriously promoting a compromise which would be un-acceptable to their respective house. In the Bundesrat, beside the embarrassment to the reporter of having to make an oral explanation to the house of a version which was offensive to a majority of its members, the result would certainly be to reflect on the judgment and capability of the Bundesrat's membership on the Media-tion Committee.

Actually in view of the tight binding of interests among every Land's Bundesrat membership, the possibil-ity of an unrepresentative representation is remote. Taking into account the necessary margin of spontaneous action which will enable the *Vermittlungsausschuss* to arrive at a workable compromise, the decisions made by Bundesrat members within the Committee should probably be understood to be what Herbert Simon calls "programed decisions."[50]

Table IV illustrates the extent to which the Bundesrat has resorted to the use of the Joint Mediation Committee during the period beginning September 7, 1949, and ending March 28, 1958. Of a total of 124 times the Bundesrat has laid claim to the Committee up to March

50. "Programed decisions" are "those decision-making situations that are governed to a considerable extent by policies, rules and operating procedures." Herbert Simon, "Recent Advances in Organization Theory," in *Research Frontiers in Politics and Government,* The Brookings Lectures (Washington, 1955), p. 39.

TABLE IV
USE OF JOINT MEDIATION COMMITTEE BY BUNDESRAT, SEPTEMBER 7, 1949–MARCH 28, 1958[a]

	Bills introduced by Federal Government not requiring Bundesrat Consent	Bills introduced by Federal Government requiring Bundesrat Consent
Total	395	385
Demand for VA by Bundesrat	19	71
No protest	17	—
Protest	2	—

	Bills introduced by Bundestag not requiring BR consent	Bills introduced by Bundestag requiring BR consent
Total	110	174
Demand for VA by Bundesrat	14	20
No protest	13	—
Protest	1	—

a Figures compiled from *Handbuch des Bundesrates*, (Teil II), 94-98.

28, 1958, 70 of them came in the first legislative period, leaving a remainder of only 54. From these figures there appears to be no basis for the assumption that increasingly the tendency has been for the Bundesrat to press for amendments in the Joint Mediation Committee.[51] Rather the reverse has been the case, that the Bundesrat has been progressively less inclined to press its case vis-à-vis the Federal Government and the Bundestag through the office of the Mediation Committee. But in any case these figures represent only a slight decrease, and this decrease was recently explained by a Bundesrat official as mainly the result of a growing tendency for the *Vermittlungsausschuss* to adopt the position of the Bundesrat on certain legal questions, and for the Bundestag to concur also, thus avoiding having to resort to the Mediation Committee in similar cases.

51. This was the conclusion, for example, of Heidenheimer in "Federalism and the Party Structure, the Case of West Germany," pp. 824-26.

It is also indicative of something that the Bundesrat offered a much greater number of objections (71) to Government bills requiring its consent and which it could have vetoed, than it did to bills which did not require its consent but which conceivably might have been "favorably improved upon" (19). These same figures suggest that the Bundesrat, while having progressively less in the way of complaints to pursue, has leaned recently toward trying to iron out these differences without unpleasant clashes with anybody. This of course can be done with the greatest facility within the protective privacy of the *Vermittlungsausschuss.*

A major problem attendant to the Committee's work as legislative mediator has been that of its acknowledged tendency to lapse into functional specialization. Such a tendency becomes a problem when the need for persons competent to deal with highly detailed points of difference overshadows a corresponding need to effect a political balance between the two houses. In cases which give rise to administrative complications, and these are likely quite numerous, the habit of the Committee has been to bring into its secret meetings specially recruited experts— *Abgeordnete* from the Bundestag and *Beamten* from the Federation and the Länder—to serve as expert counsel.[52]

During 1951 and 1952, in order to deal with Bundestag-Bundesrat conflicts over financial legislation, the Committee created eight sub-committees to make the preliminary studies necessary for a detailed agreement. Observers of the outcome of these counselling activities through sub-committees have noticed a steady increase in the influence of these specialists and a concomitant narrowing

52. The admission of such persons is expressly authorized in Article 6 of the *GeschO, Vermittlungsausschuss, Handbuch des Bundesrates.* p. 133.

of the scope of mediation, both producing a decline in "the spirit of real political mediation."[53]

In fairness one must acknowledge the Mediation Committee's success in eliminating differences between the two houses. And that is after all its purpose. Even with those bills which could not be enacted without its concurrence, the Bundesrat managed to be satisfied with all but 10 of the 71 Government bills coming out of the Committee, and all but 2 of the Bundestag measures. Thus in ten years this institution unique to German experience has salvaged most of 124 bills entrusted to it, leaving only 12 to be rescued in other ways or abandoned altogether.

EINSPRUCH

Article 77, Paragraph 3 of the Basic Law says the Bundesrat may, following the mediation procedure, enter a protest *(Einspruch)* against a measure within one week. This device exists as a corollary to the mediation procedure and as another item in the complex of compromises which were made in the Parliamentary Council by the political parties. Contrary to the mediation process, however, the *Einspruch* procedure is confined to ordinary federal laws which do not require Bundesrat approval. Too, the Bundesrat can only resort to this method after the *Vermittlungsausschuss* has met and sought to make the bill acceptable.

A similar arrangement for non-financial bills existed under the Weimar system for a *Reichsrat* protest. But unlike the earlier Land chamber, which made frequent use of the *Einspruch*,[54] the Bundesrat had used it only

53. Walter Dehm, "Vermittlungsausschuss als Schlichter," *Das Parlament,* January 22, 1958. See also Dehm, "Stellung, Aufgaben und Bedeutung des Vermittlungsausschusses," *Neue Deutsche Beamtenzeitung, Heft 1* (January, 1960), 1-3.

54. Fritz Poetzsch-Heffter reports that the Reichsrat used the protest ten times between July, 1929, and April, 1931. See Schäfer, *Der Bundesrat,* p. 85, note.

three times up to March 28, 1958. Of these three the Bundestag was unable to override the protest in only one case, the first. In the 50th meeting of the Bundesrat on February 16, 1951, the *Einspruch* was adopted for the first time against a Government price law for milk, butter and cheese. The Bundesrat protest was carried by a vote of 34 to 9, requiring thereby a two-thirds vote in the Bundestag to validate the measure.[55] When the Bundestag tried to overrule the protest two weeks later, it was unable to muster two-thirds of Bundestag membership. Only 200 Deputies voted to reverse the decision of the Land chamber. On short notice a new federal price law covering the same ground was duly passed by the Bundestag before the old one expired, this time without protest.

An interesting precedent with the *Einspruch* occurred with its use for the third time by the Bundesrat. On December 17, 1954, the Bundesrat adopted a protest against a bill by a margin of 22 votes to 16.[56] Although later during that same meeting the Bundesrat changed its vote on the matter to make it unanimous, the Bundestag had acted in the meantime and had overridden the earlier objection. President Heuss, in announcing the law, maintained the position of the Bundestag and the Federal Government, and the matter was not contested. Thereafter a gentleman's agreement was made between the presidents of the Bundestag and Bundesrat providing

55. The reason for the Bundesrat's objection, as stated by the rapporteur, was that the Bundestag had completely neglected the compromise version of the *Vermittlungsausschuss*, thus contravening the prescriptions of Article 77 in the Basic Law. The nine votes cast against the protest came from the two most agriculturally-based Länder, Lower Saxony and Schleswig-Holstein. Bundesrat *Sitzungsberichte, 50. Sitz.*, February 16, 1951, p. 150.

56. On this issue, which involved fixing an age limit for members of the federal Supreme Court, the Bundesrat had wanted it to be 68 instead of 70, which was the Bundestag's choice. *Sitzungsberichte, 134. Sitz.*, December 17, 1954, p. 381.

that each house would act upon measures coming from the other only after formal notification by the respective presidents.

A fair conclusion would be that the element of Bundesrat influence exercised through the *Einspruch* has not been impressive, although this has been a matter of choice for the Bundesrat itself. Very likely this can be accounted for by the wide expanse of legislative coverage the Bundesrat enjoys through *Zustimmungsbedürftigkeit* and for which the *Einspruch* is not applicable. But it is also true that the extraordinary success of the Joint Mediation Committee has been such as to preclude the gnashing of parliamentary teeth or other unseemly or uncooperative behavior. Beneath this success lies the fact that "time and again the will to achieve a mutual agreement overcomes all differences of opinion, however deep-seated."[57]

57. Statement by Walter Dehm quoted in Heidenheimer, "Federalism and the Party System," p. 825.

CHAPTER IV

The Bundesrat and National Party Politics

The point should be abundantly clear that the Bundesrat was planned as a truly federative body. The Christian parties of South Germany, known organizationally as the *Ellwanger Kreis*, felt that they had secured protection in the Bundesrat against the possibility of excessive control by the unitary aims of the centralized party leadership.[1] The further possibility was anticipated that the Bundesrat would be the most suitable arrangement for stabilizing a viable distribution on constitutional powers between the Federation and the Land governments; and that it would enable the Länder governments to protect their own interests as they saw fit, rather than engage in advance skirmishing for the promotion of partisan viewpoints at the national level.

Political developments since 1949 have wrought important changes which could not have been wholly anticipated. The growth of two major parties in the Federal Republic to overshadow all others has led to a virtual two-party system in Germany. The resulting situation, which has been an incidental cause for a great deal of optimism about German democracy, represents a bold contrast to the party alignments of Weimar Germany, and indeed to those existing even in 1949.[2] After the 1957

1. "Die Länder und der deutsche Staat. Die Stellung der CDU und CSU zum Verfassungsproblem," in *Die Gegenwart* (August 5, 1948), pp. 10ff.
2. See James K. Pollock, *German Democracy at Work* (Ann Arbor,

federal elections in Germany, the Christian Democratic Union (CDU) together with its Bavarian affiliate, the Christian Social Union (CSU), held an absolute majority in the Bundestag. Only three other parties continued to hold seats by 1957: the Free Democrats (FDP), the Social Democrats (SPD), and the German Party (DP). Compare this with the 1949 results, when 11 parties secured representation in the Bundestag. The CDU/CSU grew in strength from 139 seats in 1949, to 244 seats in 1953, to 270 in 1957. The SPD grew as the major Opposition party from 131 seats in 1949, to 150 in 1953, to 169 seats in 1957.[3] After 1953, the coalition of Chancellor Adenauer (CDU/CSU, FDP, DP and the Refugee Party) commanded a two-thirds majority in the Bundestag. Although this margin did not outlast the year 1956, the Adenauer regime was able to force through Parliament a number of measures requiring this extraordinary margin.

The role of the national parties and their strength in the Bundestag relative to each other were crucial after 1949 in the developing inter-relationships between the Federation and the Länder. It is particularly worth noting that after 1949 both the CDU and the SPD developed into more or less tightly organized national parties. This has been less conspicuous of the CDU than other parties, due to the heterogeneous mixture of interests within its ranks.

1955); and Harry Pross, "West Germany: Unfinished Business for Democracy," *Orbis*, II (fall, 1958), 356-71. Karl Loewenstein describes the West German party system since 1957 as "a one and a half party system" in *Political Power and the Governmental Process* (Chicago, 1957), p. 97. For a history of all major parties until 1954 see Ludwig Bergsträsser, *Geschichte der Politischen Parteien in Deutschland* (München, 1955). A good study of all major parties from 1945 until the elections of 1953 is *Parteien in der Bundesrepublik: Studien zur Entwicklung der Parteien bis zur Bundestagswahl 1953 (Schriften des Instituts für Politische Wissenschaft, Bd. 6)*, Mit Beiträgen von Max Gustav Lange et al (Stuttgart, 1955).

3. Election figures come from *Keesings's Contemporary Archives*, (London, 1949, 1953, 1957).

But even within the CDU the dominance of the Chancellor confirms that party headquarters are at Bonn, and that the power has gradually shifted from the Land party centers to the German capital.[4] The evolution of steep, nationally-oriented party oligarchies,[5] has meant a changed attitude toward the Bundesrat. To be sure this notion of a "changed" attitude is not intended to imply that the Bundesrat was originally accepted or conceived by all groups as necessary to prevent a dangerous lapse into centralism. Nevertheless, anyone with a taste for irony cannot but appreciate that the Bundesrat, as precisely the instrument designed to guarantee the participation of the Länder in legislation and in the political developments of the Federation, should become "in a grotesque inversion of its purposes, an instrument for the subordination of Land to federal policy."[6]

The "inversion" element might be characterized and accounted for as follows: the more authority the Bundesrat was given (e.g., by extending the list of *Zustimmungsgesetze*, by the proliferation of federal enactments regulating Land administrative procedures in the execution of federal laws, by introducing legislation requiring Bundesrat concurrence in order to implement interna-

4. Arnold Heidenheimer raises a contrary view;—viz., that the CDU is structurally organized according to the Länder; and that the Bonn Office, only begun in 1952, does not exercise a heavy measure of control over the Land parties. Still, he states emphatically that the flow of party finances is not from Land to Federation, but exactly the reverse! "German Party Finance: the CDU," *The American Political Science Review*, LI (June, 1957), 385.

5. The SPD has always been typically characterized as a strongly hierarchical organization. For a discussion of the hierarchy and structural integration of roles within the SPD, for the period after 1949, see Klaus Schuetz, "Die Sozialdemokratie im Nachkriegsdeutschland," in *Parteien in der Bundesrepublik*, pp. 157-275. See also the excellent survey of the SPD up to the First World War by Carl E. Schorske, *German Social Democracy, 1905-1917; The Development of the Great Schism* (Cambridge, Mass., 1955).

6. Fritz René Allemann, *Bonn ist nicht Weimar* (Köln, 1956), p. 353.

tional agreements, etc.), then the more tempting were opportunities for influencing the votes of the Länder in the Bundesrat. It was in fact its own great importance, quite in contrast to a politically emasculated Reichsrat, which caused the Bundesrat to be a threat to its own purposes. The Bundesrat after all was given not only administrative and legislative functions. It existed as well to settle particular differences among the Länder. This additional political coloration was to make of it a playground for another kind of power struggle, not between federal and Land authorities, but between different political forces at the federal level.

One writer has suggested that this could almost have been foreseen. Hans Simon observed that the issue of federalism was one ranged at the outset between the Land Minister-Presidents and national party leaders; or more realistically, between five SPD Minister-Presidents; five CDU/CSU Minister-Presidents, and one FDP Minister-President.[7] Also this same writer noted that once the slightly artificial Basic Law had been born "by caesarean operation," party forces fell to work at once seeking to secure their control over Land political leaders. In large part they succeeded in doing so.[8] One may not infer from this that members of the Bundesrat were not expected in their official capacities to have party connections. Most members of the Bundesrat do, in fact, belong to party groups and are certainly no less bound than their counter-

7. Hans Simon, "The Bonn Constitution and Its Government," in Hans Morganthau (ed.), *Germany and the Future of Europe* (Chicago, 1951), pp. 122-24.

8. *Ibid.*, p. 123. Simon prophesized that political differences between the two houses of Parliament would diminish to the vanishing point. In relation to the likelihood of "emergency legislation" to bypass the Bundestag altogether he said, "The Bundestag and the Bundesrat will become increasingly coordinated, and whoever controls the one will control the other; and for that reason it is most unlikely that that emergency power will be exercised at all, let alone misused." (p. 124).

parts in the Bundestag to instructions from the partisan formations that control their respective governments. Instructions, however, do not usually come to them from a single party, but from a coalition of parties. The only instances of one-party governments since 1949 have occurred in Baden, Hamburg, Hesse and, since 1958, Northrhine-Westphalia. In order to maximize its influence in legislation, therefore, each party in the Bundestag seeks to secure the strongest possible Landtag parties in order to have some voice, if not a controlling influence, in the party make-up of the Land Governments.

This source of influence can be of particular moment for the opposition. If it is not strong in the Bundestag, then it might strengthen its chances in the Bundesrat and develop that chamber as a bulwark against the Federal Government and the Bundestag majority. Too, interest of the opposition will be quite high if the Bundestag majority is small. The reason for this is obvious: it can weaken the Government seriously by systematic obstruction from the Bundesrat, perhaps even causing a Government crisis. The Government on the other hand seeks always to widen its influence over legislation, and this pushes the Government into a position of having to create a "friendly" Bundesrat. Essentially the same holds for the small parties, especially those in the Bonn Coalition; for they stand to enhance their status as partners when it is known that if it should become politically desirable they will form opposition governments at the Land level. For these reasons and to a considerable extent a fusion of purposes has occurred between Land and Federation under one of two party banners. And while the Bundesrat was supposed to be only a "federative" organ, this "dovetailing" of purposes has meant that Land politics has become a partisan instrument of the Federation and therefore has contributed to centralism generally.[9]

These multi-dimensional competitive tendencies compel all the actors involved—Federal Government, Bundestag, and the parties—to take an active interest in Landtag elections. As a result competing forces at the federal level carry their differences to Landtag contests and there wage a continuation of the never-ending federal election campaign. With such a development as this Land Parliament elections in the Hansa cities, in the Rhineland, and even in staunchly particularist Bavaria have become progressively less the figments of Land policy and have assumed progressively more the character of "indirect Bundesrat elections." More will be said about this later. On the basis of this scattered blueprint the course of German Land politics since 1949 can almost be plotted. Eschenburg suggests that the repeated penetration (since 1950) by national party oligarchies into Landtag election campaigns "has had a tendency to weaken the peculiar meaning and value of those elections. . . ."[10] Furthermore this kind of intrusion must be expected to encourage "electioneering feedback" in the formation of Land Governments. It is certainly tempting the fates for the Bonn Coalition parties to force the issue too strongly in a Land where a strong potential opposition bloc exists.

One further feature of the Bundesrat relates integrally to the idea of co-ordinating Land and federal party programs by building local party coalitions to parallel the one at Bonn. The Bundesrat is not a periodically dissoluble body. It is rather a "permanent" (ewige) establishment of Land representatives, and there is never a complete turnover in membership. Although every Landtag

9. In 1956 Theodor Eschenburg spoke of "dovetailing" (Verzahnung) as being more and more typical of federal and Land policies (Staat und Gesellschaft in Deutschland [Stuttgart, 1956]).

10. Ibid., p. 617.

electoral period is of four years duration, they do not all take place at the same time. There has been no single year since 1947, for example, in which at least one Landtag election did not occur. Naturally every election is an occasion for a possible change in the composition of the Bundesrat; and while only a maximum of five votes is at stake in any single change, these five votes can be decisive. An examination of Table VI will reveal the steadily diminishing number of votes in the Bundesrat which are classified under the "doubtful" category. While in September, 1949, the bulk of a total of forty-three Bundesrat votes were not clearly oriented toward any single national party, this figure grew steadily smaller with time. By October, 1952, a fair appraisal would be that all Bundesrat votes* could be anticipated on major national issues according to party positions at Bonn. It can also be seen that, except for a short time in 1954 and 1955 and after 1959, the potential party line-up in the Bundesrat was sufficiently close that any single change of a five-vote Land Government could completely reverse the whole picture.

A warning must be entered here about the use of the terms "probably" and "doubtful" in Table VI. In either case the term covers a number of possibilities, and a Land coalition cannot at any time be absolutely predicted to jump this way or that on a matter, even when party positions are strongly and clearly drawn. As already pointed out, Land Governments have almost always been coalition governments, often tenuous ones resting on "agreements to agree or not to disagree" in tieing the coalition partners together for a variety of reasons. But on issues of pronounced federal concern, such as national defense,

* With the formation of the Southwest State (Baden-Württemberg) the number of votes was reduced to 38. But after the entry of Saarland in January, 1957, it went back to 41.

foreign affairs, international economic agreements, etc., closer coordination is likely to follow between the Bonn party attitudes and corresponding party attitudes at the Land level. It is borne out below that this degree of "coordination" has at times intensified the party battle, extending even to issues which would not otherwise have aroused Land interests at all. Thus a total of twelve "Probably CDU" votes would be twelve votes controlled by Länder which are under either sole CDU leadership or coalitions between the CDU/CSU and its junior partners at Bonn (FDP, DP and the BHE[11]). On the other hand, an equal number of "probably SPD" votes would be seats controlled by the Socialists alone (i.e., the Georg August Zinn Government in Hesse, 1951-1954, or the Max Brauer Government in Hamburg after December, 1957), or by the Socialists in alliance with other parties (FDP and BHE mainly).

The term "doubtful" in Table V obviously has limited utility as a predictive category. It is intended to include votes in the Bundesrat which are instructed by Land party formations not clearly parallel to the Government-Opposition role network at Bonn. Normally a Land government resting on a partnership of the SPD and CDU, or which includes in its government ministers from those two parties, would be classified as "doubtful." As Tables V and VI indicate, this particular species of Land government after about 1951 was hard to find. Both of these tables, especially VI, are illustrative of the trend after 1950 toward the duplication of Bonn party alignments in the several Länder. Exceptions have existed, of course, reflecting as a rule efforts to create all-party governments dedicated to the minimization of partisan differences and quarrels at the Land level. The three

11. The Refugee Association: *Bund der Heimatvertriebenen und Entrechteten.*

TABLE V. PARTY COMPOSITION OF

	1949	1950	1951	1952	1953
Baden	Wohleb: CDU			Baden-Württemberg — April 25.— Maier: FDP with SPD; October 7.— Müller: CDU with FDP, SPD, BHE	
Württemberg-Baden	Maier: FDP with CDU, SPD		November— Maier: FDP with SPD		
Württemberg-Hohenzollern	Bock: CDU with SPD				
Bavaria	Ehard: CSU with SPD		January— Ehard: CSU with SPD, BHE		
Berlin	Reuter: SPD with CDU, FDP		Reuter: SPD with CDU, FDP		October— Schreiber: CDU with FDP
Bremen	Kaisen: SPD with FDP		November— Kaisen: SPD with FDP, CDU		
Hamburg	Brauer: SPD with FDP, KPD	January— Brauer: SPD with FDP			December— Sieveking: CDU with FDP, DP
Hesse	Stock: SPD with CDU	January— Stock: SPD	January— Zinn: SPD		
Lower Saxony	Kopf: SPD with CDU, Z		June— Kopf: SPD with Z, BHE		
Northrhine-Westphalia	Arnold: CDU with SPD, FDP, Z, KPD	August— Arnold: CDU with Z			
Rhineland-Palatinate	Altmeier: CDU with FDP, SPD, KPD		June— Altmeier: CDU with FPD		
Schleswig-Holstein	Dieckmann: SPD	September— Bartram: CDU with FDP, DP, BHE	June— Lübke: CDU FDP, DP, BHE		
Saarland					

CDU Christian Democratic Union
CSU Christian Social Union (Bavarian
    affiliate of the CDU)
SPD Social Democratic Party
DP German Party

LAND GOVERNMENT, 1949-1960

1954	1955	1956	1957	1958	1959	1960
		March— Müller: CDU with SPD, FDP, BHE		December— Kiesinger. CDU with SPD, FDP, BHE		July— Kiesinger: CDU with FDP
November— Hoegner: SPD FDP, BP, BHE			October— Seidel: CSU with FDP, BHE			January— Ehard: CSU with FDP, BHE
	January— Suhr: SPD with CDU		October— Brandt: SPD with CDU	December— Brandt: SPD with CDU		
	October— Kaisen: SPD with CDU, FDP				December— Kaisen: SPD with FDP	
			November— Brauer: SPD			
November— Zinn: SPD with BHE					January— Zinn: SPD with BHE	
	April— Hellwege: DP CDU, FDP, BHE		January— Hellwege: DP with CDU, SPD		May— Kopf: SPD with FDP, BHE	
August— Arnold: CDU with FDP, Z		February— Steinhoff: SPD with Z, FDP		July— Meyers: CDU		
	May— Altmeier: CDU with FDP			November— Altmeier: CDU	May— Altmeier: CDU with FDP	
September— von Hassel: CDU with FDP, BHE				November— von Hassel: CDU with FDP		
	(elections in December)		January— Reinert: CDU with FDP, SPD		April— Röder: CDU with SPD	

FDP Free Democratic Party
BHE Refugee Association
Z   Center Party
BP   Bavarian Party
KPD Communist Party

TABLE VI

LIKELY PARTISAN BREAKDOWN OF LAND
GOVERNMENTS, 1949-1960

Date	Total Bundesrat votes	Probably CDU	Probably SPD	Doubtful
September 1949	43	3	10	30
August 1950	43	12	6	25
June 1951	43	16	15	12
April 1952	38	18	15	5
October 1953	38	23	15	—
1954	38	26	12	—
April 1955	38	26	12	—
February 1956	38	21	17	—
November 1957	41	26	15	—
July 1958	41	31	10	—
May 1959	41	26	15	—
July 1960	41	26	15	—

major exceptions have been the Bremen Government
under Wilhelm Kaisen, the Baden-Württemberger Government under Gebhard Müller, and the Franz Röder
Government in Saarland. Although himself a Socialist,
Kaisen included both the FDP and CDU in his government from 1951 until December, 1959. The other two
Länder mentioned were dominated by the CDU, both by
being the largest party in the Land and as the party of
the Minister-President. But the partisan spirit of the Bonn
coalition persisted even here, and these governments
could not be fairly characterized as "doubtful" on sensitive
party matters. During the coalition years Bremen's votes
in the Bundesrat were reliably SPD if the issue were
clearly identified as one of overriding party interest.

Likewise the price of Socialist portfolios in the CDU-controlled governments at Saarbrücken and Stuttgart was a willingness not to demand votes in the Bundesrat hostile to the Adenauer Government.[12]

The fact that the predominantly Protestant CDU in Bremen could maintain amicable relations with the Socialists to some extent points up the conservative, non-militant character of Kaisen's socialism. But it also reflects the weakness of the CDU in that Land. After the elections of October, 1955, the CDU managed to secure only 18 of a total of 100 seats. The SPD won 52, the FDP 18, DP 18, and KPD 4. The mathematics of that political situation did not make CDU support a compelling necessity. An adequate SPD/FDP majority could have carried the Kaisen Government along without CDU support.

Essentially the same thing in reverse would hold for the Saarland Government, admitted to the Bundesrat with three votes in January, 1957. On the basis of the Land elections held in December, 1955, the CDU and FDP together controlled 29 of 50 seats in the Land Parliament. The SPD won only 8 seats; but a government under Egon Reinert included the Socialists in a congenial "tripartism" arrangement. One of the bases for Socialist entry into the government was reported to be its willingness not to obstruct the Saar's "friendly" position in the Bundesrat toward the Adenauer Government.[13] It was unlikely in any event that Saarland would have come into the Bundesrat as late as 1957 as a "doubtful" Land in its allegiance to Adenauer commitments. By this time the

12. By the end of 1960 only the Saar and West Berlin continued to have governments including both the SPD and the Christian Democrats, and one must conclude that the "era of slide rule politics" has yet to run its course. See Richard Hiscocks, *Democracy in Western Germany* (London, 1957), pp. 167-70.

13. *Neue Zürcher Zeitung*, January 16, 1957,

margin of doubt had been effectively stifled, and the result was a Bundesrat which appeared to correspond along party lines with the Federal Government. One may not presume from this, however, that partisan similarity let the Bundesrat into a callous disregard for the interests of the governments of the Länder. Rather the Bundesrat simply came to adjudge Land interests in the light of all-German party problems. As will be shown later the Land leaders in the Bundesrat remained in their roles as vigorous champions of their particular interests when the need arose.

The overall streamlining process of Land governments was brought about mostly between 1950 and the end of 1952. It was primarily the result of official pressure from Bonn upon Land CDU (or CSU) leaders to break up existing coalitions with the SPD and form governments instead with the Union's partners in the Adenauer government—the FDP and DP; and of similar pressures from leaders in Socialist headquarters upon their Land subordinates to form opposition governments. Klaus Schuetz, for example, reports that the Land Socialist parties were informed by party headquarters that they must consider themselves only as "stepping stones in the achievement of a higher national order" and to avoid the development of "parochial" attitudes.[14] Reasons for application of this pressure are not confined to the satisfactions of a

14. Hiscocks says, "The federal aspect of German politics has been endangered by lack of wisdom in Bonn." *(Democracy in Western Germany,* p. 170). Fritz René Allemann speaks of a "crisis in German federalism" inspired by "reckless party bosses" in Bonn *(Bonn ist nicht Weimar,* p. 356). Eschenburg, though recognizing the dovetailing process as tending to blur distinctions between the two policy levels, does not seem to consider it a cause for serious concern: "The orientation of Bundesrat votes along lines of the partisan rivalry of Bonn is visible only with great political decisions, e.g., international agreements about rearmament. . . . With the great part of decisions, party connections of the Bundesrat members play little or no role." *(Staat und Gesellschaft in Deutschland,* p. 629.)

cooperative Bundesrat. There was intrinsic merit, at least in the eyes of party agents at Bonn, in securing the highest degree of party coordination possible between Bund and Land. But that the CDU, as the party most deeply committed to the federal principle, should assume such an attitude has been deplored by some as a betrayal of the traditional German concept of a Second Chamber.

When the Federal Government must look to the Länder for the effective administration of its policies, then naturally the idea of like-minded Land administrations will always be appealing. It certainly cannot be denied that the CDU, especially Chancellor Adenauer, extended every effort to duplicate the Bonn party model whenever possible. Whereas in 1949 there were seven Land governments which included both the SPD and CDU; by November 1954, there were only two such governments, neither of which could be accurately classified as "doubtful." One interesting government change which was to cause much excitement and ultimately, in the scramble for control, a hopeless confusion of Land with federal party programs took place in Hesse in January, 1951. The Socialist leader Georg August Zinn formed for the first time a government without the CDU. On the basis of the 1950 elections, the SPD commanded 47 of 80 seats in the Landtag, the CDU and FDP combined only 25, with the Refugees (BHE) controlling the remaining 8 seats. Between the formation of this government and the Hessian Landtag elections in November, 1954, relations were stormy between the federal and Land parties. The major animus involved CDU leaders at Bonn and the supporters of Zinn's government.[15]

15. A good account of this particular campaign in its federal-Land aspects is in Arnold Heidenheimer, "Federalism and the Party System," *American Political Science Review*, LII (September, 1958), 809-30. Also the *Frankfurter Allgemeine Zeitung* carried a detailed running description of the contest. In fairness to Chancellor Adenauer, this was

Earlier there had been evidence of considerable enthusiasm within the Hessian CDU to form a coalition with the Socialists, but pressure soon developed from Bonn and from conservative Protestant members of the CDU in Hesse on these "anti-Adenauer" men. A letter to the then chairman of the Hessian CDU, Werner Hilpert, from a party colleague chastened his old-fashioned provincialism. He was quoted as saying, "Think on the federal plane! Great political decisions lie in the balance. We must simply create a parallelogram of power between the government coalition in the Bundestag and that in the Bundesrat."[16] This particular campaign, symptomatic of the change being forged between the federal and Land parties, saw the effective merger of the FDP and CDU in a "working alliance" against the "obnoxious SPD Minister-President, Georg August Zinn."[17] Whereas there is no evidence that the Socialists responded in kind, apparently relying instead on the relative success of the SPD administration since 1951, the emphatic theme of CDU election propaganda was one of federal politics. The *Frankfurter Allgemeine* reported the popular and recurrent use during the contest by Adenauer zealots of the CDU jingle:[18]

Deine Wahl im Hessenstaat
Zählt im Bonner Bundesrat

not the first time that overweening federal influence shaped the formation of a Land government. Goetz Roth has demonstrated that the government formed in Land Lower Saxony in June, 1951, was primarily the offspring of federal, not Land, intentions. (Roth, *Fraktion und Regierungsbildung. Eine Monographische Darstellung der Regierungsbildung in Niedersachsen im Jahre 1951* [Meisenheim am Glan, 1954].)

16. Letter from Erich Koehler to Werner Hilpert, May 16, 1954. Quoted in Heidenheimer, "Federalism and the Party System," p. 818. Following the CDU's embarrassing failure to defeat the Zinn Government, Hilpert was replaced by a more federally-oriented party chairman.

17. CDU Newsletter *(Union in Deutschland)*, quoted in *Frankfurter Allgemeine Zeitung*, September 16, 1954.

18. FAZ, November 24, 1954.

Regierung Zinn stützt Ollenhauer
Wählt CDU für Adenauer.

The election results were not altogether rewarding for the Bonn enthusiasts. Although the CDU doubled its Landtag strength from 12 to 24 seats, and the FDP rose from 13 to 21 while the SPD dropped three of its 47 seats; still, the "obnoxious Minister-President" was not removed. Zinn made a successful bid for the 7 votes of the Refugee Party and managed to form another government, this time in a coalition. With 51 votes of a total of 96, continued Socialist control of the Government at Wiesbaden was secured, though doubtless with added concern for Hesse's refugee population. Thus it was that by 1952 not only the formation of Land Cabinets, but Land elections as well moved in the shadow of Bonn decisions. A glance at Tables V and VI suggests that the bulk of the Land governments formed after August, 1950, bore the "made in Bonn" stamp. It has not always been easy, however, to effect the perfect symmetry of the parallelogram concept without some trouble, and in certain instances opposition groups outbid the Chancellor in securing political leases on Land Cabinets. No less contrary to the constitutional spirit of the Bund-Land system were the countermoves of the Opposition, motivated by the desire of indirectly overturning the Adenauer Government.

Probably the best example of Socialist success at weakening the hand of Adenauer by defeating CDU governments among the Länder occurred in Northrhine-Westphalia in February, 1956. It is doubtful that this action was solely, or even primarily, aimed at controlling Northrhine-Westphalia's Bundesrat votes. But once the deed was done it certainly had this effect. Adenauer's earlier performances in that Land returned to haunt him when the Bundesrat came to consider such important federal legislation as the law to implement the Common Market Agreements in 1957. The trouble in Northrhine-Westphalia might be characterized as having developed out of the friction between Minister-President Karl Arnold of the CDU's trade-union-influenced left wing, and Chancellor Adenauer himself. The Chancellor was generally associated with the right wing of his party and with the FDP. Signs of difficulty had appeared even in 1949, when Arnold's action in the Bundesrat caused him to be elected its first President. This upset Adenauer's plans for Hans Ehard and required him to reshuffle his Cabinet posts once more to admit Ehard and thereby accommodate Bavarian sensibilities. But party animosities in the Federal Capital were not yet fully developed, and congenial "tripartite" governments were still acceptable, if actively discouraged. During the early part of 1950, while other Land governments were falling into the Bonn pattern, the Arnold CDU/SPD coalition remained intact.

Following the Landtag elections in 1950, and after some unpleasantness between Arnold and Adenauer about party leadership in the Rhineland CDU, Arnold emerged as the dominant influence in his party, which in turn controlled the new Landtag. As Adenauer became less tractable on the coalition question, the differences between him and Arnold grew more obvious. An open rupture appeared likely over the issue of government formation in Northrhine-Westphalia. A strong and increasingly bitter division developed between the Arnold followers who wanted a continuation of the "Grand Coalition," and the Adenauer group which wanted a CDU government to include the Free Democrats. Numerically, either would have been feasible, based on the following election results:[19] CDU, 93 seats; SPD, 12 seats; FDP, 26 seats; Z, 67 seats; KPD, 16 seats.

It seemed for a time that the quarrelling factions of the Rhineland CDU would cause the break-up of the party. Arnold stood his ground, however, in spite of heavy pressure from Bonn on his loyalty to the trade union elements within the Union.[20] Following three months of unsuccessful and embarrassing efforts to produce a majority-supported government, Arnold announced formation of an "open-door Cabinet" to include his own party and the small *Zentrum*. With these extra 16 seats Arnold commanded a majority of 109 votes of 214. It was a big enough margin to rule popularly until the 1954 elections.

With the passage of time Arnold's resistance to the parallelogram movement eroded. Party fortunes in his Land changed with the 1954 elections, although the CDU continued to be the strongest party with 90 seats. The Center's Landtag strength slipped to 9, leaving those two parties with a combined strength of only 99 of 200 seats. The Socialists, on the other hand, jumped to 76 seats, and they became more insistent on being included in the new Government. In spite of the SPD's proclaimed willingness to accept pro-Adenauer votes in the Bundesrat if they were brought into the coalition, the new Arnold Cabinet again excluded them.[21] This came as anything but a merry surprise to the Socialists. Throughout the month of June and most of July (1954), Arnold had been treating

19. *Keesing's Contemporary Archives*, 1955-1956, p. 13804.

20. Arnold was informed by pro-Adenauer members of the Land party that his only alternative to a "Bonn-type" coalition was resignation from the party. *Union in Deutschland*, August 26, 1950.

21. According to Heidenheimer, Socialist leader Fritz Steinhoff later complained bitterly that the CDU had demanded, as the price for admission to the government in 1954, that the Rhineland SPD use its influence with the Bundestag SPD *Fraktion* to urge support for Adenauer's rearmament program. ("Federalism and the Party System," p. 821.)

with political figures commonly associated with the Adenauer group. Some, however, expressed surprise. The day following the elections the *Frankfurter Allgemeine* predicted another *Grosse Koalition* to include both the FDP and SPD.[22] From Bonn Ollenhauer even insisted that Arnold would have no choice but to accept the SPD in his government in view of the CDU's "popular rejection" at the polls, having lost 1,000,000 voters from the 1953 elections and having fallen from 48.9 per cent to 41.3 per cent.[23]

Notwithstanding Arnold's left-wing "social" orientation, his new government included the FDP in the existing SPD-Center coalition. This was widely interpreted as a swing to the right, especially in view of placing Dr. Middlehauve—a right wing Free Democrat—in the role of Deputy Minister-President. Arnold himself stated rather candidly that an important factor in bringing the FDP into his government was that "It seemed desirable to bring the Land Ministry into line with the coalition supporting the Federal Government, especially as the election campaign had been fought not only on local issues but also on the question of the Government's foreign policy."[24]

What ultimately happened in Northrhine-Westphalia in early 1956 to alter the partisan composition of the Bundesrat was almost the logical outgrowth of Arnold's decision in 1954 to join the parallelogram crowd. Since the Free Democrats were deeply involved in the whole concatenation of events at Düsseldorf, a brief explanation of that party's troubles would be in order. Being a

22. *FAZ*, June 17, 1954.
23. *Ibid.* Ollenhauer's statement about "popular rejection" probably does some violence to the facts. The CDU had performed rather poorly in every election in which Adenauer was not himself a candidate. So the drop in votes from 1953 to 1954 was not as serious as it might sound.
24. *Keesing's Contemporary Archives* 1955-1956.

Government party, the FDP found that it had a hard time at the 1953 polls distinguishing itself from the Chancellor's party. This naturally had its debilitating effects. Already weakened by the Naumann scandal involving a former Nazi's plan to gain control of the FDP,[25] badly divided on the question of Adenauer's foreign policy and in open rebellion against his electoral laws, the FDP sought to recoup its lost prestige by picking from its ranks the vigorous Dr. Thomas Dehler as president of the party in March, 1954. A strong anti-clerical, Dehler had been dropped from the Adenauer cabinet earlier, no doubt because of his aggressiveness. He was to lead his party out of its domination by the CDU, and then out of the Bonn Government. Because the Dehler group became more and more critical of the Adenauer foreign and cultural (confessional schools) policies, a *de facto* alliance emerged between the FDP and SPD, at least in these two fields.[26] Dehler had been unable to move the pro-Adenauer members of his party *Fraktion* in the Bundestag, and so the attentions of the discontented turned to Northrhine-Westphalia.

In February, 1956, the differences between federal and Land party issues completely vanished in the old Rhine province. Illustrating that their purpose was to oppose the Government in Bonn, the FDP and SPD joined forces and sustained a "no-confidence" vote against Arnold's regime. The Socialists, bitter about their exclusion from the 1950 and 1954 governments in spite of their willingness to join, were eager to strike back at Adenauer. The FDP's explanation was given by Dr.

25. A thoroughly interesting, if dramatized, narrative of the Naumann affair is in Alistair Horne, *Return to Power* (New York, 1956), pp. 160-83.
26. In this connection, see Alfred Grosser, *The Colossus Again: Western Germany from Defeat to Rearmament* (London, 1955), pp. 220-24.

Hermann Kohlhase, now to become Minister of Economics and Transport in the new government. According to Kohlhase, this action by the Free Democrats bore no specific relation to politics in Northrhine-Westphalia, but rather was believed simply to be the best way to enforce retribution upon Adenauer. All the accumulated grievances of the junior Bonn-coalition partner were ventilated, lamenting especially the increasingly open dominance of the FDP by Adenauer attested by the Chancellor's efforts the preceding month to influence the choice of the FDP chairman in the Bundestag. Most offensive to the FDP was the introduction by the CDU in December, 1955, of an electoral law that would have seriously endangered the independent existence of the Free Democrats as a party, much less as a "partner" in the Bonn coalition. Kohlhase said:[27]

The lesson of these developments was not lost on us. We do not, however, credit Minister-President Arnold with such political short-sightedness and such a crass denial of full partnership; but we are obliged to take notice of all the procedures and subtleties of the electoral law attack by the Bonn CDU leadership. A political party under present circumstances is at the same time a federal party and a collection of Land contingents. . . . If a party cannot win proper satisfaction in settlement of problems intolerable to it at the federal level—and possibly this occurred to the Minister-President—then it must serve notice to the Land branches of its Bonn partner. It does this in order to meet pressure created at the federal branch with counter pressure at the Land branch.

Thus the efforts of Chancellor Adenauer to synchronize party life and thought at federal and Land levels have in some cases come full circle. The February rebellion of the FDP in Düsseldorf was roughly the same thing, with

27. Northrhine-Westphalia Landtag *Sitzungsberichte*, February 16, 1956, pp. 1014-15.

an opposition bias, as Adenauer's actions in Northrhine-Westphalia in May, 1954, and in Hesse in that same year. It remains to be seen whether the partisan parallelism between the Federation and the Länder held up on critical votes in the Bundesrat and whether it tended to replace the concern of the Land governments for their own peculiar advantages with an all-German partisan spirit in major cases. Close examination of Bundesrat reports indicates the persistence of a strong party community to bridge the intergovernmental span only in those areas of overriding party concern, where there is a great deal at stake. Several good examples have occurred of measures appearing in the Bundesrat that should test the national party loyalties of the Land governments. Three such measures will be followed through the Bundesrat in this connection: the Federal Government's electoral law draft of 1953, which directly affected in one way or another the interests of every party, big and small; the European Defense Community legislation, which drew an unyielding line of opposition from the Socialists; and the General Codetermination Law of 1952, on which party alignments were also very distinct.

THE ELECTORAL LAW OF 1953[*]

The Federal Government's proposal for a new electoral law was submitted to the Bundesrat for First Passage on February 6, 1953. There it promptly encountered the organized opposition of a majority of Bundesrat votes. Acting on the Basis of recommendations by Dr. Zimmer, chairman and reporter *(Berichterstatter)* for the Committee for Interior Affairs, the Bundesrat rejected the Government draft and sent the measure back for one corresponding more with the 1949 law. Although no Land

[*] The 1949 law had been effective only for election of the First Bundestag.

expressed complete satisfaction with the new *Wahlgesetz,* various shades of hostile opinion tended to converge on one or two phases. Its most offensive aspect was the provision that a candidate must obtain more than 50 per cent of the votes to secure election, with an auxiliary vote *(Hilfsstimme)* where that majority was not obtained on the first ballot. On the second ballot two or more parties could combine forces in an electoral alliance on the same "ticket."[28]

The following electoral figures should be indicative as to how a Socialist or Free Democrat voter would feel about the proposed law: under the old law in 1949, only 26 deputies were directly elected by absolute majorities out of 240 electoral districts. Kurt Schumacher, leader of the SPD from Hannover, was the only Socialist deputy so elected. There were 25 CDU deputies elected in districts by absolute majorities: 8 from Rhineland-Palatinate, 8 from Northrhine-Westphalia, 4 each from South Baden and Württemberg, and 1 each from Bavaria, Lower Saxony, and Württemberg-Baden. Had the provisions of the proposed new law been in effect, 214 second ballots would have been required. The SPD would have had to enter a second campaign without allies and under a decided disadvantage to the CDU.

The new measure provided for election in electoral districts by only a simple majority, but it also provided for the possibility of a combination of several parties in the *Hilfsstimme* against the strongest party in an electoral district. It was generally recognized in this respect that

28. The most detailed discussion of the Government's draft in the Bundesrat came during first passage. In a technical sense this is the only time the Bundesrat considers the Government bills because they become "Bundestag bills" after having been discharged by that house. Still the Bundesrat normally reserves its major debate until a bill has been through the Bundestag. For the first passage discussion see Bundesrat *Sitzungsberichte, 100. Sitz.,* February 6, 1953, pp. 38-48.

the three Bonn Coalition parties (CDU/CSU, FDP, and DP) could combine against another party which was stronger than any single one of them, and this could only mean the SPD. If this possibility were to materialize the SPD actually stood to lose 64 of the 96 seats it had won directly in the 1949 elections. The *Frankfurter Allgemeine* compiled hypothetical figures, assuming such an electoral alliance, and came to the following results on the basis of the 1949 returns:[29]

	Direct seats won	
	1949 law	new draft-law
CDU	116	156
SPD	96	32
FDP	12	28
DP	5	15
BP	11	10
Ind.	2	1

Similarly, the list mandates were to increase from 160 to 242 (bringing the ratio to 50:50 for direct seats to list seats). With combinations among the Bonn Coalition parties, the overall result would be, again using 1949 figures:

	1949	1953
CDU	159	218
SPD	149	114
FDP	62	85
DP	21	28
BP	21	21
KPD	29	17
Z	15	— (victims of 5% clause)
Other	28	1
	484	484

Totalling the votes of the CDU, FDP and DP, as computed, the Coalition parties would have a two-thirds

29. *FAZ*, February 9, 1953.

majority in the Bundestag with 331 of 484 votes. One would expect loyal Socialists in the Bundesrat to beat down the law if they could. This is about what happened, with the added result that the FDP gave the Socialists wholehearted support. Strong dissatisfaction had been building up within the FDP about its subordinate role in the Bonn Coalition. Characteristic of the dissatisfied elements, Dr. Rheinhold Maier (Baden-Württemberg) pointed out that this new system would only increase the dependence of the Free Democrats on the CDU. The Socialist-dominated governments of Hamburg, Bremen, Hesse, and Lower Saxony, plus the coalition (SPD-FDP) government of Baden-Württemberg, commanding a total of 20 votes in the Bundesrat, all cast their votes to reject the existing draft and demand a new one. A proposal of Rhineland-Palatinate[30] to abstain from voting until the second passage was defeated.

Decisive in determining the Bundesrat's action were the five votes of Baden-Württemberg, which rested on a coalition of Free Democrats and Socialists under the leadership of Reinhold Maier. Himself a left-wing Free Democrat, Maier's wing of the party had consistently been one of the major sources of discontent festering within the FDP. He specifically railed against the complete domination of his party in Bonn by Adenauer and the CDU. Probably the most radical suggestion made in the Bundesrat about the electoral measure was Maier's proposal to reject the draft outright and *in toto*. This motion failed to receive a majority by 18 votes to 17, although it enjoyed the votes of most of the Socialist Länder.[31] Paradoxically, the reason Baden-Württemberg's

30. Rhineland-Palatinate was a "safe" CDU Land. Minister-President Pieter Altmeier had done his bit for the parallelogram idea in 1951, excluding the Socialists from his government. The CDU in his Landtag held an absolute majority.

31. Bundesrat *Sitzungsberichte, 100. Sitz.*, February 6, 1953, p. 46.

proposal failed was that the Socialist government of Bremen did not vote for it. Bremen was to show on several occasions that its commitment to the Socialist party line was not as rigid as that of other Länder.

The most vigorous attack on the measure was offered by Hamburg's Max Brauer, who spoke of it as "a cold political trick" and demanded that the Bundesrat reject the "horrible monster." He spoke also for the other Socialist governments in describing the 1949 law as "the ideal solution." Brauer requested the Federal Government to draft a measure which bore a stronger resemblance to the earlier electoral law.[32] To answer Brauer's criticisms Federal Minister of the Interior Dr. Lehr insisted that the hopeful aspects of the new measure had been overlooked, that the new draft was designed to introduce "integrating elements" into German party life. As if to make his welcome doubtful, Lehr bluntly denied that this law, or that any federal electoral law, required Bundesrat concurrence. Here he encountered the spirited antagonism of all Länder. Where Lehr had found no single Land that approved the law entirely and that the objections tended to be varied in content and intensity,[33] on the matter of *Zustimmungsbedürftigkeit* he received a unanimously hostile reaction.

Karl Arnold explained that this law, as any federal election law, required Bundesrat consent on the basis of Article 84 of the Basic Law. Northrhine-Westphalia's proposal for the Bundesrat's *Stellungnahme* read:[34]

(1) The electoral law must be executed by the Länder as a matter of their own concern.

32. *Ibid.*, p. 40.
33. Even the secure CDU governments of Rhineland-Palatinate and Schleswig-Holstein expressed reservations, the former about the administrative complexities of it, and the latter about the five per cent clause. Hans Ehard, Bavaria's Minister-President, spoke out sharply against the *Hilfsstimme. Ibid.*, p. 41.
34. *Ibid.*, p. 39.

(2) It requires the concurrence of the Bundesrat.

(3) But since the material regulation of the Bundestag electoral law is first of all a matter of the Bundestag's concern, the Land Government of Northrhine-Westphalia proposes that the *Stellungnahme* relating to substantive objections to the existing draft be postponed until the Second Passage.

The first two points of Arnold's proposal, which were taken over by Rhineland-Palatinate and introduced as a motion *(Antrag)*, were passed unanimously; and Dr. Lehr's objections were thus summarily dismissed. The last point received only the favorable votes of Northrhine-Westphalia and Rhineland-Palatinate.

After the rejection of Baden-Württemberg's extreme plan to dismiss the draft outright, the recommendations of the Committee for Interior Affairs remained intact. These recommendations, which had been worked out in consultation with the Judiciary and Finance Committees also, were to disapprove the principle of combining and exploiting two distinct electoral systems at the same time; and to reject the *Hilfsstimme* on grounds that ultimate election to the Bundestag would be based not on voters' choices but on agreement among the party leaders. All three committees expressed further dissatisfaction with the administrative difficulties *(verwaltungsmässige Schwierigkeiten)* that would develop in the proper distribution of votes. Sträter reported that the Interior Committee voted 6 to 2, with 2 abstentions, on the first question: a resolution whereby the Bundesrat sends an unfavorable report; 5 to 0, with 5 abstentions, on the second question: to ask the Federal Government to formulate an electoral law corresponding more closely with the 1949 law; and on the third question, 7 to 1, with 2 abstentions, to reject the second ballot altogether. Examination of the committee

Protocols reveals the following breakdown among the Land governments:[35]

No. 1: vote for an unfavorable *Stellungnahme:*

Baden-Württemberg	Abstained
Bavaria	For
Berlin	For
Bremen	For
Hamburg	For
Hesse	For
Lower Saxony	For
Northrhine-Westphalia	Abstained
Rhineland-Palatinate	Against
Schleswig-Holstein	Against

No. 2: vote to ask the Government to pose a reformulation of the law along the lines of the 1949 law:

Baden-Württemberg	Abstained
Bavaria	Abstained
Berlin	For
Bremen	For
Hamburg	For
Hesse	For
Lower Saxony	For
Northrhine-Westphalia	Abstained
Rhineland-Palatinate	Abstained
Schleswig-Holstein	Abstained

No. 3: rejection of the second ballot:

Baden-Württemberg	For
Bavaria	For
Berlin	For
Bremen	For
Hamburg	For
Hesse	For
Lower Saxony	For
Northrhine-Westphalia	Abstained

35. Bundesrat Committee for Interior Affairs, *Protokoll,* 29th Meeting, January 29, 1953.

| Rhineland-Palatinate | Abstained |
| Schleswig-Holstein | Against |

Although the committees had expressed some professional (i.e., administrative) concern about deficiencies and awkward aspects of the measure, the Land votes even in committee correlated with party interests. The two apparently non-polar Länder, Baden-Württemberg and Northrhine-Westphalia, can be explained simply. The Maier Government at Stuttgart, destined not to last out the year, was subject to pressure from both ends and could ill afford to alienate the SPD partner. The controlling influence of the CDU in the Duesseldorf Government of Karl Arnold was insufficient to justify a departure from the friendly relations Arnold had had with the Socialists in his Land.

On June 26, 1953, a compromise version known as the "Onnen Draft" was adopted over the objections of Adenauer and the bulk of the CDU. Described by Deputy Onnen as *"Verhältniswahl auf Mehrheitsbasis,"* the new draft passed the Bundestag with the support of the Socialists, Free Democrats, and a few CDU Deputies from the Rhineland. It passed by a vote of 202 to 175, and on that same day it was again referred to the Bundesrat Committee for Interior Affairs. Dr. Zimmer noted approvingly that the most odious phases of the law had been deleted from it: the "integrating elements" of a combined direct seat-list and second ballot system which would enable the Government parties to eliminate the Socialist Party as a strong opposition force in the Bundestag. The *Hilfsstimme* had been abolished; and the form of the 1949 law was restored essentially, albeit with a stronger proportional representation bias.

The new electoral law had a ratio of 50:50, for seats won by direct election to those won by PR. The new anti-splinter-parties provision established that a party would have to win at least five per cent of the overall federal vote to secure its proportionate number of seats in the Diet.[36] On the matter of Bundesrat concurrence the Chamber accepted the committee's recommendation not to demand a meeting of the *Vermittlungsausschuss* in the view of the need for haste (the elections were only six weeks off). The transmission of Bundesrat concurrence was quite clear, according to Article 84, Para. 1 of the Basic Law, and even accepted that regulations based on law *(Rechtsverordnungen)* according to Article 80, Para. 2, could be issued by the Federal Interior Minister without Bundesrat concurrence.[37] The Länder Chamber did insist, however, that this law required Bundesrat concurrence because it contained provisions concerning establishment of (Land) administrative agencies and their procedures in executing *this* federal law.

A reasonable inference here, aside from purely technical and administrative aspects, would be that Land attitudes on the 1953 Electoral Law correlated roughly with the attitudes of the party Fractions in the Bundestag. This is probably no less true of the CDU-dominated Länder than of the Socialist-dominated Länder. Since the beginning of the Weimar Republic the Socialists have been ideologically committed to the "electoral justice" of a scheme allowing proportional representation. The CDU, on the other hand, has leaned in the direction of the American predilection for the single member district system. The evidence in both cases is convincing that each was advancing the cause which stood to win it the greatest number of seats. In the early elections held in the British and American zones of occupation, the CDU

36. The 1949 law had provided also for the five per cent minimum, although the five per cent figure had previously meant that amount in any single land.

37. Bundesrat *Sitzungsberichte, 112. Sitz.,* July 3, 1953, p. 335.

had emerged stronger where the single member plurality constituencies were used. The Socialists on the other hand, because of the heavy concentration of their voters in urban industrial centers, regained strength when proportionality was re-introduced into electoral laws.

The Land party leaders' failure to vote in the Bundesrat exactly according to the decisions of their counterparts in the Bundestag (e.g., Bavaria, Northrhine-Westphalia) partially reflects the disparity between the interests of a Land party and those of the federal party, but it also reflects the strategic defenses of the Bundesrat for protecting this disparity. The differences in voting behavior can best be explained not so much by an ideological commitment of the Land parties to their "autonomy of approach" to electoral problems, as by the overriding need for each Land coalition to satisfy the electoral demands of its supporting elements. For example, the Ehard government in Bavaria (CSU), which had vigorously resisted the *Hilfsstimme* concept as likely to lead to unnecessary disruptions of a large and isolated party, rested on the votes of the SPD and Refugee Association. In fact, the combined SPD and BHE vote in the Bavarian Landtag totalled 89. With the 64 seats of the CSU this gave Ehard a majority of 153 of 204 seats, a safe one if carefully cultivated. While normally a loyal supporter of the CDU/CSU program, Ehard would understandably shy away from a choice that could estrange his government's support when Bavarian interests were at stake. There were of course other considerations as well. Dr. Ringelmann, speaking in the Bundesrat for Bavaria, criticized the cumbersome and complicated "auxiliary vote" for the directly-elected seats, pointing out that it would impose an impossible burden on the administrators of the law.[38] If, as Ringelmann said, there

38. *Ibid.*, p. 339.

was just cause to be apprehensive about the administrative complexities of a second ballot in every constituency that did not return a majority, this problem alone would give a Land leader basis for resistance, regardless of his party label.

EUROPEAN DEFENSE COMMUNITY LEGISLATION

Another national issue of the first rank, and one which inspired a relatively clear division of party opinion, was in the field of foreign affairs. The European Defense Treaties, inseparably linked to the Contractual Agreements returning German sovereignty to the Germans, were signed on May 26, 1952. The following twelve months were occasion for an uninterrupted series of partisan attacks and counter-attacks. It was perhaps inevitable that levels of party differences should become indistinguishable, especially in view of the enormity of the involvements—German rearmament and commitment to the western alliance system. The Treaties sailed through the Bundestag on March 19, 1953, by a vote of 226 to 166, with surprising calm after the stormy debates that had characterized their first reading the preceding December. The Bundestag President promptly passed them on to the Bundesrat for its approval, while the Socialist Opposition sought new ways to obstruct successful ratification. Once the EDC Treaties appeared in the Federal Chamber, that body became the center of public scrutiny. The President of the Bundesrat was Reinhold Maier, described by a British correspondent as "a typical Swabian liberal of the old school."[39] Besides playing a strategic role as President of the Chamber, Maier also found himself in the pivotal role of controlling, albeit not independently, the five votes of his Land, Baden-Württemberg.

A glance at Table VI indicates that if the Land votes

39. Horne, *Return to Power,* p. 155.

in the Bundesrat held to their party allegiances at the federal level, then the vote in the Bundesrat could be unfavorable. The votes of CDU-controlled Länder totalled 18, including Bavaria, Northrhine-Westphalia, Rhineland-Palatinate, and Schleswig-Holstein. For the Socialists, 15 "sure" votes could be counted in Hesse, Lower Saxony, and the two Hansa cities. The only Land whose government was not clearly dominated by one of the two major parties was Baden-Württemberg. It has already been pointed out *(above)* that Maier ruled in Stuttgart in coalition with the Social Democrats. His SPD allies were pushing him in the direction of opposition to the Agreements, despite his prominent membership in the FDP—a party identified as in support of the EDC.

Maier's position was particularly difficult in view of the relative strength between his own party and that of the SPD in Baden-Württemberg's Landtag. The combined vote of the FDP and BHE, on the basis of Land elections in March, 1952, was only 29, as compared with the 50 seats of the SPD. The Socialists made it abundantly clear that a pro-EDC vote by Maier's government in the Bundesrat would result in his downfall.[40] These must have been unpleasant weeks for Maier, for he was made the target of a barrage of demands by his own party members within the Federal Cabinet. Maier had even been brought under pressure earlier from the American High Commissioner when, on February 19, Mr. Conant closeted the Bundesrat President for an hour and a half to convince him of the urgency of the Treaties.[41]

The Socialist position was that the Bundesrat should take no formal position on the Treaties until legal clarification was made about whether the Agreements required a constitutional amendment. This approach was appar-

40. *FAZ*, March 23, 1953.
41. *Ibid.*, February 20, 1953.

ently undermined when the Constitutional Court at Karlsruhe, after hearing what Wilhelm Kaisen called "about 25 pounds of legal argumentation," issued a 50-page ruling.[42] Its decision was that it was not permissible for any party to hinder passage of a measure through Parliament on the grounds of suspicions of unconstitutionality; and that the Court could not pass judgment until the bill had been passed through both Houses.[43] Although the delays caused by the Social Democrats were indirectly to result in the defeat of the EDC by sowing the seeds of doubt in France about German sincerity, the issue for German ratification at least was thought to be settled. The presumption in Bonn now was that Dr. Maier, who had taken the Socialist line that parliamentary outcome of the Treaties must depend on clarification by the Court at Karlsruhe, would come around. He had told High Commissioner Conant that he would cast his Land's vote for them in the Bundesrat if Karlsruhe said they were in order.

The Treaties entered the Bundesrat formally for debate on April 24, 1953, in the form of four separate bills. They were registered on the Daily Calendar as Points One and Two. President Maier raised both points at the same time because together they encompassed the necessary legislation to implement German acceptance of the Treaty-complex. The first two parts dealt with the relations between Western Germany and the Three Powers of Occupation (termination of the Occupation Statute), and with financial arrangements for the pro-

42. Bundesrat *Sitzungsberichte, 105. Sitz.,* April 24, 1953, p. 185. The sudden concern of the SPD for constitutional form was probably, at least on the face of it, a trumped-up basis on which to explain its strictly partisan opposition to EDC. For a thorough and lucid account of the whole controversy, see Karl Loewenstein, "The Bonn Constitution and the European Defense Community Treaties, a Study in Judicial Frustration," *Yale Law Journal,* LXIV (May, 1955), 805-39.
43. *Die Welt,* March 9, 1953.

jected military forces. The last two points concerned the agreement between the United Kingdom and the EDC countries, and the establishment of EDC forces in Europe. Speaking through his Land Minister of Justice, Dr. Renner,[44] Maier chose a course of action which was felt by some to have been pulled out of thin air for the specific purpose of avoiding the anticipated unpleasantness of having to make a decision. The proposal of Baden-Württemberg, around which the Bundesrat debate settled, was to abstain from taking a position on the Agreements until the Constitutional Court had passed on the constitutionality and *Zustimmungsbedürftigkeit* of the ratification-laws.

Dr. Renner delivered himself (and Maier) of a long statement pointing out that in the absence of an authoritative decision from the Court the Bundesrat could do nothing. "No one is more qualified and competent to answer this question (of constitutionality) than [members of] the Federal Constitutional Court. It was for this very reason that the Judiciary Committee . . . declined to arrange a statement on the constitutionality of these laws for the Plenum."[45] Hence, it followed that it would be neither "purposeful nor proper" for the Bundesrat to effect a decision on the matter. In the same speech, and in one of those rare instances when a member of the Bundesrat refers, however indirectly, to partisan differences, Renner made a clean breast of it. It is worth quoting because it makes a convincing argument for the point of this chapter:

> I will speak quite openly and not subtly. We have (in Baden-Württemberg) a coalition among the FDP, BHE and SPD. This Coalition has been effective in building up the new Land of the Federation and has worked well. But on these

44. As Bundesrat President, Maier did not authorize himself to make a formal recommendation to the *Plenum*.
45. Bundesrat *Sitzungsberichte, 105. Sitz.*, p. 179.

Agreements we are certainly not of one opinion. This fact cannot be ignored. The SPD is against them. The other two parties in the Coalition are for them. The Opposition in our Land has pathetically demanded from the [Land] government a "Bekenntnis" to the Agreements. One should be most cautious with use of the word "Bekenntnis" in the political sphere. It has its appropriate place in the religious field, but not in the political arena. For us it is not a matter of a "Bekenntnis," but of reasonable consideration and careful judgment.

The Minister-President of Land Baden-Württemberg explained last week in an article that has received much attention that he would concur with the Agreements if the Federal Constitutional Court held them to be compatible with the Basic Law. If we in Baden-Württemberg are to fall victims to division on this matter, then we would at least like to know we are not contributing simply to an academic quarrel. If we should now resolve our internal differences, and the Federal Constitutional Court found the Agreements contrary to the Basic Law, then to use a term that has lately become famous, we would have fallen out over nothing.

(Laughter and applause)

Surely nobody who thinks fairly and impartially could expect us to do such a thing.

Whether or not the decision of the Southwest State would have been specifically for or against, had there been a ruling from the Court, is open to conjecture. Under the circumstances it is easy to understand, if not be sympathetic with, Maier's reluctance to commit political suicide. In fact his unique solution was to cost him his job anyway. In the October elections, having effectively estranged all major party groups, he was swept from office and temporarily eliminated as a political influence in western Germany.[46] It is also easy to understand how Minister-President Ehard of Bavaria, relatively secure

46. See the comments on Maier's subsequent fortunes in Grosser, *The Colossus Again*, pp. 222-24.

from the dangers attending the Stuttgart government, could insist on maintaining the integrity of the Bundesrat. Ehard spoke first for the supporters of the Treaties in the Bundesrat. He deplored the legal muddle which had enveloped the whole controversy but urged that the Bundesrat not abandon its constitutional responsibility as a legislative force. Affirming the Bundesrat's desire to accept its role in legislative processing, he said:[47]

But the process of legislation cannot be completed if the Bundesrat does not act on a bill. It is very instructive, what the Court has said in its ruling: that the process of legislation must be concluded before it is possible to determine its constitutionality. . . . It is provided—and that is certainly the sense of the Constitution—that the Bundesrat has the right, but also the duty, of participating in legislation. . . . It can approve, or it can reject. But it cannot in my opinion refuse to say anything. That would be contrary to the Constitution. . . .
The Bundesrat cannot shirk its obligation; it must have the courage to make a decision. . . . A great deal affecting the destiny of Germany hangs in the balance. We can decide in favor of the East, or we can decide in favor of the West! But to avoid the choice is out of the question! I must make it quite clear on behalf of my Land, that we cannot accept this resolution [the proposal of Baden-Württemberg to postpone a decision].

Perhaps the most interesting and in this context the most revealing statement was that made by Wilhelm Kaisen, the Socialist *Bürgermeister* of Bremen. Kaisen

47. Bundesrat *Sitzungsberichte, 105. Sitz.*, p. 183. The Standing Orders of the Bundesrat are also instructive in this regard. Section 13, paragraph 2, says: "In legislative procedure . . . the voting on a matter must be formed in such a way that there is no doubt about the reply, whether it be to (1) introduce a measure for the first time; (2) assume a formal position on a Government bill in first passage; (3) concur with a law passed by the Bundestag; (4) deny concurrence; (5) demand a meeting of the *Vermittlungsausschuss;* or (6) enter a protest to a bill." See *Geschäftsordnung des Bundesrates* in *Handbuch des Bundesrates, Teil I*, (Darmstadt, 1958), p. 127.

made explicit his concurrence with the Adenauer Government in the need for a German commitment to general western security, as well as in the utility of the European Defense Community as a good beginning toward the ultimate military integration of Germany into a broader collective security system, which he also approved. But Kaisen insisted that Germany's new democracy must not lose sight of the necessary vitality of a Government-Opposition arrangement; and that unanimous adoption of the Chancellor's position would raise justifiable suspicions. Whereas Kaisen himself professed sympathy with the Argeements he felt that he could only vote against them as a member of the Opposition Social Democrats. In this curious attitude, Kaisen said that the resolution of Baden-Württemberg returned the initiative to the Federal Government, and to the Bonn Coalition he addressed the remark: *"Ich wünsche euch alles Gute!"*[48]

With the votes of Bremen and Baden-Württemberg settled, all other votes went as expected. The result was to adopt Maier's resolution by 20 votes to 18. The Socialist Länder (Bremen, Hamburg, Hesse and Lower Saxony) plus Baden-Württemberg voted to postpone a final vote until the legal issue had been cleared up definitively, and the EDC episode was thus brought to a complete impasse. In some hasty dealings to bring the Bundesrat around to a more realistic frame of mind, Adenauer was reported by *Der Spiegel* to have entered negotiations a few days later with the Refugee leader Waldemar Kraft to form a government in Land Lower Saxony with the CDU, thereby replacing the five Socialist votes of Herr Hinrich Kopf with five pro-EDC votes and guaranteeing its passage regardless of the decision of Maier's Cabinet at Stuttgart.[49]

48. Bundesrat *Sitzungsberichte, 105. Sitz.,* p. 185.
49. *Der Spiegel,* May 14, 1953.

On May 15, after a veritable avalanche of criticisms directed at him, Dr. Maier felt constrained to reintroduce the Agreements, this time with a different plan. His new plan, as reported out of the Foreign Affairs Committee, was to vote favorably on those two parts dealing with financial aspects and with establishment of European Defense forces, then to discharge the rest of it with no action. This seems to have satisfied both sides, although partisan jockeying within the Bundesrat continued. After it was clear that Maier had contrived the Bundesrat's "new look" at the Agreements to give his own government a face-saving device, the Socialist Länder continued their efforts to force him into a position of having to vote against them again. Evidently Maier had already secured agreement within his own coalition about the new proposal, the main proviso being that the Bundesrat would not specifically pass on the basic Agreement per se, but confine its approval to those parts of the legislation which would require without doubt the approval of the Bundesrat in any case. Herr Brauer and Herr Zinn, of Hamburg and Hesse respectively, sought to have the issue of *Zustimmungsbedürftigkeit* settled on all four points before the committee proposal was voted on.[50] To avoid being trapped Maier called for a vote on the voting priority of the committee proposal and carried it by 23 to 15. In the voting that followed Baden-Württemberg cast its votes with the pro-EDC Länder, and only the 15 votes of the Socialist Länder remained opposed.

This rather ineffective outcome was satisfactory to both contesting parties at the federal level. The Adenauer Government was pleased because it had insisted all along that these were the only two parts directly affecting the

50. Bundesrat *Sitzungsberichte, 107. Sitz.*, May 15, 1953. Brauer's statement is on p. 233, Zinn's on pp. 234-35. Formally the issue of *Zustimmungsbedürftigkeit* was raised by a motion of Bremen. See statement by Senator Ehlers, pp. 232-33.

Länder and which therefore required Bundesrat consent. Ollenhauer expressed the SPD's gratification with the results because he was confident that the Constitutional Court would eventually rule that the whole Treaty structure required approval of both Houses; and that the whole process would have to be begun anew.[51] Thus Germany became the first power to complete ratification of the EDC Treaties. Bundesrat vacillation and then its attenuated confirmation left the flavor of doubt about that chamber's authority in treaty affairs, while leaving no doubt about party control of Bundesrat votes in such matters. Opinion varies as to whether the Bundesrat EDC actions weakened its ability to give the Länder a firm grip on their interests through legislative controls, but it is obvious in this particular instance that the Bundesrat ceased to be an agency for preserving the proper federal-Land equilibrium and became an uncertain tool of the national political parties.

THE GENERAL CODETERMINATION LAW OF 1952

In view of the more extensive discussion of the codetermination issue in a later chapter, from a different point of view, the problem will be brought up here only to illustrate another type of partisan conformity among the Land governments to national party attitudes. The issue in this case was purely domestic, albeit one of the most important and controversial ones since the war. The term "codetermination" *(Mitbestimmung)* refers to the right of the industrial workers to share in the administration and policy-making processes of German industry. Vigorously promoted by the largest trade union federation in western Germany, the *Deutscher Gewerkschaftsbund* (DGB), union leaders believed that codetermination

51. *FAZ*, May 17, 1953.

would give the unions a stronger hold on the affections of the working classes and advance them toward the goals of "the future society" sought by the working class movement. Whereas the DGB was deemed to have won an impressive victory in the Codetermination Law for the iron and steel (and coal) industries in 1951, it suffered a severe defeat in the General Codetermination Law the following year.

The DGB's proposal to extend the earlier law to German industry in general was adopted unchanged by the SPD and introduced into the Bundestag. It was the Federal Government's draft, however, much less favorable to the unions, which was enacted into law on July 19, 1952. In the Bundestag it received the votes of the bulk of the CDU and the DP and Center Party, while the SPD voted against it almost to a man. The Free Democrats either voted against it or abstained. A handful of CDU deputies also abstained, these being mostly from industrial areas and having strong trade union connections. Whereas the 1951 law gave equal representation to labor on the Supervisory Councils, authorized considerable union influence in the plant Works Councils, and made the law's provisions applicable to all concerns employing 300 workers or more, the 1952 law reduced worker representation on the Supervisory Councils to one-third, virtually eliminated union influence in making worker nominations, and established a minimum employee figure at 500 for the law's provisions to take effect.

By the time the Bundesrat Labor and Social affairs Committee met on July 24, 1952, to consider the bill just released by the Bundestag, the position of most parties on the bill was fairly clear. The Socialists and Communists constituted a solid front of opposition to its existing form, and all the others (excepting the FDP) were in favor. Chancellor Adenauer's persistent support for the bill tended to obscure a generally uncertain attitude among CDU leadership toward the broader codetermination question. Adenauer was distinctly unenthusiastic about trade unions, and the party's position was inclined to vary somewhat, depending on coalition necessities. Because the CDU had forced through the *Mitbestimmungsgesetz* for iron, coal, and steel during the preceding year, it had seriously jeopardized its good relations with the Free Democrats, always implacable opponents of the trade unions. By the end of 1951, party *Weltanschauungen* and tactical considerations created strong dispositions toward the measure which permeated all levels of political life.

The General Codetermination Law* came before the Bundesrat Plenum for debate on July 30, 1952. Dr. Oechsle, *Berichterstatter* for the Labor Committee, announced the recommendation of that committee to demand a meeting of the *Vermittlungsausschuss* in order to incorporate a number of proposals for change that had been worked out in committee. Because the recommendation of the Bundesrat committee in this instance was rejected by the Plenum—an unusual occurrence—and because the issue at hand was charged with strong partisan feeling, the possibility of deviant committee decisions should be examined.

Every Land, regardless of the number of votes it commands in the Bundesrat, has one vote in each committee. Ignoring for a moment the fact that deputy committee members, as a rule civil servants of the Land governments, often attend the committee meetings in place of the regular committee members, it can occasionally happen that the distribution of votes within the committee, reflecting party considerations again, will be contrary to what the Bundesrat ultimately decides. An

---

* *Betriebsverfassungsgesetz.*

example would be: should the 4 Länder that command 5 votes apiece vote together in plenary session, then their total of 20 votes could carry a Bundesrat *Stellungnahme* or *Beschlussfassung* by defeating the 18 votes of the other 6 Länder. This could happen, of course, only after the creation of the Southwest State (Baden-Württemberg) in 1953 and then prior to the admission of Saarland in 1957. But this would not necessarily be true within the committees, each Land (including West Berlin) having one vote. The other Länder can outvote them by 6 to 4 if they are united on a party issue. This result would carry also a considerable distortion of relative popular strength since the 4 dissenting Länder controlled 364 of 487 seats in the Second Bundestag. But such an eventuality is remote, not to mention unimportant on crucial party issues, because these four Länder were controlled by the same party only for about 18 months between 1955 and the entrance of Saarland into the Bundesrat with 3 votes in January, 1957.

Dr. Oechsle, Bavaria's Minister for Labor and Social Welfare, took the position of an honest broker and made a representation for his committee, although his Land voted to reject most of the bases for calling the *Vermittlungsausschuss* and then cast its votes against calling it at all. From beginning to end the committee itemized nineteen recommended changes to justify calling the Joint Mediation Committee, of which only three were to be accepted by the Bundesrat as a basis for voting. Most of these proposals concerned procedural and conceptual refinements in the measure and sought to eliminate obvious inconsistencies within the bill. Five of them departed substantially, however, from the Bundestag version, and they deserve careful examination. What is most striking about them is that they either paralleled exactly the codetermination hopes of the SPD and DGB or went beyond them in establishing provisions even more advantageous to organized labor. Briefly they are:[52]

Section one: to incorporate both the public and private sectors of the economy under application of the law and to eliminate differences between them as far as codetermination was concerned; also to take away from the Labor courts *(Arbeitsgerichte)* the authority to arbitrate conflicts between administrative agency heads *(Dienststelle)* and the Works Council *(Betriebsrat)*. This was distinct from the Bundestag version, in which the public services were not brought under the law's application in anticipation of another law dealing specifically with them.

Section four: to give the franchise for Works Council elections to all employees who had been employed by the enterprise for at least six months. The period provided in the Bundestag measure was for one year, which had been part of the CDU's original demands. The Socialists wanted a six-month qualification period.

Section fifteen: to enable the Works Councils, by a simple majority, to elect workers to the Supervisory Councils *(Aufsichtsräte)*, rather than have elections by the workers at large on a proportional basis. The Bundesrat change was essentially a return to the plan of the SPD, which had sought to give the unions greater control over the Supervisory Councils on the reasonable assumption that union influence in the Works Councils would be easier to maintain than control of the workers at large.

Section sixteen: to enable trade unions, as well as the Works Councils and workers, to make nominations for membership in the Supervisory Councils. The Bundestag draft had consciously left the role of unions minimal in this regard and had expressly excluded their participation in nominations.

52. Bundesrat *Drucksache* 311/1/52; see also the existing terms as they entered the Bundesrat in *Drucksache* 311/52, *Entwurf eines Betriebsverfassungsgesetzes,* July 21, 1952.

Section eighteen: to subject corporations with a minimum of 300 employees to these provisions, instead of the 500-minimum figure given in the Bundestag version.

In the final vote all five of these were rejected by the Bundesrat Plenum, and in fact only three of the Labor Committee's nineteen recommendations were adopted at all. Two of them dealt with subtle conflicts in the legal definition of the term *"Angestellten"*; and the other was to accept essentially the Bundestag's change of the Bundesrat's original proposal to raise the numerical membership of the workers on the Supervisory Council; that is, to leave labor representation at a figure which was to be "at least one-third," but not the originally requested ratio of one-half.[53] Dr. Oechsle did not specify in reporting out his committee's proposals, as the *Berichterstatter* is sometimes inclined to do, how the voting went within the committee. Nor is there record of a vote in the committee minutes. The political importance of the issue, however, supports the party factor as the most compelling, in spite of the variance between the committee's suggestions and official Bundesrat action.

Even had there been a preponderance of deputy committee members on the committee, these are usually instructed by their ministers and follow the instructions closely. More likely there was a preponderance of SPD Ministers in the Land Ministries of Labor who also served, as is the rule, as regular members of the Bundesrat Labor Committee. During July, 1952, the SPD was represented in every Land government except three; and even where the CDU was the dominant party, it was most likely to extend concessions to the Socialists in the labor field. With the Socialists tending to pre-empt the Labor Ministry portfolios, and with the SPD controlling West Berlin, Bremen, Hamburg, Hesse and Lower Saxony, a

53. *Ibid.*

majority existed within the committee. Furthermore the Karl Arnold government in Düsseldorf (Arnold was present at this Bundesrat meeting), resting as it did on the support of the Christian trade unions, could hardly afford to be trapped into taking an anti-labor position with no ready explanation. Thus even if the basis for consideration in the committee were the same as in the Bundesrat Plenum (i.e., partisan), the results would be different. The weighted-vote system could and did effectively shift the margin of a slender majority.

The record vote on the committee's recommendation to demand a meeting of the *Vermittlungsausschuss*, even on the limited basis of the rump proposals, failed passage with only three Länder openly opposing the motion. The voting went as follows:[54]

Berlin	Abstained
Baden-Württemberg	No
Bavaria	Abstained
Bremen	Yes
Hamburg	Yes
Hesse	Yes
Lower-Saxony	Yes
Northrhine-Westphalia	Abstained
Rhineland-Palatinate	No
Schleswig-Holstein	No

Since Bundesrat resolutions require at least a majority of the total votes, the abstentions of Bavaria and Northrhine-Westphalia killed it. "Yes" votes totalled only 15. Having established that the Bundesrat declined to demand a meeting of the *Vermittlungsausschuss*, President Kopf next called for a vote of Bundesrat concurrence with the measure. A roll-call had the following results:

Berlin	Abstained
Baden-Württemberg	Yes

54. Bundesrat *Sitzungsberichte, 90. Sitz.,* July 30, 1952 p. 355.

Bavaria	Yes
Bremen	No
Hamburg	No
Hesse	No
Lower-Saxony	No
Northrhine-Westphalia	Yes
Rhineland-Palatinate	Yes
Schleswig-Holstein	Yes

In this way the *Betriebsverfassungsgesetz,* which had been described by Chancellor Adenauer as "a major step enjoying the sponsorship of his government," was passed.[55]

At least one further point deserves to be clarified. In view of the observations about Northrhine-Westphalia's vote in the Labor Committee, does it not seem strange (and inconsistent) that Arnold should cast his Land's votes for concurrence with the measure? This might be considered strange only in the sense that Arnold probably felt considerable strain on his concurrence-vote from the strong labor wing of his party. Typically members of the Bundesrat make every effort to avoid the appearance of obstructing the work of the government. Once the issue of the *Vermittlungsausschuss* had been settled negatively, a show of strength for the measure should occasion no surprise. To this extent the preliminary voting can be more important than that on the actual issue of concurrence. Even so, as this case illustrates, where a strong partisan commitment promotes party conformity in the Bundesrat the Plenum vote will probably be about as divided as the party make-up of the various Land Governments. In both of the two record votes involving the *Betriebsverfassungsgesetz,* the Socialist-controlled Länder voted en bloc.

The outcome of the General Codetermination Law in the Bundesrat adds force to the argument that at least on

55. *FAZ,* July 17, 1952.

major matters of national scope the party contest among the *Parteifraktionen* will be repeated in the Land Chamber, albeit with the solemn dignity and decorum of experts. Eschenburg acknowledged the development and "promising vitality" of this phase of Bundesrat behavior for "Government-Opposition role politics." He said it was clearly observable only with "the gravest problems of foreign affairs, such as rearmament."[56] The evidence suggests, however, that any all-German issues on which the major parties have taken strong stands will produce a high degree of party conformity in the absence of other, stronger factors. Certainly the 1953 Electoral Law bore no implicit or direct relation to foreign affairs, whereas its immediacy for party interests was quite clear in every Land.

Occasionally a Land government is so deeply committed to the role of Government or Opposition in one or more particular fields that its votes are determined in other fields by that same role. A conspicuous example is that of Hesse during the Bundesrat debates on the Federal Government's Volunteers Bill *(Freiwilligengesetz)* in the summer of 1955. It will be recalled that the 1954 Landtag elections had been vigorously contested in that Land by Adenauer's party in an effort to unseat the Socialist government of George August Zinn; and that the campaign emphasis, at least for the CDU, had not been confined to issues of Land concern. The campaign was particularly bitter and the recriminations exchanged scarcely made for smoother relations between the Zinn Government and political leaders at Bonn. Zinn might have reasoned that since Adenauer's proclaimed goal was to replace his government with one whose Bundesrat votes would be more friendly to Adenauer policies, it was

56. Eschenburg, *Staat und Gesellschaft in Deutschland,* p. 628.

only just that Zinn respond in kind and assure Adenauer of four unfriendly votes.

When the Volunteers Bill entered the Bundesrat for first passage on June 10, 1955, the question to be voted on in the Bundesrat as developed in the committee stage was confined to constitutional and administrative aspects of the measure.[57] The Bundesrat issue was not whether the Land chamber could concur with the Paris Accords or with political angles of establishing a German military contingent. It was couched in terms raising doubts about the constitutionality and administrative feasibility of the Government's initial measure to implement those Agreements. But Land Hesse had taken a position against the Accords, pursuant to the Socialists' attitude in the 1954 election toward rearmament. Subsequently in the Bundesrat Herr Zinn expanded the basis for his Land's objections. He said:[58]

The Representatives of Land Hesse have taken a position against the Paris Accords. Hence it follows that they cannot give their consent to laws executing the Paris Accords, or any such laws that seek to implement the military sections of those Agreements. It is not now the moment to set forth the basis for this outlook and attitude; that was taken care of earlier. But for those who give consent to the Accords, without reservation as to their urgency and prompt execution, the question raises itself whether in this first move toward new German legislation on defense matters, political or even foreign policy considerations may have—or are even allowed to have—precedence over the issues of constitutional law and constitutional policy. And this question I answer emphatically in the negative.

For the rest Zinn joined the chorus of criticisms from all others in the Bundesrat about the reckless haste and badly

57. Hesse's stand was exactly the same in second passage on July 22, 1955, when the other difficulties had been removed.
58. Bundesrat *Sitzungsberichte, 142. Sitz.,* June 10, 1955, p. 140.

considered judgment of the Government in advancing such a bill with obvious intentions of forcing it through the legislative mill. In the record vote on the Bundesrat's *Stellungnahme*, which implied acceptance of the Paris Agreements, Land Hesse voted alone to oppose it. The resulting vote was 34 to 4. It is interesting that only Hesse of the Socialist governments actively played the Opposition. Of course this was during the period of months in which the Adenauer Government enjoyed a two-thirds majority in both houses of Parliament. The only "safe" SPD votes in the Bundesrat were the 12 of Hesse, Bremen and Bavaria. That the other two Länder were less militant in their opposition role no doubt is partially reflective of their better fortunes in getting along with the Adenauer regime. But it also invites the suspicion that both Kaisen (who was head of a coalition in Bremen which included the CDU and FDP) and Hoegner (Minister-President of Bavaria) were inclined to gravitate toward a sympathetic attitude with respect to the developing commitments of the Federal Republic.[59] Furthermore the Land governments had no intrinsic regard for the Paris Agreements *als eigene Angelegenheiten.*

From all the above it should be reasonably clear that in certain important cases the Bundesrat becomes an agency for the subordination of Land to federal policy. As a corollary to this, Bundesrat members can also be expected in these cases to speak the same partisan language of the Fractions in the Bundestag, though phrased in administrative expertise. One further point remains to be made in this connection that points up the

59. Kaisen, like his counterpart in Hamburg before December, 1953, Max Brauer, was consistently found somewhat out of line with his party's line on foreign affairs. Both these men, for example, made it abundantly clear they had wanted to vote for the EDC Treaties, "but the iron discipline of the party made them toe the line." See Karl Loewenstein, "The Bonn Constitution and the European Defense Community Treaties."

invidious potential of a "split-level politics" such as has emerged via the Bundesrat. Occasionally evidence appears that conscious efforts are made by Bundesrat representatives from a Land to embarrass the Federal Government when no other advantage besides embarrassment is to be gained. This applies of course only to the opposition parties. Within the Bonn experience that could only have been characteristic of the SPD and, after February, 1956, the FDP. But the same could hold true for Government parties as well, if circumstances were reversed.

This seems to be what happened in July, 1957, when the Bundesrat was giving its second and decisive consideration to the Common Market Treaties. In first passage the Bundesrat had insisted on being able to send 11 of 36 German members to the Consultative Assembly of the Community.[60] Following some assurances from the Federal Minister for Bundesrat Affairs, Herr Merkatz, that the Government would take into account the Bundesrat's wishes when the matter of selecting delegates was to be decided, the majority of the Bundesrat appeared satisfied. Merkatz left little room for honest doubt when he said:[61]

The selection of German delegates to the Common Assembly requires special legal regulation, whereby the desired connection between the Common Assembly of the Consultative Assembly of the European Council and the Assembly of the West European Union is to be duly taken into account. According to the opinion of the Federal Government the Bundesrat should be appropriately represented in the Common Assembly. The draft law to be proposed by the Federal Government for selecting German delegates to the Common Assembly will correspond with this declaration and will be formed so that the wishes of the Bundesrat can be easily accommodated.

60. Bundesrat *Sitzungsberichte, 176. Sitz.*, May 3, 1957, pp. 610-11.
61. Bundesrat *Sitzungsberichte, 181. Sitz.*, July 19, 1957, p. 746.

Despite the strength of this commitment before the Bundesrat the Socialist-controlled Länder, exclusive of Bremen, supported a motion of Northrhine-Westphalia to invoke the *Vermittlungsausschuss* in order to establish a legal guarantee for the Bundesrat's demand. Certainly the Socialists, with the possible exception of Bavaria, had no outstanding brief for federalism or Land particularism, nor for the intrinsic merits of Land representation in the Common Assembly. Still the motion won the fourteen votes of Northrhine-Westphalia, Bavaria, and Hesse. Berlin also supported the motion. It would be no serious hazard to suppose that Steinhoff's Socialist government realized the actual futility of making the proposal, but reasoned that it would force the CDU Länder to vote against the *Vermittlungsausschuss* motion in order to avoid another delay. Their negative votes would ostensibly put them in a position of opposing the efforts of the Socialist governments to protect or extend the rights of the Bundesrat and, thence, the interests of the Länder.

From all this the conclusion is inescapable that national party life in the new Germany is "split-level"; and that the federal chamber, though probably through nothing of its own doing, exists to perpetuate this fact. It should also be clear that neither major party has had a reserve on the type of political behavior which encourages it. If the interventions of the Bonn Coalition parties in Land politics in 1950-1954 were "contrary to the system," then no less so were the actions of the SPD and FDP in Düsseldorf in 1956 to strike at Adenauer by overthrowing Arnold's Government.

By the end of 1960 the synchronization of party life and thought in the Federal Republic had not come to rest. In July, 1960, one of the last remaining Grand Coalitions disappeared when Minister President Kurt Georg Kiesinger of Baden-Württemberg announced in a speech to the Landtag that the SPD was being dropped from the government, having been part of the Stuttgart government since 1953. Only the Saar Government remained as a CDU-SPD coalition, and Minister-President Röder's controlling CDU is in no way threatened with rebellious SPD delegates to the Bundesrat. Kiesinger's remarks are instructive:[62]

I have always represented the opinion, and I do now, that participation by the greatest opposition party in one or more Land governments could be useful in the political climate of the Federal Republic. But certainly one should have no illusions that such participation has distinct limitations in view of the unique structure of our federal state. The Länder, more exactly the Land governments, share in the formation of the federal will in comprehensive ways, primarily in legislation.

No one who takes his party program seriously could voluntarily contribute to the danger that his policy could be blocked in the Bundesrat by an opposition majority. If we had a federal structure as in Switzerland or the United States, where the member states do not take part directly in federal policy, then the problem of forming governments in the Länder would be much simpler.

Some recent writers suggest that this trend is leading the German Republic toward a serious crisis in federalism.[63] Generally the critics say that the German federal structure was not given sufficient protection against its friends, and that economic realities and the changing exigencies of party needs have proved the ability of the

62. *Staatsanzeiger für Baden-Württemberg*, July 9, 1960.
63. See Richard Hiscocks, *Democracy in Western Germany*, pp. 166-70; Fritz Allemann, *Bonn ist nicht Weimar*, pp. 352-56; Arnold Heidenheimer, "Federalism and the Party System," p. 828. For a recent and forceful expression of the contrary view, that German democracy is made secure only when the forces of Land particularism have been domesticated by strong central leadership and parties, see Friedrich A. v. der Heydte, "Föderalismus, Volkssouveränität und Parteien," in *Presseveröffentlichungen über den Bundesrat*, Nr. 126, March 20, 1961.

Bundesrat to maintain the federal balance to be illusory. To this one might add that these "encroachments," while visible enough to justify the term "trend," could hardly have been successful had the federative constitutional structure corresponded with a strong federal consciousness among the Länder themselves. Only a few could have appreciated how it was all "contrary to the system" to associate and intermingle permanently both levels of policy-making.

There can be no reasonable doubt that this tendency does predispose the Republic to move in a centralist direction. But again that fact cannot be ascribed solely to the subversion of the Bundesrat, nor to the "dovetailing" of party purposes between Federation and Länder. In fact the argument can fairly be made that the methods used by the CDU and SPD leaders at Bonn have strengthened the small life-energy of the Länder, which had hitherto been suffocating on the fringes of decision-making. From this it would follow that only by the "parallelogram of power" did the Länder come to have some impact on the process of making important policy decisions for Germany.

CHAPTER V

Federalism

Demonstration has been offered that the Bundesrat, through the process of party synchronization at Land and federal levels and its resulting conflicts, is often caught in a squeeze play of political forces. Proper emphasis has already underscored the fact that the Federal Chamber has been partially subsumed under the partisan symmetry of Federal Government-Opposition Bloc politics. One might fairly conclude this was the logical consequence of healthy interplay among contestants for power, and that no less logical a result would be a substantial dilution of the Military Governors' story-book version of federalism when these competing forces were left to their own devices.

On the other hand a wealth of evidence exists to reverse the image of political centralization in western Germany. The first hypothesis holds that the Bundesrat does act specifically to protect governmental integrity at the Land level and does maintain a sensitive and protective attitude toward Land interests. The assumption of this hypothesis is that a "protective attitude" of Bundesrat members toward their respective governments, if the attitude is shown to be reasonably effective, is enough to justify description of the Second Chamber as having a "federal" orientation. A difficult terminological and analytical issue is involved in this hypothesis—the question of what constitutes a Land's "interest." The debate would be endless whether such a thing as a pure "states' rights" principle exists opposed to national power, or if this sentiment is merely an ideological contrivance by which specific and identifiable "interests" pursue their common or diverse goals. While the effort to distinguish between genuine regional identifications and the "unprincipled interests" of parties and groups controlling Land votes in the Bundesrat would be a worthwhile effort, it is not a serious concern here. Should a Land's Bundesrat position be different from that of the national party or of other Länder and justified on grounds of the peculiarity of that Land's problems, then it can be understood as defensive of its own interests *as these are judged by its Cabinet*. No attempt will be made to probe this question further to determine if that action was truly representative of that Land's interests in a "pure" or "rational" sense.

The further point should be made that nothing in this hypothesis is altogether incompatible with the power configuration in the Bundesrat induced by federal party conflicts in Landtag elections and Land government formation. On some crucial issues of party concern that which constitutes the interests of a Land may be determined in part by factors that are not reducible to terms of Land interest versus national power. Nor must anything be inferred about implicit conflicts of interest among the several Länder or between the Land governments and the Federal Government, since such conflicts must depend on the nature of an issue and its anticipated consequences.

Confirmation of the first hypothesis is being sought in two ways. The first is to establish that every Land government's Bundesrat votes are cast in a manner reflecting the particular sentiments of that Land when an issue comes up involving a distinct separation of interests among the Länder. The second means is to establish that the Bundesrat as a whole consistently resists efforts of the Federal Government to extend its authority vis-à-vis the Land governments. Greater attention is given to the first of these two because, among other things, the Bundesrat has adopted an increasingly cooperative spirit toward the Federal Government, making its "resistance" thereto a thing subtly handled and difficult to assess. Furthermore since what is being sought is the isolation of the Bundesrat's manifest role as a vehicle for mobilizing several particular Land interests, then the empirical results should be the same in either case. If the performance of a Land's members in the Bundesrat indicates a primary motivation regularly to be concern for the desires and problems of their own government, then this factor should remain roughly constant in all contingencies regardless of the source of opposition.

The research dualism of the first hypothesis is arbitrary, of course, and to some extent artificial. The distance between the general (i.e., theoretical) protectiveness of Land interests by the Bundesrat and particular protectiveness of Land interests by the Bundesrat is partially contrived. Simply to acknowledge that the appearance of general protectiveness of Land interests by the Bundesrat stems from a coincidence of all particular interests does not by any means tend to invalidate that generality. If, for example, repeated instances forming something of a pattern can be observed in which the Bundesrat took a position in firm defense of Land administrative or legislative rights, one might fairly conclude that this pattern justifies the federalism hypothesis in a theoretical sense. It is not necessary to presume the existence of a "states' rights" tradition in Germany, although at least some evidence of it exists in south Germany.[1] The troublesome nature of this elusive distinction between theoretical and particular Land protection points up the difficulty of likening German federalism to the vertical "checks and balances" variety in the United States. Although the American doctrine of "states' rights" has always paralleled the contours of sectional politics, there developed around it in the nineteenth century a trend in constitutional interpretation which extended theoretical legitimacy to particularist sentiments. The absence of a similar development in Germany is accounted for mostly by the distinctive German type of federalism.

Fritz Allemann recently said the express purpose of the federal arrangement, as embodied in the Bundesrat, is to oppose the one-sided concentration of power. He further said, "But the German public simply feels this purpose to be a complication of the mechanism of government, forced on them from the outside. What obstructs the flow and development of power is wrong in their eyes."[2] Whether the Bundesrat organizes and articulates the pressures of particularism at the level of federal union, Allemann's statement notwithstanding, deserves close examination.

One final point ought to be made. The presumption of identity between general and particular Land protectiveness does not prejudice the varying emphasis of this "concern" for Land affairs. Obviously the reaction of the Bundesrat to apparent encroachments upon Land affairs would be stronger at some times than at others, depending on the magnitude of the intrusion and the strength of its

1. A good recent summary of German federal traditions and habits, especially related to southern Germany, is in Olle Nyman, *Der Westdeutsche Föderalismus* (Stockholm, 1960), esp. pp. 7-39. Robert R. Bowie discusses federal legislatures in Robert B. R. Bowie and Carl J. Friedrich (eds.), *Studies in Federalism* (Boston, 1954), pp. 3-63.
2. Fritz René Allemann, *Bonn ist nicht Weimar* (Köln, 1956), p. 353.

source. But having acknowledged the varying strength of the concern, it should not be necessary to assign it a definite value. The point to be made is more simple: that members of the Bundesrat either do act whenever possible in a way to sustain their Land interests, or that they do not do so. Stating the hypothesis in this way has the advantage of being more "operational" while at the same time avoiding a confused and unnecessary proliferation of categories along a federalism—non-federalism continuum.

INDIVIDUAL LAND PROTECTIVENESS

To validate the first phase of the federalism hypothesis, primary consideration has been given to a series of refugee-expellee[3] measures relating to resettlement. Specifically these were government programs to promote and subsidize official transfers of large numbers of refugees from one part of the Federal Republic to another part. The resettlement measures have a built-in technique for testing the tenability of the federalism hypothesis generally. There was a natural division of the Länder into those despatching refugees (*Abgabeländer*) and those receiving them (*Aufnahmeländer*), giving those Land governments within each group a strong common bond in refugee affairs.

These refugee resettlement measures[4] in every case

3. The terms "expellees" and "refugees" are used interchangeably here. "Expellees" are persons of German origin who were, by terms of the Potsdam Agreement, expelled from areas east of the Oder-Neisse Rivers and from Czechoslovakia, Hungary, Poland, and other eastern European countries. "Refugees" are German citizens who left their homes in the Soviet Zone of Occupation and in East Berlin.

4. Most of these measures were not laws passed by Parliament. Of the four resettlement programs put under way between November 29, 1951, and June 5, 1956, only the law of May 22, 1951, inaugurating Program II was not a *Verordnung* of the Federal Government. But they all required Bundesrat concurrence, and there was little doubt that they raised major policy issues at both the federal and Land levels.

provided for the official transfer of a specified quota of refugees from Bavaria, Lower Saxony, and Schleswig-Holstein to the remaining Länder of the Republic within a limited time. Since they required the consent of the Bundesrat in every case,[5] it was expected that the resources of the Länder would be used to the fullest extent in the Bundesrat to protect their own particular interests. A thorough résumé of refugee and expellee conditions in post-war Germany would be completely unmanageable in view of the general "nomadization" of Europe after 1945 and the shifting, indeed sometimes conflicting, statistics dealing with refugee matters.[6] For the purpose here it will be sufficient to characterize the refugee resettlement issue and the distribution of its intensity among western German areas.

Approximately 12,000,000 persons entered western Germany from the outside after 1945, mostly into rural districts, creating a resettlement problem arising from inequitable population density almost unimaginable in its proportions. Because the towns and many of the villages were already over-crowded with evacuées from the larger heavily bombed cities, nearly all refugees were directed to agricultural districts. Many of them had to be

5. In the case of the Second Resettlement Program of May, 1951, the law was unanimously declared to be a *Zustimmungsgesetz* by the Judiciary Committee of the Bundesrat. See Bundesrat *Sitzungsberichte,* 52. *Sitz.,* March 16, 1951, p. 210. For the other three programs explicit Bundesrat consent is made necessary in Article 119 of the Basic Law: "In matters relating to refugees and expellees, in particular as regards their distribution among the Länder the Federal Government may, with the consent of the Bundesrat, issue ordinances *(Verordnungen)* having the force of law, pending settlement of the matter by federal legislation."

6. Except for research currently in progress, not much is available in the way of a complete, detailed work on the refugee problem in Germany since 1945. See, however, P. J. Bouman et al, *The Refugee Problem in Western Germany* (The Hague, 1950); also the section dealing with the whole range of refugee matters in *Deutschland Heute* (Wiesbaden, 1954), pp. 150-78. A number of regular issues and releases are made by the Federal Ministry for Refugees, Expellees and War Victims in Bonn.

placed in emergency camps, and often in abandoned army barracks and mud-huts far removed from industrial centers with employment potential. In a typical camp in Lower Bavaria thirteen Silesian families were housed in a single room, sleeping in multiple-tiered bunks and with a narrow bay as living space for each family. These new arrivals were rarely able to find the type of work for which they were prepared and were usually employed only under sub-standard conditions. Furthermore, the social-psychological dangers of uprootedness to the expelled population were a constant threat to the stability of a crowded area. If one had grown up in the mountains of the Sudentenland, he would feel strange in the swampy meadows of Schleswig-Holstein. If one had been born and bred on the Pomeranian plain, he could not easily become accustomed to the Bavarian plateau. The necessary result was to strengthen latent feelings of nostalgia and hinder the integration process.

The refugee problem was not uniformly shared by all the west German Länder, however; and the three Länder Bavaria, Lower Saxony and Schleswig-Holstein, all predominantly rural, contained the bulk of the refugee masses. These three Länder with less than 40 per cent of the population of western Germany, contained roughly 70 per cent of all expellees and refugees. Considering the danger to German social stability in these areas caused by a large and demoralized minority, many of whom were unemployed, the Federal Government responded to articulate pressures by programming a number of resettlements.[7] To do this the Federal Government was

7. In their Stuttgart Charter of 1950, the refugees and expellees solemnly announced their wish to be integrated into the social and economic life of the Federal Republic and urged the Federal Government and all Land governments to help them be located in an environment suitable for achieving this goal. (Hans Wallenberg, *Report on Democratic Institutions in Germany* [New York, 1956], pp. 58-59.)

given authority in Article 119 of the "Transitional Provisions" of the Basic Law to issue the necessary *Verordnungen* to effect an equitable distribution of expellees among the Länder pursuant to their successful integration.

Beginning in 1949, a series of four resettlement measures was started projecting the ultimate transfer of over a million refugees. In a *Verordnung* of November 29, 1949, pursuant to Article 119 of the Basic Law, the Federal government created the first program for 300,000 refugees. From Schleswig-Holstein should come 150,000 refugees, and 75,000 each from Lower Saxony and Bavaria. The distribution key was as follows:[8]

Bremen	2,000
Hamburg	5,000
Hesse	8,000
Northrhine-Westphalia	90,000
Rhineland-Palatinate	90,000
Baden	48,000
Württemberg-Baden	8,000
Baden-Württemberg	
Württemberg-Hohenzollern	49,000

Before this program was successfully completed a second resettlement campaign was instituted through the law enacted on May 22, 1951. This law provided for the settlement of another 300,000 refugees from the original three *Abgabeländer*. The idea was motivated by the unanimous decision of the Bundestag on May 4, 1950, to resettle an additional 600,000 (totalling 900,000) refugees. To avoid aggravating the problems attendant to this plan in the financing of homes, the Federal Government issued ordinances fixing termination dates for the fulfillment of resettlement obligations in stages. By the end of 1952,

8. Germany, Federal Republic, Bundesministerium für Angelegenheiten der Vertriebenen. *Vertriebene, Flüchtlinge, Kriegsgefangene, Heimatlose Ausländer, 1949-1952* (Bonn, 1953).

200,000 refugees were to be resettled, and an additional 100,000 by mid-1953. Resettlement quotas were fixed as follows:

Baden-Württemberg	79,000
Bremen	4,000
Hamburg	11,000
Hesse	7,000
Northrhine-Westphalia	179,000
Rhineland-Palatinate	20,000

On February 13, 1953, the first segment of a third resettlement program was put into force, which together with the second segment projected the transfer of another 315,000 persons. The emphasis of the first half was on alleviating the concentration of crowded refugee camps in Schleswig-Holstein, Lower Saxony, and Bavaria by moving 150,000 refugees from them. The second half, which became effective on January 19, 1955, would move another 150,000 refugees and 15,000 evacueés from the larger cities.[9] Distribution of the refugee and evacuée transfers under the third program was to be:[10]

Baden-Württemberg	71,500
Bremen	3,500
Hamburg	31,000
Hesse	15,000
Northrhine-Westphalia	182,500
Rhineland-Palatinate	11,500

Finally, on June 5, 1956, the Federal Government decreed a final installment on its long-range program for equalization of refugee density. The fourth resettlement plan was inaugurated to include 135,000 refugees from the

9. Evidently the decision to include 15,000 evacueés from Schleswig-Holstein and Lower Saxony was made just prior to the delivery of this *Verordnung* to the Bundesrat. (Bundesrat *Drucksache* 267/54: *Entwurf einer Verordnung zur Umsiedlung von Vertriebenen und Flüchtlingen aus überbelegten Ländern,* January 19, 1955.)

10. Bundesministerium für Vertriebenes, *Geschäftsstatistik über die Umsiedlung* (February 13, 1959), p. 2.

same Länder, to be recruited primarily from among refugees who had had family members resettled earlier to other areas under a specified quota. The distribution breakdown on this measure was as follows:

Baden-Württemberg	29,300
Bremen	6,000
Hamburg	17,150
Hesse	10,550
Northrhine-Westphalia	67,500
Rhineland-Palatinate	4,500

TABLE VII
OVERALL RESETTLEMENT PROGRAM (UNTIL 1956)

Program	1949-51	1951-52	1953	1954	1955	1956
First	300,000	—	—	—	—	—
Second	—	200,000	100,000	—	—	—
Third	—	—	150,000		165,000	—

The criteria used by the Federal Government in determining the various resettlement quotas to be adopted by each receiving Land were (1) smallness of the refugee portion of overall population and (2) ability of a Land to offer job opportunities. The figures in the above tables indicate the relative imbalance in refugee population immediately after the war, and the gradual and partial equalization of refugee density by officially sponsored transfers. Thus the heaviest quotas in every case were affixed to the two Länder Northrhine-Westphalia and Baden-Württemberg, both heavily industrial and both having low percentages of refugee population. If the first hypothesis is to be verified, these two Länder must make a strong representation in behalf of their own problems.

The first law affecting resettlement was debated by

the Bundesrat on May 22, 1951.[11] An important point of reference concerns the partisan make-up at that time of the two distinct Land groups, with the CDU dominant in Schleswig-Holstein, the SPD dominant in Lower Saxony, and a CDU-SPD alliance dominating Land Bavaria. Apart from this, it is noteworthy that all three governments included the Refugee Party as well. The *Aufnahmeländer* were also characterized by diffuse partisan composition. Northrhine-Westphalia was being ruled by the CDU government of Karl Arnold, and Württemberg-Hohenzollern (soon to be subsumed under the new *Südweststaat*) by the CDU-SPD coalition government of Gebhard Müller. When the Bundestag announced on May 4, 1950, that 900,000 refugees must be resettled, this proclamation was supported by all party Fractions. Similarly, the Bundestag's passage of the May, 1951, law was unanimous; so that consensus on the matter was strong among party groups at the national level.

Since the resettlement issue pertained to federalism by affecting particular interests of the Länder differently, it is not inconsequential that it was an *Initiativgesetz* of the Bundestag. For one thing the measure went to the Bundesrat with the full support of the people's representatives in the popular house already on the record, making a contrary attitude by the Bundesrat considerably more difficult.[12] Secondly the lack of a Bundesrat first passage

11. The first program begun on November 29, 1949, was based on a Government enactment and covered only a part of the year 1951. The Federal Minister for Refugees Affairs, Herr Lukaschek, informed the Bundesrat: "The Federal Government was unanimously of the view that after the difficult experiences of the preceding years . . . , a law drawn from the political will of the Bundestag would be better for this year." (Bundesrat *Sitzungsberichte, 52. Sitz.,* March 16, 1951, p. 217.)

12. On Bundestag bills the Bundesrat can have changes made only by demanding a meeting of the *Vermittlungsausschuss* according to Article 77, para. 2 of the Basic Law. Since this action must result in slowing down the legislative machinery and requires a duplication of

on the measure lessened the possibility that the permanent staff members of the Bundesrat Refugee Committee might shuffle the quota figures around before the bill reached the Bundestag, and eliminated the advantage to the Bundesrat of having on hand a formal explanation by the Federal Government. Most important, since the measure appeared only once before the Bundesrat—after its release from the Bundestag—this was the only chance the adversely affected Länder would have to make a strong case for themselves in an effort to modify the measure. No doubt this fact was partially responsible for causing the Adenauer government to permit the second resettlement program to be proposed by the Socialist Fraction in the Bundestag.

The *Berichterstatter* for the Bundesrat Committee for Refugee Questions was Herr Albertz, the Refugee Minister for Lower Saxony.[13] Albertz announced that the Refugee Committee voted by majority to recommend giving the law the concurrence of the Bundesrat and not invoking the Mediation Committee. Unanimous agreement was reached in the committee that the costs of resettlement, which officially became a federal concern with this law, be supported wholly by the Federation. According to Albertz, "The issue of cost is regulated in such a manner that the costs are to be supported by the Federation within the framework of the first Transition Law *(Überleitungsgesetz)*." That particular law was due to expire on March 31, 1951, however, and there was no direct mention made of its expiration in the 1951 *Umsiedlungsgesetz*. From which Albertz concluded that in view of the express wishes of the Länder concerning the

---

efforts by the Bundestag, the idea of calling the *Vermittlungsausschuss* is stigmatized as reflecting an "uncooperative" spirit. See Chapter III.

13. In every refugee resettlement measure discussed in plenary meeting between 1951 and 1956, the reporting member of the Refugee Committee was from one of the *Abgabeländer*.

financial aspects, the clear intent of the omission was "to avoid prejudicing a later judgment, which must follow in a second *Überleitungsgesetz.*"[14] Within the Refugee Committee a series of Land amendments had been presented, covering the numerical quotas, the financial settlement, and the right of the Federal Government to issue individual instructions to Land authorities. These proposals were overridden by a clear majority, composed of both *Abgabeländer* and *Aufnahmeländer.*[15] As spokesman for the committee Albertz made a point of representing both sides and recognized the difficulties from all angles. For the *Aufnahmeländer* he said: "The *Aufnahmeländer* can point out rightfully that it is something quite different to absorb refugees in the year 1951 from what it was under the massive trans-migrations of 1945-46 under the bayonets of Military Government." On the other hand Albertz' words in favor of the plan evidently represented the views of the Refugee Minister for one of the *Abgabeländer* when he said:[16]

It is altogether clear to all Länder and to the representative of the Federal Government that such a law will remain little more than a piece of paper if it is not supported by the good intentions of the Federal Government and all Länder. It is further clear that the re-settlement only partially depends—and I need to emphasize the word 'partially'—on the question how financial means for social home-building *(sozialer Wohnungsbau)* might be made available to the *Aufnahmeländer. . . .*

The *Abgabeländer* must state emphatically that the numbers now being re-assigned in no way represent a real help. In all three *Abgabeländer* the number of persons who have had to be received by way of reuniting families and

14. Bundesrat *Sitzungsberichte, 52. Sitz.*, March 16, 1951, p. 210.
15. Bundesrat *Drucksache Nr. 236/51: Entwurf eines Gesetzes zur Umsiedlung von Heimatvertriebenen aus den Ländern Bayern, Niedersachsen und Schleswig-Holstein,* March 9, 1951.
16. Bundesrat *Sitzungsberichte, 52. Sitz.*, March 16, 1951, p. 210.

because of the continuing influx from the Soviet zone as well as from the German areas beyond the Oder-Neisse, surpasses by far the number of people now to the resettled.

Following the Albertz report each Land delegation expressed its views on the substance of the measure. The only Länder openly opposing passage in its existing form were Northrhine-Westphalia and the three *Südweststaaten* (Baden, Württemberg-Baden, and Württemberg-Hohenzollern). Speaking first was Northrhine-Westphalia's Minister for Housing and Reconstruction, Dr. Schmidt. The official disapproval of this law by that Land was prefaced with a statement by Dr. Schmidt acknowledging that refugee resettlement was a necessary and decisive issue which had to be resolved. He said:

Land Northrhine-Westphalia recognizes that the *Abgabeländer* must be relieved of their ... homeless ... and that it is more appropriate and from the standpoint of cost more realistic to create homes where jobs exist rather than jobs where homes exist. It is a difficult burden to accept 172,500 resettlers in a year. But in order to serve this great cause, we do not resist in any way the high quota of 57.6 per cent as a burden to Northrhine-Westphalia.

Having acknowledged the equitable distribution of quotas, Schmidt denied the possibility of meeting the law's terminal dates for all resettlements, i.e., 200,000 by September 30, 1951, and the remaining 100,000 by December 31. Of the first 200,000 resettlers, Northrhine-Westphalia's share was set at 115,000. This was, according to Land Minister Schmidt, manifestly impossible.

Every expert knows that the necessary housing, even if we were to build according to a 'crash program', could not be created in six months. Next, the real estate must be arranged, and the requisite legal settlements must be made. Every expert estimates the time interval from plan-to-completion to be at least nine months. This law provides six months. But furthermore there are another 100,000 persons to be resettled by 31 December.[17]

So the Arnold government of Northrhine-Westphalia (CDU) was willing to cooperate only under radically altered conditions. Probably the strongest protest by Land Minister Schmidt was about the financial coverage of the law, and here evidences of bitterness crept into his words. In fact, except for those fragmentary funds already available,[18] the language of this law did not make it clear that the necessary federal funds for housing construction would be promptly put at the disposal of the *Aufnahmeländer*. On this ambiguity Schmidt had the following to say:[19]

> Section 17 of the law ignores the problem of finance. That was part of the plan. The framers of this law were fully aware that a decision according to the motion of Northrhine-Westphalia would make necessary a clear decision about where the money is to come from. Since a proposal dealing with this aspect of the issue could not be made the matter has been passed over in silence. Now we are told: well, just move these people into mass-quarters! I strongly believe that we should reach a decision based on the interests of the refugees rather than on political considerations.

All the protests lodged by Northrhine-Westphalia in the Bundesrat were gathered and submitted to the Bundesrat Plenum as a formal proposal to demand a

17. *Ibid.*, p. 213.

18. According to Schmidt, all estimates of the cost of transporting and building homes for 300,000 refugees converged on the figure 600,000,000 DM. Only 155,000,000 DM was already on hand, specifically 95,000,000 from the Main Office for Immediate Assistance, 50,000,000 from the Federal Housing Ministry, and 10,000,000 from the Immediate Assistance sources of the French zone. *Ibid.*, p. 214.

19. *Ibid.*, p. 212. Section 17, para. 2 of the law said Federal budgetary allowances would be made available to the *Aufnahmeländer* to alleviate their task in housing construction, "soweit die nachstellige Finanzierung nicht aus anderen öffentlichen Mitteln gedeckt werden kann." (*Drucksache 236/51.*)

meeting of the Joint Mediation Committee in order to effect the desired changes. Schmidt's plan was to keep the refugees in their camps another 3 to 6 months until a satisfactory money settlement could be reached. Otherwise the result would be that "the incompetence of bureaucracy is denounced, and our young democracy looked upon as an unfit and malicious form of government. Such a responsibility Northrhine-Westphalia does not accept." Responding to Schmidt's adverse comments, the Finance Minister for Schleswig-Holstein, Waldemar Kraft, posted a reminder that in the face of overwhelming misery among hundreds of thousands in his Land it seemed awkward and improper to quibble over the element of timing. He particularly criticized Schmidt's remark about the law's disservice to "our young democracy," pointing out that the young democracy would be best protected "if we eliminate distress from the distress-centers as soon as possible." Then directing his words at Northrhine-Westphalia's plea for more time, Kraft said:[20]

Resettlement is not an event that pounces on the unsuspecting Land government of Northrhine-Westphalia from one day to another. If it is argued therefore that 9 months are necessary instead of 6—to build homes—then I must say from my knowledge of things: first, that Northrhine-Westphalia has had plenty of time to face this problem . . .

(agreement in the chamber)

and moreover that Northrhine-Westphalia has all along been the only Land in position to undertake the necessary construction. The remaining Länder can only plan, and not build—although people are waiting for it—since the financial means are not available.

A bit of unpleasantness followed between Kraft and Dr. Schmidt over something the latter had said. In

20. Bundesrat *Sitzungsberichte, 52. Sitz.*, March 16, 1951, p. 213.

Schmidt's initial criticism of the law, he had made the following statement:

Gentlemen! Yesterday evening I had occasion for discussion with an expelled colleague—a lawyer colleague from the East Zone. I tried to make clear the problem with this law. He said, "That reminds me of the Soviet Government's methods, by which a planned obligation, a plan not possible of fulfillment, is laid down. Then everyone is pleased afterward if the plan is accomplished by 70% or 80%." So it is with us here.

At Kraft's suggestion President Ehard asked Minister Schmidt if he cared to withdraw that particular analogy. Schmidt did not so wish, and Ehard officially scolded him from the chair, with the stricture that Bundesrat members were expected to behave in the most exemplary manner and avoid "catchwords." Schmidt was not to speak again, but the cudgels were picked up by other members of the Bundesrat from Länder having high resettlement quotas, and the argument continued. Now and then the sober, businesslike atmosphere of the plenum was disrupted by a brisk exchange of words. When the third spokesman for the *Abgabeländer*, Dr. Oberländer from Bavaria, rose to express his Land's satisfaction with the law, he had some trouble speaking over the protesting interjections from Gebhard Müller of Württemberg-Hohenzollern.[21]

I must say that the *Abgabeländer* were unanimous today in not making any new claims. Rather they were satisfied with the existing quotas in the hope that the law would be unanimously passed. . . . Bavaria today has a quota of 65,000. I can easily demonstrate that last year alone over 65,000 men migrated to Bavaria—

(Müller: But they immediately migrate farther!)

—but that is not fully correct and moreover that quota will be accounted for exactly by the *Aufnahmeländer*.

(Müller: We already have, in a half-year, 2,400 emigrants from Bavaria!)

21. *Ibid.*, p. 214.

In contrast with 65,000 that is a trifling matter.

(Müller: But we are a small Land!)

We cannot account for those who crossed the border, only those who are officially given transportation.

This type of verbal interaction, which is more or less characteristic of the Bundestag, rarely colors the business of the Bundesrat. Such exchanges can be expected only when vital interests are at stake. However, when the refugee resettlement issue was debated in the Bundestag the deputies from Northrhine-Westphalia and the Southwest areas were silent. The force of party discipline in the popular house foreclosed any opposition to the measure from troubled sources. The Refugee Committee reporter in the Bundesrat, Herr Albertz, later said the comments made by representatives from Northrhine-Westphalia and others were inspired by "an irresponsible and selfish provincialism" which had no place in matters of pressing national concern, such as the refugee issue. Noting the harshness of the reaction to this law in the Bundesrat, Albertz said:[22]

I have been 'pastoral' heretofore in my report. Now I must speak more sharply and state that the representatives of the *Aufnahmeländer* in the Bundestag have been silent. There would have been the place to speak. The *Abgabeländer* have made long statements in the Bundestag Committees as well as in the Plenum. That is where the views should have been expressed which are being given here in the Bundesrat.

Albertz of course was wrong. In view of the oligarchial controls held by party leaders in the Bundestag little opportunity existed there for dissident deputies to speak out against decisions of their party leaders. A general tendency of the party hierarchy to be unresponsive to rank and file opinions is characteristic of German party

22. *Ibid.*, p. 216.

politics. On the other hand regional dissatisfaction with a law can find easy expression in the Bundesrat, where party influence is dominant only when it converges in some way with Land interests. So it is difficult to agree with Herr Albertz, at least on the point that the Bundesrat is an improper place for exposing important federal legislation to disharmonies among the western German Länder.

The Federal Minister for Expellees, Dr. Lukaschek, who had heard the whole debate, summed up the attitude of the Federal Government and the *Abgabeländer* when he said that a meeting of the *Vermittlungsausschuss* could serve no useful purpose. Recognizing that the resettlement problem was extraordinarily difficult and that housing was the chief issue, Lukaschek nevertheless insisted it was a matter of democracy and not primarily of money. Lukaschek pointed out the difference between 3.7 persons per dwelling in the *Aufnahmeländer* and 6.1 persons per dwelling in the *Abgabeländer*. This disparity created an urgent social necessity for the *Abgabeländer,* and recognition of the unalterable priority of this necessity was expected of every Land. The Federal Expellee Minister said also he understood perfectly why the *Aufnahmeländer* "should point out the existing difficulties," but that in the interests of creating a measure of social equilibrium with the Republic, the law must be passed.

In the record vote on the law as unchanged, the Länder split as follows:

		(Quota)
Berlin	Yes	—
Bavaria	Yes	—
Bremen	Yes	1.3%
Hamburg	Yes	3.7%
Hesse	Yes	2.3%
Lower Saxony	Yes	—

Northrhine-Westphalia	No	59.7%
Rhineland-Palatinate	Abstained	6.7%
Schleswig-Holstein	Yes	—
Baden	No	
Württemberg-Baden	No	} 26.3%
Württemberg-Hohenzollern	No	

Thus the law carried, with 24 in favor, 15 opposed and 4 abstentions; and it was proclaimed into force on May 22, 1951. Later developments showed that the *Aufnahmeländer* were not, as Lukaschek had optimistically described them, simply "pointing out the existing difficulties." They meant to put the Bonn Government on notice that they had no intention of sharing the burdens of Schleswig-Holstein in the absence of ironclad financial coverage and guarantees from the Federal Finance Ministry. On June 6, 1951, Northrhine-Westphalia, Rhineland-Palatinate and the three Southwest Länder announced that despite the honorable claims of the May law they could execute their resettlement quotas only within the limits of then existing housing space. Hence they were prepared to accept a total of only 100,000 refugees instead of the required 300,000.[23]

In the Bundestag session the following November 12, Deputy Dr. Edert (CDU, from Kiel in Schleswig-Holstein) confronted the Federal Expellee Ministry with an interpellation that drew stark contrasts between the legally established resettlement obligations and the actual rate of absorption by the *Aufnahmeländer*. Reading from a report issued by the *Abgabeländer* on October 1, 1951, Edert said that of 300,000 expellees only 11,500 had been resettled by August 31.[24] Edert concluded from this that "the will of the people is being ignored. The trouble, I think, lies in the selfish attitude of the *Aufnahmeländer*

23. *Die Betreuung der Vertriebenen,* (Bonn, 1959), pp. 38-39.
24. *Das Parlament,* November 15, 1951.

and otherwise in the deficient and halting issuance of instructions by the Federal Expellee Ministry." Deputy Edert's major complaint, which went unchallenged by other members of the Bundestag, was that the *Aufnahmeländer* saw the problem as essentially financial and not a human one. The fact that Dr. Edert was a member of the CDU criticizing the inaction, or action, of governments controlled by the CDU makes his words worth quoting:[25]

The excuses of Northrhine-Westphalia [CDU and Z], Baden [CDU], Württemberg-Hohenzollern [CDU and SPD], Württemberg-Baden [FDP, CDU and SPD] strike me as threadbare. Of all of them, Baden's reply has been most shocking: that it could exercise no appreciable influence on its own administrative services for the acceleration of home-building—a typical reply.

Edert's remarks were no different from others being made, especially by political leaders in the three *Abgabeländer* who felt the pressures of extremely bad refugee conditions. As Schleswig-Holstein sought through the coercion of legal devices to escape the popular appellation of "poor house of the Federal Republic," the more prosperous and industrial Länder of Northrhine-Westphalia and the Southwest States successfully resisted the dangers of creating economic disequilibrium within their borders from mass resettlements. The provisions of Article 37 of the Basic Law, authorizing federal compulsion in case a Land is delinquent in its legal obligations, became highly academic in view of the fact that the *Aufnahmeländer* comprised 2/3 of the overall population of western Germany. In the fall of 1951, when the whole range of related issues in the refugee-expellee problem was dealt with in the *Bundesvertriebenengesetz,*[26] representatives of

25. *Ibid.*
26. Bundestag *Drucksache 2872: Entwurf eines Gesetzes über die Angelegenheiten der Vertriebenen und Flüchtlinge (Bundesvertriebenengesetz),* November 26, 1951.

the *Abgabeländer* evidently found it useful to be more conciliatory toward their colleagues in other Land governments. Dr. Oberländer (Bavaria), as *Berichterstatter* for the Refugee Committee, while finding it regrettable that "the 1951 program has been so poorly implemented," nevertheless showed markedly more reserve in addressing the *Aufnahmeländer* than had been the case in March. Oberländer joined Federal Minister Lukaschek in hailing this new law the "Basic Law for the Rights of the Expellees and Refugees" and urging every effort to adopt its spirit.[27] In the resettlement field the *Bundesvertriebenengesetz* only affirmed that Bavaria, Lower Saxony and Schleswig-Holstein would be relieved of their disproportionate burden by refugee transfers and that these would be effected by *Rechtsverordnungen* issued by the Federal Government with Bundesrat consent.[28]

This law provoked one of the longest debates the Bundesrat had had up to that time and, unlike most Bundesrat discussions, covered nearly 20 pages of double-columned stenographic reports. This fact is much less attributable to its controversial nature, however, than to its length, comprehensiveness, and complexity. The only excitement created about the resettlement issue was a result of consolidated efforts of the *Abgabeländer* to strengthen the affirmation of legal commitments in Section 38 of the law, the only part dealing exclusively with inter-Land resettlement. A proposal of Dr. Ringelmann (Bavaria), which was rejected, would have changed the fourth paragraph of Section 38, to read:[29] "The Federal Government, in case of non-fulfillment of the resettlement plan may by *Verordnungen* with Bundesrat concurrence, order financial compensation to be made." Ringelmann's

27. Bundesrat *Sitzungsberichte, 70. Sitz.,* October 12, 1951, p. 701.
28. Bundestag *Drucksache* 2872, Section 38.
29. Bundesrat *Sitzungsberichte, 70. Sitz.,* October 12, 1951, p. 709.

proposal secured only the 14 votes of the three *Abgabe-länder* and was defeated 29-14. As with the previous case in May, the alignment of Land votes for or against the change proposal was determined by Land interests strictly. The proposal of Bavaria was one which would accrue solely to the advantage of the *Abgabeländer*.

By early 1952 it was obvious the resettlement plan of the May law had been a failure. Furthermore the representations of the *Aufnahmeländer* had indicated their intentions not to comply with its terms. The result was the introduction of another bill by the Federal Government the following spring purporting to rectify the embarrassing inadequacies in fulfillment of the 1951 quotas. In its 81st meeting on March 28, 1952, the Bundesrat considered the Government draft in first passage. This time the *Berichterstatter* was Herr Asbach, Refugee Minister for Schleswig-Holstein. He reported the bill favorably out of the Refugee Committee with the recommendation that the Bundesrat give its concurrence. The gist of committee talks had been that the terminal dates of September 30, 1951, for 200,000 refugees and December 31, 1951, for another 100,000 could not be observed because of the housing problem in the *Aufnahmeländer;* and to that extent the law was not realistic. According to Asbach, "This law recognizes the dependence of population equalization on the construction of housing, adapts the law to . . . new conditions, and officially recognizes the actual state of affairs in the *Aufnahmeländer*."[30] The statement of purpose and explanation *(Begründung)* of this bill acknowledged that the majority of the anticipated resettlements did not take place in 1951, and affirmed that the last phase of that law involving 100,000 persons would have to be begun from the beginning.

30. Bundesrat *Sitzungsberichte, 81. Sitz.,* March 28, 1952, p. 144.

Two things about this draft invite comment relevant to the experience of 1951 and to the first hypothesis of this study. First, the Federal Government carefully avoided a strict commitment in the text of the bill to terminal dates for fulfillment of quotas. It was specified simply that the Government would later determine by issuance of *Rechtsverordnungen* not later than May 31, 1952, to what time limits the *Aufnahmeländer* would be held.[31] In view of the effective obstinacy of some of the *Aufnahmeländer* in refusing to observe the time limits in 1951, the purpose of this provision was evidently to enable the Lukaschek Ministry to assess the willingness and capability of the affected Länder to absorb their refugee quotas before fixing a time limit. Second, the Federal Government was careful to close the biggest part of the distance in the financial sphere. Now a sum of 150,000,000 DM was made available to the *Aufnahmeländer*, an average of 1,500 DM for each refugee. This money was to be spent exclusively in the building of homes for resettled refugees. The view of the Federal Government, according to Asbach, was "that by the end of [1952] . . . most of the resettled refugees should have work and lodging."[32] Although the money provision did not meet head-on the demands (i.e., of Northrhine-Westphalia) for 2,000 DM per refugee, it at least took a big step toward recognizing the Federal Government's major responsibility in the matter. It was furthermore an admission that the "humane basis for the resettlement program" argument used by the Federal Government, the *Parteifraktion* leaders in the Bundestag and by the *Abgabeländer* leaders was inadequate to

31. Bundesrat *Drucksache 123/52; Entwurf eines Gesetzes zur Änderung und Ergänzung des Gesetzes zur Umsiedlung von Heimatvertriebenen aus den Ländern Bayern, Niedersachsen, und Schleswig-Holstein,* March 20, 1952.
32. Bundesrat *Sitzungsberichte, 81. Sitz.,* March 28, 1952, p. 145.

produce a complaint pattern of behavior by resisting Land governments.

These two points are convincing evidence that a federal minority, representing but 14 votes in the Bundesrat, can effectively stalemate certain types of federal legislation and force the majority (and the Federal Government) to meet its own terms. The point needs to be made, however, that resistance to this legislation was not necessarily made effective by the means of resistance within the Bundesrat. Rather its effectiveness was due to "foot-dragging" in execution of the law. If the 1952 Supplementary Law demonstrated anything clearly, it demonstrated an acknowledgement by the Adenauer Government that it could not enforce policy execution on an uncooperative Land, at least not without recourse to radical measures by way of "federal compulsion."

When, therefore, the third resettlement program was begun in February, 1953, the Government *Verordnung* activating the program made explicit that the 225,000,000 DM appropriated by the Bundestag the preceding summer would be devoted entirely to home-construction and distributed proportionately among the *Aufnahme-länder* according to the size of their quotas.[33] Of 150,000 resettlers in the first segment of the third program, the largest quotas again went to Northrhine-Westphalia (87,000 or 58.0%) and to the Southwest Länder, now consolidated as Baden-Württemberg (40,500 or 27.0%). Accordingly, they received the lion's share of Federal funds on the established formula of 1,500 DM per resettler. Specifications about time limits were left up to the Federal Government at a later date.

As of January 1, 1959, the overall resettlement idea

33. Bundesrat *Drucksache 22/53: Entwurf einer Verordnung zur Umsiedlung von Vertriebenen aus Flüchtlingslägern und Notwohnungen in den Ländern Bayern, Niedersachsen und Schleswig-Holstein*, January 14, 1953.

could be described as having had a fair success. As indicated in Table VII, 940,746 or 89.6 percent of a projected 1,050,000 persons in four programs had been resettled by December 31, 1958. So the conclusion is forced that differences among the *Aufnahmeländer*, the *Abgabeländer* and the Federal Government have been worked out satisfactorily since 1951. A further point would be that the strength of Land particularism, even in Länder lacking cultural traditions, can seriously affect the formulation and execution of legislative policy in Germany. Members of the Bundesrat in the above instances did act in a manner representative of the views and interests of their own Länder as interpreted by the Land Cabinets. The actions of the Bundesrat on these resettlement measures served to bring the effective resistance of particular Land governments to articulation and to point up the Bundesrat as the mobilizer of a federal consciousness in this respect.

GENERAL LAND PROTECTIVENESS

Having tentatively established that members of the Bundesrat do act to protect the specific interests and preserve the governmental integrity of their own governments, thus encouraging federalism, it remains to be demonstrated whether the Bundesrat persists as an instrument for the protection of Land government interests *generally* in legislative affairs. The point has been made above that in the tradition of German federalism, the Second Chamber cannot be typified as an enthusiastic defender of Land legislative prerogatives vis-à-vis the Federation. On the other hand the proposition might well be demonstrated that members of that body regularly press their case for requiring Land participation in and approval of federal legislation through the Bundesrat. If members of the Bundesrat have sought in the recent past to extend the range of legislation coming under the category of *Zustimmungsbedürftigkeit* (see Chapter III), the inference is that this action constitutes an effort to guarantee to the Länder a protective shell against federal action that lacks the consent of the Land governments themselves.[34]

To illustrate the attitude of the Bundesrat toward the question of the need for its concurrence to federal laws, four measures have been selected covering four entirely different policy areas, but which are by no means atypical as bills. The 1951 Refugee Resettlement Law, the Electoral Law of 1953, the General Codetermination Law of 1952, and the law to implement the Common Market Agreement in 1957 will be examined briefly. All came at different times and affected the Länder in different ways. Bundesrat plenary reports show that in any given year something of a pattern develops in the Bundesrat's attitude to most laws, regardless of type, and whether they require Bundesrat consent. Admission must be made that elements figuring in the Bundesrat's efforts to extend the limits of its influence in legislation are not always easily identified. But since the fortunes of that chamber are inextricably tied up with those of the Länder as federal legislative policy determinants, the empirical results are the same whatever the case.

In both the case of the 1951 Refugee Resettlement Law and the Common Market implementation law of 1957, the legal necessity for Bundesrat concurrence was simply affirmed by the reporting committee member and

34. The view is quite common that the future of federalism in Germany must correlate directly with the coverage of the *Zustimmungsgesetze*, and that through them the Bundesrat has managed to keep a watchful, if usually approving eye on federal legislation. See, e.g., Jakob Kratzer, "Zustimmungsgesetze," *Archiv des Öffentlichen Rechts*, Bd. 77, 271.

was not challenged. As a rule, although each committee dealing with the matter will have an eye on the issue of *Zustimmungsbedürftigkeit,* the Judiciary Committee *(Rechtsausschuss)* carries the major responsibility for inclusion of a measure among the *Zustimmungsgesetze,* and its recommendation is apt to be adopted unanimously by the Bundesrat as a whole. With the refugee measure, the Bundesrat's unanimous decision was to identify the law as a *Zustimmungsgesetz* and to point out that its formal proclamation had therefore to be changed to include the phrase: "with the consent of the Bundesrat."[35] This decision was taken as a matter of course, and it was essentially the same in 1957.

The Common Market Treaties were debated in first passage on May 3, 1957.[36] Dr. Weber, Senator of Hamburg and *Berichterstatter* for the special Bundesrat committee established to study these economic treaties, reported the conclusion of the committee that this ratification-law was a *Zustimmungsgesetz.* Evidently there was unanimity within the committee in view of Weber's statement: "That the Treaties require the consent of the Bundesrat cannot be denied." The basis in the Basic Law for this conclusion was Article 84, paragraph 1, dealing with the law's administration and the financial angle of it arising from Article 105, paragraph 3. Professor Hallstein, State Secretary in the Federal Ministry for Foreign Affairs, very discreetly declined to take issue with the question of *Zustimmungsbedürftigkeit.* The case for Land rights was carried a big step further in this instance. Both Dr. Weber and Hesse's Minister-President Zinn emphasized that a partial abandonment of western Germany's sovereignty

35. Bundesrat *Sitzungsberichte, 52. Sitz.,* March 16, 1951, p. 210.
36. Bundesrat *Sitzungsberichte, 176. Sitz.,* May 3, 1957. Bundesrat *Drucksache 146/57: Entwurf eines Gesetzes über den Vertrag vom 25, März 1957 zur Gründung der Europäischen Wirtschaftsgemeinschaft und der Europäischen Atomgemeinschaft.,* April 21, 1957.

through a supra-national economic community would considerably affect Land rights and involve the Länder directly. After rejecting a motion of Northrhine-Westphalia to convene the *Vermittlungsausschuss,* the Bundesrat adopted the recommended *Stellungnahme* of Dr. Weber to insist on sending 11 (of 36) German members to the Consultative Assembly of the Community from among the Bundesrat's members and otherwise to raise no objections to the Treaties. The law returned to the Bundesrat for second passage on July 19. This time Dr. von Merkatz, the Federal Minister for Bundesrat Affairs, was on hand to offer the formal assurances of the Federal Government that when membership in the Assembly came up for legal regulation the wishes of the Bundesrat would be recognized and the Bundesrat "appropriately represented."[37] The reaction of the Federal Government in this case justifies the conclusion that the Bundesrat's persistence as protector of rights of the Länder was effective, and the kind of representation sought by the Land governments would probably not have been forthcoming without the strong position taken in first passage. In early 1961, the proposed law incorporating Bundesrat representation had not been passed by the Bundestag, although it was brought in by the Federal Government.

When the General Codetermination Law, a much more controversial measure, was debated and voted on in the Bundesrat, a representative from the Federal Government was present to contest the issue of *Zustimmungsbedürftigkeit.* A brief interplay took place on the floor of the chamber:[38]

Dr. Spiecker (Northrhine-Westphalia): I would like to draw your attention to the fact that the Judiciary Committee considers this law a *Zustimmungsgesetz.*

37. Bundesrat *Sitzungsberichte, 181. Sitz.,* July 19, 1957, pp. 745-46.
38. Bundesrat *Sitzungsberichte, 90. Sitz.,* July 30, 1952, p. 356.

President Kopf: The Judiciary Committee considers this law a *Zustimmungsgesetz*.

Sauerborn (State Secretary in the Federal Labor Ministry): On behalf of the Federal Government I must point out that after an exhaustive examination of the legal bases for this measure, the Federal Government does not share the view of the Bundesrat Judiciary Committee about the *Zustimmungsbedürftigkeit* of the General Codetermination Law. But in view of the extensive calendar which you face, I will forego a description of the individual reasons for this view.

(Kaisen [Bremen]: It would be well if you stated them!)

I am prepared to do exactly that!

Renner (Baden-Württemberg): After this explanation of the Federal Government representative has been given, I must make it clear as chairman of the Judiciary Committee that that committee must insist on its viewpoint. The reasons for it have been stated in detail. Up until just now there has been no such categorical denial of the *Zustimmungsbedürftigkeit* of the law. There are contained within this law clear administrative instructions to the Land authorities.

(Sauerborn: Shall I state the reasons?)

President Kopf: No!!

(Applause and cheers)

The fourth instance cited in which the question of obligatory Bundesrat concurrence was raised resembles the codetermination debate except in one major respect. When the Electoral Law draft proposed by the Federal Government early in 1953 went to the Bundesrat for first passage, it encountered a storm of criticism. Unlike the codetermination issue, however, the question of *Zustimmungsbedürftigkeit* with the Electoral Law became a *cause célèbre* and was lengthily discussed, mainly because of the implications the decision would have for all subsequent electoral laws. It was pointed out in an earlier chapter that the Bundesrat voted unanimously to

establish the *Zustimmungsbedürftigkeit* of that law. It
was not pointed out, however, that in addition to the
arguments of Federal Interior Minister Lehr against
construction of this law as a *Zustimmungsgesetz*, one of
the Bundesrat members had reservations as well, albeit of
a general nature. Dr. Spiecker of Northrhine-Westphalia
was actually opposing a motion of Rhineland-Palatinate
to the effect that *any* federal electoral law would necessarily be *zustimmungsbedürftig*.[39] According to Spiecker,
the question of requiring Bundesrat concurrence to a
federal law hung on the contents of the law. Whereas
this one he felt to be *zustimmungsbedürftig*—even if it
should be found unconstitutional—Spiecker denied that
all federal electoral laws would be such in all cases, and
he cautioned the Bundesrat against closing off the
possibility of a different finding with a future electoral
law.

Spiecker's arguments against the generality of the
issue and Minister Lehr's arguments against the specific
necessity for concurrence to this one were essentially the
same, that a law providing for elections to the Bundestag
should not be considered a simple administrative act to
execute a federal law. Rather it was " . . . ein einheitlicher
Organisationsakt des Bundesvolkes, gerichtet auf die
Wahl eines Bundestages."[40] The Federal Government was
not sustained, however, and the Bundesrat resolved that
this electoral law required the consent of the Land government representatives in the Bundesrat. Apparently the
Bundesrat never voted on the motion of Rhineland-
Palatinate, and the question of a blanket requirement of
Bundesrat concurrence with federal electoral laws remains
an open one. These matters can only be settled in the final
instance by the Federal Constitutional Court.

39. Bundesrat *Drucksache Nr. 32/3/53,* n.d.
40. Bundesrat *Sitzungsberichte, 100. Sitz.,* February 6, 1953, p. 43.

The record of the Bundesrat on these four measures is indicative of a strong preoccupation with the rights of the Land governments in federal legislation. A cursory examination of plenary discussions of almost all federal legislation would reinforce this impression, whether the law under consideration dealt with incorporation of a national television network, legislation affecting the allocation of federal tax revenues, or an act to dispose of valuable pre-war Prussian book and art properties. It is an easy matter to establish within the Bundesrat a coming together of several distinct attitudes into a single posture of support for Land rights generally. To assess the weight of this single factor relative to other attitude-determinants operating within that chamber and in the Land Cabinets would be considerably more difficult. Succeeding chapters develop more perspective on the totality of Bundesrat action.

The conclusion from all the above evidence, within the limits of the research inventory, is to confirm the first hypothesis: that the Bundesrat does in fact act specifically to protect governmental integrity and freedom of action at the Land level and does in fact maintain a sensitive and protective attitude within the Federal Parliament toward Land government interests.

CHAPTER VI

Legislation, Bureaucracy, and Anonymity

The relationship between democratic order and bureaucracy constitutes one of the enduring problems of modern political science. A major cause for many haunting jeremiads about democratic politics in the twentieth century springs from a professed fear of an advancing monopoly of power by government bureaucracies.[1] The problem, if it exists, would seem to take on even greater importance in the German Federal Republic because the bureaucratic element is directly integrated into the legislative process itself through the Bundesrat, instead of being external to the legislative body as in the United States and Great Britain. There has in fact been considerable concern among West German liberals about the influence of a highly competent bureaucracy, placed foursquare within the Federal Parliament, on the development of democratic impulses. In western Germany the Bundestag is democratically organized, in the sense that it

1. Since the initial stimulus by Weber and Michels, the list of systematic studies of bureaucratic institutions has become legion. Particularly well known are the arguments of James Burnham, Ludwig von Mises, Friedrich A. Hayek, and Gordon (Lord) Hewart. Some more recent contributions include Herbert Simon, *Administrative Behavior* (New York, 1958); Peter Blau, *Bureaucracy in Modern Society* (New York, 1956); and Philip Selznick, *TVA and the Grass Roots* (Berkeley and Los Angeles, 1949). An effort to combat the despair of bureaucracy analysts is in Alvin W. Gouldner, "Metaphysical Pathos and the Theory of Bureaucracy," *American Political Science Review,* XLIX (June, 1955), 496-507; see also S. M. Lipset, *Political Man: The Social Bases of Politics* (Garden City, N. Y. 1960), esp. pp. 21-30.

reflects popular pressures, public opinion, and party conflicts. The Bundesrat is chosen and staffed in quite different ways and according to different criteria.

A cursory examination of current Bundesrat tendencies, which in turn could only be reinforced by earlier legislative habits that activated bureaucratic influences, supports the idea that formal administrative personnel as well as informal tendencies toward bureaucratization play a vital role in determining the official parliamentary attitude of the Upper House.[2] The main points to be examined here are: first, to what extent is the Bundesrat an instrument through which the administrative pressures and points of view of the professional bureaucracy brought to bear in the legislative field on policy-making in general? Second, to what extent do the Land government ministers in the Bundesrat, who after all are mostly party politicians responsible for their actions to partisan legislative bodies at the Land level, seek to avoid the strains of party strife by reducing problems of political conflict to those of administrative routine?

Because the German Land bureaucracies are given official prior access—in the first passage—to bills emanating from the Federal Government, characterization of the Bundesrat's legislative role must be closely related to the simple facts of legislative procedure. Correspondingly, a legislative case was selected for examination which was a *Gesetzentwurf* of the Federal Government, and which would thereby maximize the Bundesrat committees' share of time allocated under the Basic Law for "prior con-

2. The coöptation of career civil servants into the second legislative chamber had been a sensitive matter of debate during the plenary meetings of the Parliamentary Council. See especially the criticism by Dr. Rudolf Katz (SPD) in the *Stenographische Berichte, 7. Sitzung,* October 21, 1948, p. 91. See also John Ford Golay, *The Founding of the Federal Republic of Germany* (Chicago, 1958), pp. 41-58; and Arnold Brecht, "Personnel Management," in E. H. Litchfield (ed.), *Governing Postwar Germany* (Ithaca, 1953), pp. 263-93.

sideration" of such bills. Once the German leaders had decided in 1949 to require politically responsible Cabinet ministers to attend plenary meetings, then presumably it would not matter so much that senior administrators *(Beamten)* from appropriate Land ministries could be appointed to serve on the Bundesrat standing committees as "deputy committee members." As a matter of fact it mattered rather much.

For one thing it would be difficult to over-emphasize the influence of committee work on the Bundesrat's parliamentary role, despite the fact that on most important questions Land Cabinet discussions had already been held and decisions reached on broad outlines. Only rarely does the Bundesrat deviate from committee recommendations, and these few instances are those particularly sensitive issues on which party interests and commitments are pre-emptive.[3] Second, the regular committee member, who is also a "regular" or "deputy" member of the Bundesrat and thus a member of his Land Cabinet, is under too much pressure for time to attend his committee meetings regularly, leaving important discussions and arrangements in committee to be handled on behalf of his Land by an administrative expert. Every Land—including West Berlin—is represented on every standing committee by one of its Bundesrat members or "someone else acting as an agent of the government." A

3. On the basis of information gained through conversations held in the summer, 1960, between the author and committee secretaries, members and former members of the Bundesrat, there is general consensus that "all but a negligible number" of legislative actions taken by the Bundesrat are based on adoption of committee reports. A close examination of Bundesrat *Sitzungsberichte* is further indicative of the almost complete monopoly which committees hold over Bundesrat votes. In the first major work dealing with the political position of the Bundesrat, Karlheinz Neunreither reports that in cases where there was no conflict in committee reports, only one per cent failed of adoption. (Neunreither, *Der Bundesrat Zwischen Politik und Verwaltung* [Heidelberg, 1959], p. 42.)

common observation made about Bundesrat committees is that the bulk of the work there is handled by career civil servants, many of whom enjoy a strategic importance by virtue of their permanent residence in Bonn.[4] The importance of this observation and its relevance to the Bundesrat as a legislative institution are especially enlarged since the policy was early adopted by the Bundesrat of giving the interested committee virtually all of the three-week period to study a first passage bill.

Table VIII illustrates the ratio of ministers to civil servants serving on ten Bundesrat committees between 1949 and 1961. Since every land has one representative (and one vote) on each of these committees, it was represented in every case by either a minister or an administrative specialist, barring a few failures to be represented at all. The table figures clearly point to a developing preponderance of professional administrators in the committees, with the ratio of preponderance advancing steadily from 1949 until about 1955 and levelling off thereafter. It is also true that a high percentage of ministers recorded as present for a meeting remained only for consideration of one bill and then left their government interests to be safeguarded by a specialist. These considerations must not be construed to

4. Although the only deputy committee members having a permanent Bonn residence are those on the staffs of the Land *Bevollmächtigten,* most of the preparation for committee work is done in the Land ministries, which send their representatives to sessions of the Bundesrat committees. These representatives are usually delegated by the Länder as deputy members of the committees. If these administrators are unable to attend the meetings, they at least advise the Bonn staffs by letter or by telephone. On the influence of civil servants generally within the Bundesrat committees, see Hans Schäfer, *Der Bundesrat* (Köln, 1955), pp. 49-61; Olle Nyman, *Der Westdeutsche Föderalismus* (Stockholm, 1960), pp. 146-48; and Neunreither, *Der Bundesrat Zwischen Politik und Verwaltung,* pp. 30-36. Werner Weber describes the Bundesrat committees as "a world of bureaucracy with its own laws." (*Spannungen und Kräfte im westdeutschen Verfassungssystem* [Stuttgart, 1951], p. 92).

TABLE VIII

CIVIL SERVANTS IN BUNDESRAT COMMITTEE MEETINGS, 1949-1960

Committee meetings	1949	1950	1951	1952	1953	1954	1955	1956	1957	1958	1959	1960[b]	Total
A. Committee for Agriculture													
All civil servants[a] or all but one	0	6	4	3	3	6	4	9	12	2	8	3	60
More than ½ civil servants	4	24	27	22	15	16	13	18	15	11	11	5	191
Less than ½ civil servants	0	1	0	0	0	0	0	0	0	0	0	0	1
No civil servants (all Ministers) or only one	0	0	0	0	0	0	0	0	0	0	0	0	0

[a] The term "civil servant" applies to persons not in their Land Cabinets. In cases where State Secretaries are members of their Cabinets, a practice permitted in Bavaria and Baden-Württemberg, they were considered Ministers.
[b] Until July.

B. Committee for Economics	1949	1950	1951	1952	1953	1954	1955	1956	1957	1958	1959	1960	Total
All civil servants or all but one	0	4	7	8	10	7	6	8	4	8	3	3	68
More than ½ civil servants	2	16	28	21	15	16	15	17	14	14	12	9	179
Less than ½ civil servants	1	1	0	0	0	0	0	0	1	0	0	0	3
No civil servants (all Ministers) or only one	0	0	0	0	0	0	0	0	0	0	0	0	0

C. Committee for Labor and Social Affairs	1949	1950	1951	1952	1953	1954	1955	1956	1957	1958	1959	1960	Total
All civil servants or all but one	0	5	3	3	4	4	2	7	6	4	6	4	48
More than ½ civil servants	2	17	22	19	18	14	14	17	15	14	13	8	173
Less than ½ civil servants	0	0	5	1	0	0	0	0	0	0	0	0	6
No civil servants (all Ministers) or only one	0	0	0	0	0	0	0	0	0	0	0	0	0

D. Committee for the Interior	1949	1950	1951	1952	1953	1954	1955	1956	1957	1958	1959	1960	Total
All civil servants or all but one	0	11	21	14	10	17	15	15	14	11	13	10	151
More than ½ civil servants	1	26	29	22	21	17	17	16	15	11	13	10	198
Less than ½ civil servants	1	1	1	0	0	0	0	0	0	0	0	0	3
No civil servants (all Ministers) or only one	0	0	0	0	0	0	0	0	0	0	0	0	0

E. Finance Committee	1949	1950	1951	1952	1953	1954	1955	1956	1957	1958	1959	1960	Total
All civil servants or all but one	0	0	0	0	0	0	0	0	0	0	0	0	0
More than ½ civil servants	1	8	20	12	12	10	10	10	10	6	7	8	118
Less than ½ civil servants	4	13	9	12	6	6	4	8	5	7	5	1	80
No civil servants (all Ministers) or only one	0	0	0	0	0	0	0	0	0	0	0	0	0

F. Judiciary Committee	1949	1950	1951	1952	1953	1954	1955	1956	1957	1958	1959	1960	Total
All civil servants or all but one	0	1	19	25	15	12	7	6	2	0	3	5	95
More than ½ civil servants	7	38	32	33	17	16	15	19	14	14	12	9	226
Less than ½ civil servants	0	0	0	0	0	0	0	0	0	1	0	0	1
No civil servants (all Ministers) or only one	0	0	0	0	0	0	0	0	0	0	0	0	0

TABLE VIII (Cont.)

Committee meetings	1949	1950	1951	1952	1953	1954	1955	1956	1957	1958	1959	1960b	Total
G. Committee for Traffic and Post													
All civil servants or all but one	0	3	7	15	5	5	4	5	6	5	3	2	60
More than ½ civil servants	2	15	15	21	12	7	8	11	12	7	8	5	123
Less than ½ civil servants	1	0	0	0	0	0	0	0	0	0	0	0	1
No civil servants (all Ministers) or only one	0	0	0	0	0	0	0	0	0	0	0	0	0
H. Committee for Cultural Questions													
All civil servants or all but one	0	0	0	1	2	3	3	1	3	3	2	1	19
More than ½ civil servants	0	1	3	4	4	5	4	1	3	4	3	1	33
Less than ½ civil servants	0	3	1	2	2	1	0	2	0	0	0	0	11
No civil servants (all Ministers) or only one	0	0	0	0	0	0	0	0	0	0	0	0	0
I. Committee for Refugee Questions													
All civil servants or all but one	0	4	3	7	6	1	6	9	5	4	9	3	57
More than ½ civil servants	1	12	16	12	13	7	8	12	6	6	9	3	105
Less than ½ civil servants	1	1	0	0	0	0	0	0	1	0	0	0	3
No civil servants (all Ministers) or only one	1	0	0	0	0	0	0	0	0	0	0	0	1
J. Committee for Reconstruction and Housing													
All civil servants or all but one	0	0	2	4	4	6	4	8	9	7	4	0	48
More than ½ civil servants	0	5	8	14	10	8	10	11	9	9	7	4	95
Less than ½ civil servants	0	1	1	0	0	1	1	1	0	1	0	0	6
No civil servants (all Ministers) or only one	0	0	0	0	0	0	0	0	0	0	0	0	0
K. Committee Meetings for Ten Standing Committeesc													
All civil servants or all but one	0	34	66	80	59	61	51	68	61	44	51	31	606
More than ½ civil servants	20	165	197	180	133	113	113	127	105	93	90	61	1399
Less than ½ civil servants	8	15	17	15	13	11	10	16	15	12	10	5	147
No civil servants (all Ministers) or only one	1	0	0	0	2	2	0	0	1	0	0	0	6

c The three main "political" committees—Foreign Affairs, Defense, and All-German Questions—are classified, and their protocols are not generally available. A reasonable assumption would be that a higher proportion of Land Ministers regularly attend meetings of these committees. Neunreither has indicated this for the year 1955 in *Der Bundesrat Zwischen Politik und Verwaltung*, p. 35.

mean that the votes of a Land in the Bundesrat are formally bound to committee recommendations. Bundesrat members are bound only to votes made within their Cabinets, and the work in committee is of a "preliminary" nature. The significance of these data lies rather in the factual persuasiveness of the expert views of deputy committee members on parliamentary action taken by their formal leaders in the plenum. This unstructured element of coerciveness relates directly to the simple routine steps in the passage of certain bills, and specifically to the peculiarities of first passage.

Examination of committee protocols and recommendations made to the plenum is revealing. Considering the table figures and the predisposition of the Bundesrat plenum to adopt committee reports unchanged, one can conclude that at least with first passage bills, the recommendations of administrative specialists are crucial.[5] This exercise of positive influence within the Federal Parliament by Land ministerial bureaucracies constitutes a manifest element of bureaucratization. The net result is that the Bundesrat in its first impulse to action on Government bills tends to seek less to redirect or clarify the course of policy or of its aims, than to reduce that policy to fixed processes of administration according to local convenience and "internal criteria of correctness."[6]

5. The committees' importance, however, must be recognized as subordinate in those sensitive policy areas in which federal and Land party attitudes have "dovetailed." For the influence of federal political parties on Bundesrat voting see Arnold Heidenheimer, "Federalism and the Party System," *American Political Science Review*, XLI (September, 1959), 809-30; Weber, *Spannung und Kräfte*, pp. 92ff.; and Theodor Eschenburg, *Staat und Gesellschaft in Deutschland* (Stuttgart, 1956), pp. 615ff.

6. The idea of applying "internal criteria of correctness" as a test of the desirability of a measure (bill, ordinance, etc.) irrespective of its broader purposes does not force judgment about the possibility of compartmentalizing so-called administrative decisions, thus separating them generically from so-called policy decisions. See Simon, *Administrative Behavior*, pp. 52-59.

In addition to the nexus between the procedural component of first passage and a manifest element of bureaucracy, a closer look at the habits and apparent biases of these federative legislators supports the idea of a latent tendency toward bureaucratization growing out of the political responsibilities and professional background of "regular" Bundesrat members. Every person appointed to the Bundesrat is also a member of his local Cabinet with direct responsibility for administration of federal laws in a given policy area. It would be no surprise if these Ministers should feel it necessary to be constantly alert to problems that might arise in the execution of laws, or even if they should betray a visibly keener interest in protecting Land ministerial independence of action than the general legislative prerogatives of the Länder. The point has already been made that West German federalism is predicated on a system of policy determination at the center with field administration in Land and local offices.

The idea of a latent bureaucratic function in federal legislation does not presume on the analytical merits of separating policy from administration, their separation being a highly questionable matter. Still the artificiality of the distinction in no way alters the possibility that Bundesrat members seek to perform just such a separation. By being "administration-oriented" rather than "policy-oriented," by trying to convert issues of controversy and dissent into those settled and routine affairs of state familiar to the practiced eye of a professional administrator,[7] even regular members show latent tendencies toward bureaucratization of the legislative

7. Recognition of this tendency has led Alfred Grosser to describe the federative chamber as "an assembly of wise men that operates to counteract the centralism of the Federal Government and the demogoguery of the Bundestag." (Grosser, *Die Bonner Demokratie* [Düsseldorf, 1960], p. 84.)

process in western Germany. Thus a bureaucratic point of view, in the Weberian sense of "routinization of duties," might be seen operating in every phase of Bundersat actions.

The second phase of the second hypothesis is approached irrespective of the idea that mobile pressures from the professional bureaucracy are brought into play during first passage. That is, Land ministers in the Bundesrat might be demonstrated to reveal in their general orientation a tendency to reduce policy questions to administrative and procedural ones. Here plenary discussions are relevant that handle federal laws in second passage, where one would not necessarily expect a bureaucratic bias. In this way the tactical advantage of administrative careerists on the committee staffs can be temporarily overlooked, and a closer examination made of Bundesrat members acting in a strict parliamentary capacity during second passage. It might be recalled at this point that regular Bundesrat members, having distinct ministerial portfolios in their respective governments, must necessarily maintain a permanent interest in the enforcement phases of federal laws and the anticipated problems attendant to their enforcement. This fact raises several possibilities about official Bundesrat behavior that could yield a unique characterization for it as a legislative chamber.

One of the most frequently acknowledged attributes of German political life has been its tendency to convert all major political issues into compartmentalized problems of public administration and jurisprudence, and to assign a heavy share of public influence to "non-political" office holders.[8] A bibliography of twentieth century German

8. Herbert Spiro in *The Politics of Codetermination* (Cambridge, 1958), pp. 5-15, notes this tendency in all phases of German social activity. Spiro speaks of a German yearning for a thorough "compartmentalization of public life" and of the popular methods used for

works in political science reveals a preponderance of studies dealing with jurisprudence and administration indicating a tendency to ignore the "non-rational" or purely "politics" aspect of social action. Official German state functionaries are often found to believe that the legitimate sphere of public activity is inside the limits of already existing legal regulations, and that the order prescribed by concrete laws is equivalent to order in general. The German political scientist Max Weber spoke often and critically of his countrymen's "passion for bureaucracy." His words in this regard are instructive:[9]

It is as if in politics the spectre of timidity—which has in any case always been rather a standby for the Germans—were to stand alone at the helm; as if we were deliberately to become men who need "order" and nothing but order, who become nervous and cowardly if for one moment this order wavers, and helpless if they are torn away from their total incorporation in it.

As a contemporary of the Bismarckian state renowned for its bureaucratic milieu, Weber was here exhorting his students "to challenge the unquestioning idolization of bureaucracy." The problem of course is more complex than a mere preoccupation with the routine duties of political life. It has become a general axiom of social psychology, for example, that people, especially public

---

overcoming spontaneous political action in "a calculated effort to effect a reduction of politics." This point is also a major theme of Friedrich Meinecke, who speaks of the substitution of *homo faber* for *homo sapiens* in the German emphasis on the over-rationalized but technically proficient man. See Meinecke, *The German Catastrophe* (Cambridge, 1950), esp. pp. 7-25 and 34-39. Also John Hallowell, *The Decline of Liberalism as an Ideology* (Berkeley and Los Angeles, 1934), pp. 14-20; Hans Rosenberg, *Bureaucracy, Aristocracy and Autocracy: the Prussian Experience* (Cambridge, 1958), pp. 232-38; and Talcott Parsons, "Democracy and Social Structure in Pre-Nazi Germany," *Journal of Legal and Political Philosophy*, I (1942), 96-114.

9. J. P. Mayer, *Max Weber and German Politics* (London, 1944), pp. 127-28.

functionaries, have a low tolerance for ambiguity and for unstructured situations, and hence they naturally gravitate toward elimination of the ambiguity by way of social order.[10] The question might be asked: is this deliberate structuring of order evident in the approach to legislation of German Land executives and high-ranking administrators?

THE PROCEDURAL COMPONENT: MANIFEST BUREAUCRACY

With these considerations in mind examination of the Bundesrat in its bureaucratic context can proceed by a breakdown of Bundesrat debates on legislative cases selected for their appropriateness to the subject. The subject of German rearmament represents an issue of sufficient political disagreement among German leaders to cause intra-parliamentary controversy, and the Bundesrat's participation should be revealing. Particular attention is given here to the Volunteers Bill of the Adenauer Government because that measure was the first rearmament bill, and because it encountered strong disapproval from several different sources for different reasons. The peculiar characteristics of the Bundesrat's reaction to it are useful especially for confirming the correlation between the procedural involvements of first passage and the Bundesrat's bureaucratic bias.

Ratification by West Germany of the Paris Accords in March, 1955, included German acceptance of the Saar Statute, West European Union, the presence of foreign troops on German soil, and West German entrance into NATO.[11] It also meant acceptance by the Germans of a

10. Hadley Cantril, *The Psychology of Social Movements* (New York, 1941), pp. 54-60; also R. K. Merton, *Social Theory and Social Structure* (rev. ed.; Glencoe, Ill., 1957), pp. 196, 204.
11. A concise description of the West German rearmament issue as a domestic controversy is by Gordon A. Craig, *NATO and the New German Army* (Memorandum Number Eight), Center for International

plan for raising and maintaining a military establishment of 500,000 officers and men, including both volunteers and conscripts. The months immediately preceding and following the signing of these Accords gave convincing evidence of an intense feeling of anti-militarism in West Germany, particularly among the draft-age youth. In the spring and summer of 1954, government spokesmen were jeered at by young Germans in public meeting-halls, and at Augsburg a group of students met the Federal Defense Minister with hostile shouts and a barrage of beer mugs.[12] This feeling doubtless reflected a preoccupation with Germany's unhappy past experiences with military adventure.

Parliamentary energies during the spring and summer of 1955 were absorbed with crucial questions arising from the projected rearmament program, mainly with the important question of the proper relationship between civilian and military authorities in the Federal Republic. This was especially true of the SPD Fraction in the Bundestag. Although the Socialists opposed building a new army and entrance into NATO as obstacles to Germany's ultimate reunification, they acknowledged the inevitability of it and were active in the debates trying to anchor the military establishment to strict parliamentary control.[13] The importance of the task of parliamentariza-

Studies (Princeton, 1955). See also Hans Speier (ed.), *West German Leadership and Foreign Policy* (Evanston, 1957); and Norbert Tönnies, *Der Weg zu den Waffen: Die Geschichte der deutschen Wiederbewaffnung, 1949-1957* (Köln, 1957), esp. pp. 176-80. A series of highly colorful and forthright commentaries on the projected German army was written by Adelbert Weinstein, the military expert of the *Frankfurter Allgemeine Zeitung*, throughout 1955 (hereafter cited as *FAZ*).

12. Craig, *NATO and the New German Army*, p. 5. On May 28, 1955, the day that the Volunteers Bill was sent to the Bundesrat by the Federal Government for first passage, the *Deutscher Gewerkschaftsbund* (DGB) announced again its unqualified opposition to rearmament in any form.

13. See, for example, excerpts from the speech of Fritz Erler, the

tion of the army was stated aptly, if cautiously, by Dr. Richard Jaeger (CSU), Vice-President of the Bundestag and chairman of the European Security Committee, during the first Bundestag debate of the Volunteers Bill. Jaeger said:[14]

We face an unusual situation. Germany has always had a good army. Today we have beyond a doubt the beginnings of a good democracy, and one that is developing well. But we have never had in Germany at the same time a good army, and a good democracy, and a suitable relationship between them such as other democracies know. Ladies and Gentlemen, this seems to me to be the essence of the problem: to create a *Bundeswehr* which is the equal of former German armies in striking power but which is not only well integrated into the democratic state—without becoming a state within a state—but supports and maintains this democratic state out of inner conviction. That is the problem we face.

The sensitiveness of the rearmament issue, aggravated by a general belief that in the event of war Germany would become a nuclear battleground, affected all political groups. It was therefore surprising, though characteristic, that Chancellor Adenauer's preliminary handling of the matter was so arbitrary and hastily conceived.[15] His plan was to abandon for the time being a comprehensive law regulating the details of military affairs and to introduce immediately a brief skeleton-bill which would authorize establishment of the necessary

SPD's defense expert, in *FAZ*, June 30, 1955, and in *Das Parlament*, July 20, 1955.

14. Bundestag *Verhandlungen, 93. Sitz.,* June 28, 1955 *(Stenographische Berichte Band 26),* Bonn, 1955, p. 5228.

15. Chancellor Adenauer's difficulties in this case are not always appreciated. The Paris Treaties did not go into effect until May 5, 1955; and to engage in active preparations before that time would have invited the charge of militarism from other countries. On the other hand, once the Treaties had been ratified Dr. Adenauer was anxious to demonstrate to Germany's new allies her readiness to accept an obligation to the new security concept. See Richard Hiscocks, *Democracy in Western Germany* (London, 1957), pp. 286-89.

cadres and courses of instruction while the permanent legislation was being worked out. The stop-gap Volunteers Bill *(Freiwilligengesetz)* was sent to the Bundesrat for first passage on May 28, 1955. There it ran into the first organized resistance, which ultimately forced the Chancellor to make several important concessions. There had already been strong indications of disapproval of Adenauer's plans, but the Chancellor gave no indication from his handling of the matter that he expected disapproval from the Bundesrat.

The Volunteers Bill consisted of but three short sections with these essential provisions:[16] the conscription of military forces would begin with enlistment of voluntary soldiers; pending special legislation their status would be that of Civil Servants on Probation *(Beamten auf Probe)*, and the same legal regulations governing civil servants would apply to the soldiers; the Federal Government would determine through *Rechtsverordnungen* how the soldiers would fall into civil service grades according to a fixed formula. Other than these provisions, the bill simply stated that it would expire upon effective promulgation of the comprehensive Soldiers Law, not later than March 31, 1956. The abbreviated measure was promptly referred to the newly constituted Bundesrat Committee for European Security Questions and was considered in three different meetings of that committee before its discussion in the plenary session on June 10, 1955. Subsequent to its referral to the Security Committee, the bill also went to the Finance and Judiciary Committees. The report of these committees, which was adopted unchanged by the plenum, contained the recommended formulation of a reply by the Bundesrat that

16. Bundesrat *Drucksache 172/55, 28. Mai 1955; Entwurf eines Gesetzes über die vorläufige Rechtsstellung der Freiwilligen in den Streitkräften (Freiwilligengesetz).*

was mutually acceptable to all three committees. The reporter was unusually apologetic and his report unusually long.

Committee reaction turned on two central criticisms: first, that the existing draft opened the door to formation of large volunteer contingents and would thereby prejudice the question of administration by "necessitating the creation of a large administrative apparatus," for which no provision existed in the Basic Law. Second, extending the status of *Beamten auf Probe* to the volunteers, temporarily integrating military with civil administration, would be repugnant if not dangerous to sound standards of administrative management. The reporting member of the *federführende* Security Committee, Dr. Artur Sträter of the CDU government of Karl Arnold in Northrhine-Westphalia, also expressed the committees' embarrassment at having to be "as much concerned with fundamental questions of defense as with the specifics of the Government's first bill of defense."[17] The general lack of advance information concerning the new bill made it necessary for the Bundesrat committee to meet head-on the principles of policy in the rearmament field. Sträter gave ample demonstration that the examining committees abhorred having to adventure into the unknown.

The peculiar position of the Security Committee was made doubly uncomfortable, according to Sträter, "because the mysterious *Drei-Paragraphen-Blitzgesetz* simply permits no knowledge of what concept of military organization really lies at the base of it all." The necessary outcome was that even with a maximum effort on everybody's part the allotted time was hardly enough to complete satisfactory consultations on the matter. This was especially regrettable to Dr. Sträter in view of the fateful rearmament issue involved, "which is likely to

17. Bundesrat *Sitzungsberichte, 142. Sitz.,* June 10, 1955, p. 134.

be . . . the outstanding problem of the next few years."
Furthermore the Security Committee emphasized that it
was not being "dilatory or obstructive," but that it wanted
to proceed properly and assume its own fair share of the
responsibility. For the Bundesrat has always considered it
an obligation, not only to take a formal position on the
material content of a bill, "but also to take care that
completed laws have administrative firmness and are able
to withstand close examination by the Constitutional
Court."[18] The crucial point of agreement among all three
participant committees concerned the likelihood of prejudicing later measures and thereby forestalling the
desired results (*das gewollte Entgültige vorwegnehmen*).
All these objections were presented orally to the
assembled Security Committee during its meeting of
June 3.

Before the plenum heard the committee report these
three committees held long and searching meetings, and
consensus was then reached that West German defense
policy must "proceed from a political decision containing
absolute clarification of all constitutional and legal
principles," and that such clarity was lacking. At least to
this extent the bill was found deficient. Still the conciliatory tone of the Bundesrat committees did not disappear altogether until the morning before the plenary
meeting, and the overall committee reaction was not then
unsympathetic. Conclusions reached tentatively on the
earlier date were to accept the intentions of the Federal
Government and to approve the Government's proposal to
create promptly the pre-conditions necessary for material-
ization of a defense contribution appropriate to the Paris
Accords; but also to announce: "The Bundesrat expects
the Federal Government to complete the draft law, to
create the legal pre-conditions for its practicability, and

18. *Ibid.*, p. 135.

to make known the principles of its defense policy."[19] Other than this the committee wanted the Bundesrat to insist that *Rechtsverordnungen* issued for transitional regulations could be permitted only with the concurrence of the Bundesrat; and that the volunteers would perform strictly military duties, leaving administration to the civil authorities. This was the situation on June 3.

On the date set for full Bundesrat discussion of the rearmament measure an embarrassing discrepancy came to light between the statement of the Federal Chancellor's intentions and an open letter of the Federal Finance Minister to the Budget and Security Committees of the Bundestag. Upon an invitation from Bundesrat President Peter Altmeier (CDU, Rhineland-Palatinate), Chancellor Adenauer offered his personal reaction to the tentative committee recommendations. Adenauer's main point was that federal law-makers would not be hindered in any way by this bill in their attention to permanent defense legislation. He said, "The Volunteers Bill is a strictly preliminary measure. I positively confirm that the decisions to be made in matters of military organization and administration, especially the administrative competence and participation of the Länder, will not be prejudiced by this law. These questions must yet be discussed."[20]

But the Chancellor's reassurances seemed to conflict with the letter from the Federal Finance Ministry to the Budget and Security Committees of the Bundestag. Finance Minister Schäffer explained on June 9 that the subordinate authorities and services of the anticipated defense administrative hierarchy might be created right

19. *Ibid.*, p. 136.
20. The text of Adenauer's letter is in *ibid.*, pp. 127-38. The Chancellor had also given previous assurance to the Bundesrat that its committee recommendations would be given the closest attention. (*FAZ*, June 4, 1955.)

away, and that the sum of 83,000,000 DM was to be provided to get started. Express mention was made in Schäffer's letter of the following offices: Military Affairs Administration, Military Allowances Office, Headquarters Administration, Military Replacement Office, and about half a dozen others. The haste involved here was offensive to the Bundesrat committees and the amount unaccountably large, especially in view of Defense Minister Blank's explanation before the Bundesrat Security Committee that his projected ministry would need less than 100 new positions and no important new administrative machinery.[21] The Security Committee of the Bundesrat had become highly suspicious. Dr. Sträter pointed out the stark inconsistencies between the Finance Ministry's proposition and the promises of Chancellor Adenauer a few days earlier. Despite the remonstrances of both Blank and Adenauer that the Volunteers Bill would in no way anticipate the structure of military administration, the feeling on the Bundesrat committee after June 9 was that 83,000,000 DM could pay for a large volume of administration and that this would anticipate the question quite a bit. One member of the committee was quoted as saying that the Bundesrat was now confirmed in its demand to require full clarification on all points and in its indication that the contrivance of a Federal defense administration was without support in the Basic Law.

The final committee report therefore was considerably more strident than earlier committee discussions would indicate, and all three committees converged on the two major complaints. The committee staffs, according to Sträter, had been especially impatient with the *Beamten auf Probe* approach and were strongly inclined to the view that the use of civil service law for soldiers must fail in every respect. Expert opinion within the committees felt

21. *FAZ*, June 4, 1955.

that the "awkward application" of the many civil service guarantees to military personnel could lead to "impossible consequences." To aggravate an already "awkward" situation the committees felt that the Government had left purposely vague how the authorizations for civil service officials might "appropriately" (*sinngemäss*) cover identical matters in the military sphere. That same day the Bundesrat voted 38-4 to adopt the committee recommendations and to send these to the Federal Government as the *Stellungnahme* of the Bundesrat.[22] This statement announced the essential concurrence of the Bundesrat with the Government's intentions to implement the Paris Accords, but demanded that the Government give thorough consideration to the report of the Bundesrat Security Committee. The essence of the Bundesrat's position was to find that the Volunteers Bill attempted regulation of a part of the problem without clarification about defense in a broader sense and without the legal possibilities for its execution. Students familiar with German legislative habits would recognize this first passage action as a particularly strong representation *vis-à-vis* the Federal Government, in spite of the fact that only the votes of Land Hesse were cast against the Bundesrat's essential agreement to rearmament.

The results of committee and plenary Bundesrat action in this case indicate an overriding concern for the danger of pre-empting the whole field of defense administration prematurely for the Federal Government, and the danger of prejudicing future defense legislation by ill-conceived programming, particularly with the "Civil Servants on Probation" solution. A fair conclusion would be that the committee viewpoint was decisive, and that by adopting

22. The four dissenting votes were those of Land Hesse, controlled by an all-Socialist government and opposed both to rearmament and to the Paris Accords.

without change the committee recommendations the Bundesrat gave official vitality to the pressures and points of view of the professional bureaucracy. At least in this instance the Bundesrat did fulfill the administrator's role of bureaucratic supervision. That the Judiciary Committee should direct its criticisms of the mechanics of the measure to their "awkwardness," for example, is indicative of a tendency to find "unawkward" ways of accomplishing the same thing. It is of course true that the demands of the participating committees for modification raised constitutional-political issues of a distinctly controversial nature, as evidenced by the partisan support given the Bundesrat's views when the bill was debated by the *Parteifraktionen* in the popular chamber.[23] Still the fact remains that no member of the Bundesrat, excepting those from socialist Hesse, made suggestions about the formulation and direction of defense policy as such. The basis for the complaint and the whole thrust of the discussion, which in turn were based on the committee's report, revolved about administrative feasibility and management.

Before turning to instances of Bundesrat action in second passage, one further look might be taken at decisions made in first passage in connection with rearmament. On the same day that final action was taken on the Volunteers Bill and the law creating the Personnel Screening Board *(Personal-gutachterausschussgesetz)*, the Bundesrat plenum considered in first passage the Federal Government's permanent remilitarization measure, the Soldiers Law *(Soldatengesetz)*.[24] This was a comprehen-

23. The opposition in this case was not confined to the SPD. It included the FDP and influential deputies of the CDU/CSU as well, such as Dr. Richard Jaeger and Franz Joseph Strauss. Bundestag *Verhandlungen, 93. Sitz.,* June 28, 1955 *(Stenographische Berichte Band 26)*, Bonn, 1955, pp. 5223-31; 5261-91; and 5237-44.

24. Bundesrat *Drucksache 211/55,* June 1, 1955; *Entwurf eines Gesetzes über die Rechtsstellung der Soldaten (Soldatengesetz).*

sive, 48-page bill covering, in Herr Blank's description, "every conceivable loose end relating to the new citizen-army." By this time the rearmament business had become the most sensitive issue in West German political life. To complicate matters for the Adenauer-Blank defense strategy, the Soldiers Law appeared almost simultaneously with the disturbing revelation of the results of the great American air maneuvers known as "Operation Carte Blanche." Despite the vigorous reassurances of Generals McAuliffe and Gruenther, most Germans were alarmed on finding that 335 "bombs" had been dropped in the crowded area between Hamburg and Munich and that 1,700,000 Germans were "killed" and 3,500,000 "wounded."[25] So that at the time the Soldiers Law was being considered by the Bundesrat, the broader issue of German survival as a nuclear battlefield had assumed enormous proportions.

When Dr. Sträter reported to the Bundesrat plenary session, the issue of rearmament as such was not brought up, except in tangential and perfunctory ways. The whole focus of the Security Committee's recommendations was on technical (e.g., vocabulary) deficiencies in the bill and on problems of administration raised by it. It was the view of the Security and Judiciary Committees—and this was their major criticism—that the constitutionally required preconditions for execution of the law were lacking, since "administrative competence of the Federation in this field is not anchored in the Basic Law."[26] In this connection, it was not the opinion of Sträter's committee that executive power over the Soldiers Law should remain confined to the Länder; rather there was general agreement that "The Armed Forces should be a federal concern under federal direction." Because the committee

25. Craig, *NATO and the New German Army*, p. 26.
26. Bundesrat *Sitzungsberichte*, 145, Sitz., July 22, 1955, p. 231.

believed it not possible to distinguish the question of administration from the Soldiers Law itself, the conclusion was to find the measure incomplete in this respect. There was, according to Sträter, no way to deduce federal administrative competence *aus der Natur der Sache*. Therefore, "The regulations of this bill can be made to conform to the Basic Law only by an appropriate change in the Basic Law."[27]

For the rest the Security Committee was content to recommend changing the bill only in minor and insubstantial ways, and its recommendations were approved by the Bundesrat and forwarded to the Federal Government. The Bundesrat *Stellungnahme* was to point out the incompatibility between the bill and the Basic Law, but to point out also that a change in the Basic Law would legitimate the purpose of the measure.

The only effort made to relate the Bundesrat's position on this bill to the broad constitutional and democratic problems of building a new German army was made by Hesse's Deputy Minister-President, Herr Franke, and one could reasonably associate these broader observations of the Hessian member with the strong socialist commitments of the government of Herr Zinn. Without prejudice to the political bearing of the Hessian Government as

27. *Ibid.*, p. 232. This change was achieved on March 19, 1956, one day before the Soldiers Law went into effect. Article 87B says: "The administration of the Federal Defense Forces shall be conducted as a Federal administration with its own administrative sub-structure." This constitutional change passed the Bundesrat unanimously in its 155th meeting at Berlin on March 16, 1956, even though the CDU did not then control a strict two-thirds majority in the Bundesrat. The SPD Minister-President of Hesse, Herr Zinn, pointed out that concurrence with this constitutional amendment did not indicate approval of rearmament. According to Zinn, it was obvious that the Soldiers Law would be enacted anyway unless the *Vermittlungsausschuss* were convened. Zinn felt that there was no chance of effecting "a desirable reorientation of defense policy" in that way, and so he cast his Land's votes in favor of both the constitutional amendment and the Soldiers Law. (Bundesrat *Sitzungsberichte, 155. Sitz.*, March 16, 1956, p. 82.)

expressed on the Volunteers Bill, Hesse concurred with the proposals of the Security Committee in so far as they made some technical improvements. Still, Minister Franke left no doubt that his Land disagreed with the basic proposition underlying the bill. Franke's viewpoint was "that everything depends on integrating the new German Wehrmacht into the constitutional-democratic order of the Federal Republic; but this draft passes over that problem in silence." He found it regrettable furthermore that the bill's silence on such important questions should be treated in the Bundesrat "with more silence." As a consequence, Franke said, "The honorable intentions of many civil servants engaged in its being worked out must be taken for granted." It was Hesse's hope[28]

that during the further legislative handling of this bill one does not confine oneself to the correction of trifles, but that the Bundestag particularly think through the broad questions on a new basis. In this way it will obviate the internal political dangers which until now have been connected with establishment of a *Wehrmacht* in Germany.

Even with this apparently partisan remonstrance, Franke was constrained to admit that the strict limits of time in first passage prevented giving the bill a thorough going-over within the committee except in some technical details. This had in fact been roughly the reason advanced by Sträter for confining his report to the "essentials." Sträter's explanation had been that the contents of the Soldiers Law were well-known and had received generous discussion in the press, so the committee had made better use of its limited time by looking to the questions of administrative competence and technical detail.

The general inattention of the Bundesrat to the issue of rearmament per se can be best understood in terms of that chamber's primary concern with the question of

28. Bundesrat *Sitzungsberichte, 145. Sitz.,* July 22, 1955, p. 232.

constitutional correctness and administrative competence, both of which seriously touch upon the political integrity of the Land governments as autonomous agents of German field administration. The tendency of the Bundesrat to push matters of purely administrative direction into the foreground must also, however, be looked at in the light of the interested committees' obvious advantage in first passage. Again in this case plenary action, as well as Sträter's report, support the conclusion that the Bundesrat is not inclined to discuss first passage bills except as the discussion is set by the appropriate committee.

PARLIAMENTARY ACTION: LATENT BUREAUCRACY

To test the durability of the Bundesrat's administrative bias outside the procedural component of first passage, attention is now turned to final action on the Volunteers Bill in the Bundesrat, in second passage. The professional background of regular Bundesrat membership would be relevant here. Of 41 members in the summer of 1955 (exclusive of Berlin), 26 had previously served in a professional capacity in either a Land bureaucracy or the federal bureaucracy. Of the remaining 15 more than half had been in a ministerial post for over five years.[29] With these backgrounds and with such a heavy volume of administrative duties in the Land governments, the Bundesrat might have been expected to show some regard for the needs of administrators, even when professional civil servants on the committee staffs had no earlier opportunity to make their persuasive views known.

29. Short biographical sketches of Bundesrat members appear in *Handbuch des Bundesrates, Teil II* (Darmstadt, 1958), pp. 135-80. Additional personal information was obtained from Walter Habel (ed.), *Wer ist Wer* (Berlin, 1955); and from Horst Kliemann and Stephen S. Taylor (eds.), *Who's Who in Germany* (Munich, 1956).

The reaction of the Federal Government to the Bundesrat's unfavorable reception of the Volunteers Bill was to announce its intention of submitting the bill to the Bundestag as it was, but to accelerate plans for producing permanent defense legislation. Following the growth of opposition to the bill, not only in the Bundesrat but from the Opposition SPD and even from within the Bonn Coalition, Defense Minister Blank said the Government would seek "a compromise solution ultimately" but for the time being would persist in its support of the existing draft. Blank explained the coincidence in time of the now-famous proposal of the Finance Ministry with introduction of the Volunteers Bill as "purely accidental."[30] When the bill was received by the Bundestag a strong consensus there, along the lines of the Bundesrat attitude, was that defense legislation had to be bound up with a clear account of questions of military administration, supreme command, emergency powers, soldiers' status, and the composition and powers of the projected Personnel Screening Board.

In the organized protests which came from the Bundestag in the first reading of the Volunteers Bill on June 28, the opposition took over exactly the same arguments used by the Bundesrat. Once again the major criticism was that the proposal attempted to regulate a part of the problem without clarification of defense policy as a whole and without the legal basis for its execution, and furthermore that this bill directed the administrative development of the Bundeswehr into certain definite channels which might later prove objectionable. Long prior to first reading of this bill in the Bundestag, the *Frankfurter Allgemeine* reported that parliamentary opinion in both houses seemed to confirm that "rough-

30. *FAZ*, June 13, 1955.

shod" *(ungebildet)* provisional solutions would not be satisfactory.[31]

By the middle of the month the pressures originated in the Bundesrat against the bill had developed enough momentum in the Bundestag to prompt action by the Defense Ministry. Dr. Richard Jaeger sharply criticized Blank in the Bundestag and credited him with having created "the present unhappy arrangement" with the Volunteers Bill, "which could not conceivably pass in its present form." The reaction of the Government was for Herr Blank to appear before the Bundestag and explain the Government's long-range defense plans. After offering a detailed exposition of all phases of defense policy, Blank said that the Federal Government would persist in its promotion of this temporary measure as "a prelude to definitive legislation and [as something] . . . which makes it possible for the Federal Government to begin with the first measures for selection and training of volunteers."[32] Blank did not share the Bundesrat's anxieties about making the volunteers "Civil Servants on Probation," nor did he agree that military administration was pre-judged in any way by this measure. He did make it plain, however, that his speech was primarily in response to the request first made in the Bundesrat for clarity about principles.

Herr Blank's efforts to rescue the Volunteers Bill were only partially successful. Although the bill managed ultimately to weather the storm the version sent to the Bundesrat for second passage bore only a faint resemblance to the original one. The leader of opposition to its original form within the Coalition group was Richard Jaeger, who affirmed that a desire to meet Bundesrat

31. *Ibid.*, June 11, 1955.
32. Bundestag *Verhandlungen*, 92. *Sitz.*, June 27, 1955, p. 5214.

objections was largely responsible for the changes. He said:[33]

> We have particularly regretted that the Federal Government has failed to submit this short law in a modified form after the thorough critique which it experienced in the Bundesrat. It is perhaps a tribute to the law-makers in that House that it has been given credit for undertaking these changes, which lawyers in the Federal Government obviously did not care to worry about. But . . . respect for the Second Chamber has, in my opinion, made it necessary to discuss the question of a general revision of the bill.

Meanwhile the Defense Ministry had been busy setting straight the problems of permanent legislation, so that when the Volunteers Bill was debated in first reading in the Bundestag, the Bundesrat had already received in first passage the comprehensive Soldiers Law. The three-week interval expired on July 22, the same day that the Bundesrat gave final consideration to the Volunteers Bill. Thus it was possible, as the result of a notable exertion on the part of the Government to be cooperative, for the Bundesrat to dispose of both bills in the same meeting, one in first and the other in second passage.

The new version of the Volunteers Bill made several vital changes covering the major complaints of the Bundesrat. This time it was a much longer bill, making explicit several things which had before rested only on verbal pledges. A 6,000-man limitation was expressly written into the measure, and the tasks to which these early volunteers might be assigned were listed: attachments to international headquarters (NATO), acceptance of foreign military assistance, training of military recruits, and purely military functions of the Federal Defense Ministry.[34]

33. *Ibid.*, *93. Sitz.*, June 28, 1955, pp. 5223-24.
34. Bundesrat *Drucksache 274/55*, July 16, 1955: (title not given).

The problem of the volunteers' legal status was cause for an interesting bit of circumlocution. Whereas in the original plan they were sworn in under oath as soldiers "serving in the capacity of Civil Servants on Probation," now they simply "accepted an engagement as employees" of the Defense Ministry. The first four months of civil service were to serve "as a period of aptitude training." Until permanent legislation took effect, the legal prescriptions binding on enlisted soldiers "*shall be equivalent* to that of Civil Servants on Probation."[35] The new version also made express reference to the projected Personnel Screening Board, which was established by law on the same day, for service grades of Colonel (*Oberst*) and higher. Most important for the Bundesrat, it specified that "substantial" changes or expansion of defense administration would require "special legal regulation."

In the Bundesrat Dr. Sträter announced his committee's approving acknowledgment of the changes that had been made. He said he was highly gratified "that some of these changes can be traced to stimuli from the Bundesrat." From the previous month's fears of the Security Committee that the Volunteers Bill authorized Blank to create an operative army whose legal and administrative governance was left vague, had come a law making unmistakably clear that only with specific preliminary precautions and according to established codes of field administration should the establishment of German military forces be begun. After a brief recapitulation of first passage talks, Sträter pointed out how these had been responsible, point-by-point, for the changes and how these changes met the Bundesrat's complaints. The reporter's remarks on these points put some perspective on the attitude of the Bundesrat now in its conclusive action on this bill.

35. *Ibid.*, Section 3.

First, the problem of prejudicing the issue was dealt with satisfactorily. The absolute limitation of 6,000 volunteers more or less settled the questions, and additionally "the remaining sections of the law emphasize the preparatory character of this first measure. Herewith, the dangers of prejudicing the issue are minimized as far as possible if the establishment of military forces is to begin."[36] Second, the Bundesrat's active concern about regulating a part of the problem with no clarification of overall military organization had met with desirable results. It had not been the Bundesrat's intention to expect the military organization to be explicitly anchored in the Basic Law prior to issuance of the first preliminary measure. According to Sträter, it had simply wanted to remind the Federal Government that "problems suddenly appeared in the field, for solutions to which . . . [the Bundesrat] would have to share responsibility; and it had only wanted to know the direction of things." With the extensive account given in the Bundestag by Herr Blank on June 27, this consideration was believed effectively met.

Third, the Bundesrat had emphasized that the earlier draft sought to govern a part of the problem without creating the legal possibilities for its execution. This factor achieved special prominence after the proposal of the Finance Ministry was made known. This proposal had been withdrawn, and the Defense Minister had hurried to point out that he is not authorized to erect a centralized federal administrative apparatus. The new law prohibited setting up authorities of a military type. Fourth, there had been serious misgivings in the Bundesrat about the "appropriate" application of the civil service law and against the anticipated authorization of "Civil Servants on

36. Sträter's committee report is in Bundesrat *Sitzungsberichte, 145. Sitz.*, July 22, 1955, pp. 226-27.

Probation" status for volunteers. This matter was given detailed consideration in the Bundestag committees, where Land delegates participated in the talks. The new law embodies, in fact, a suggestion by Land Northrhine-Westphalia that the "volunteer" concept be as civilianized as possible under the temporary measure. Accordingly, a suitable and temporary status "sui generis" for the soldiers was created, not by making them "Civil Servants on Probation," but simply by making applicable to them also the legal prescriptions for Civil Servants on Probation. In this way, the status problem was believed avoided. The remaining two points were presumed secure, dealing with parliamentary control through the Personnel Board and the necessity for Bundesrat concurrence to salary regulations. Dr. Sträter's recommendation was to accept the law and not to call the Mediation Committee in accordance with Article 77. This was the decision of the Bundesrat, the only dissenting votes being those of Land Hesse.

On the basis of these developments in the Bundesrat with the parliamentary handling of the rearmament bills, one or two inferences may be drawn. With the administrative technicalities and impediments settled to the essential satisfaction of the Bundesrat this second and final action would have been the appropriate time to remove treatment of the rearmament issue from its technical and legalistic aspects. The Bundesrat committees did not now have the tactical advantage they normally enjoy during the three-week interval of first passage. But the combination of factors that make the Bundesrat a bureaucracy-oriented chamber accounted for final action on the Volunteers Bill. The gist of the plenary resolution was to express satisfaction that the previous legal-administrative vagueness surrounding the earlier bill had given way to a measure "making unmistakably clear" that only according to established codes of German field administration should the enlistment of military forces be begun. The reluctance of the Chamber to approve a measure when "the direction of things" was unknown is scarcely an indication of boldness, or even of a sensitiveness to the developing substance of policy in this field. Nor does it reflect any particular willingness to take a strong stand in favor of relating this policy goal to the ultimate goals of policy in other fields.

The decision of the plenum was to drop the matter and raise no further questions, the only dissenting votes being those of Land Hesse. Evidently the position of the Bundesrat in its conclusive action on the bill in second passage was determined by its earlier representations and by the extent to which the Government complied with its initial demands. What happened between first and second passages was not a retreat or a re-orientation of defense policy by the Adenauer Government. The change in civil service status for the volunteers, for example, represented mainly a tightening of the terms of accountability in more detail along lines readily recognizable to professional administrators.[37] It had all along been the intention of Adenauer and Blank, according to their own repeated statements, to keep this temporary military contingent under the close civilian control of the Federal Defense Ministry. Rather the satisfaction of the Bundesrat in July sprang from a rearrangement of the techniques by which this policy was to be carried out. The approval of the Bundesrat was based on implementation of the original

37. This should not obscure the consideration that the Federal Government's original plan for temporarily integrating the volunteers into the ordinary civil service would have had important consequences for many Land civil servants. In conversations with the author, members of the Bundesrat Secretariat staff were quick to point out the natural interest of the Länder in matters affecting civil service personnel.

goals and directives, as left unchanged, according to acceptable and standardized procedures.

To amplify still further the possible variations that Bundesrat actions might take in this same regard, one other rearmament bill is relevant. The Military Personnel Screening Board Bill *(Personalgutachterausschussgesetz)*,[38] which was part of the original rearmament legislation complex, was introduced by the Bundestag in a concerted effort by all major party fractions to stabilize parliamentary control over the military. Being an *Initiativgesetz* of the Bundestag there was no first passage, and the bill went to the Bundesrat for the first time in second passage. Since in this case, as in most second passage cases, the committee staff careerists had no particular advantage in access to the measure, Bundesrat members were acting in a strict parliamentary capacity. The bill went directly to the plenum.

The issues raised by this bill were clear enough. It sought to preclude the re-emergence of an Officer Corps with a Prussian mould independent of civilian authority by establishing an autonomous, civilian Board to select all senior officers and "to lay down guiding principles according to which all remaining service personnel are to be examined." The Board was to have access on demand to all classified papers, and its members were not bound to any instructions. When the second and third readings took place in the Bundestag on July 15, 1955, they were the occasion for a renewed debate on the merits of rearmament and on the broader implications and possible consequences of trying to make an incorruptible institution of this type.[39] Although the Defense Ministry had

38. Bundesrat *Drucksache 267/55,* July 15, 1955: *Entwurf eines Gesetzes über den Personalgutachterausschuss für die Streitkräfte (Personalgutachterausschussgesetz).*

39. Bundestag *Verhandlungen,* 99. *Sitz.,* July 15, 1955. See speeches

consistently denied the need for such a special law, this bill was supported by every party except the *Deutsche Partei*. It was to be coterminous with the Volunteers Bill, both of which would be replaced by the Soldiers Law.

In the Bundesrat there was virtually no debate, and consideration of the bill could not have taken more than fifteen minutes. The Security Committee Reporter was Herr Farny (Baden-Württemberg), whose report to the plenum consisted mainly of (1) a bare acknowledgement of the principle of parliamentary control and (2) recommendations first to require Bundesrat consent and then to give that consent.[40] Farny expressed the disappointment of his committee, which had met only that same morning, that the earlier suggestion of Northrhine-Westphalia to appoint three Bundesrat members to the Personnel Screening Board was not adopted. He also raised the point, although not so strongly as to question the bill's feasibility, that the provision authorizing the Bundestag to approve the Federal Government's appointments to the Board might be "a constitutionally impermissible restraint by the Legislature on the Executive."[41]

Other than these comments, only one aspect of this bill stirred comment in the Bundesrat. Section One stipulated that the Screening Board "shall consist of thirty to forty members." Although declining to demand a meeting of the *Vermittlungsausschuss*, which in this case would have be the only recourse short of rejection, the general consensus was that this provision constituted a noticeable flaw in the bill. Not only were the figures too large, but the uncertainty of its size was considered undesirably vague and conducive to "unpleasant consequences." No

by Mellies (SPD), pp. 5532-39; Berendsen (CDU/CSU), pp. 5535-38; Dr. Mende (FDP), pp. 5534-36; and Schneider (DP), pp. 5533-34.
40. Bundesrat *Sitzungsberichte, 145. Sitz.,* July 22, 1955, p. 228.
41. *Ibid.*

one gave any clear indication what unpleasantness might occur, but quite probably the idea was prompted by fears that this elasticity and bulk would promote quibbling, not only in appointments to the Board but among members of the Board itself.[42] Certainly one primarily concerned with competent and regularized direction in the handling of political problems would want to avoid leaving such a matter to later, informal determination.

The conclusion forced by these cases of second passage Bundesrat action is that motivation to participate in policy-making in the broad sense is scarcely stronger than in first passage. Bureaucratic influence thus also develops irrespectively of the tactical advantage enjoyed by administrative careerists during first passage. In the instance of the second passage of the Volunteers Bill, members of the Bundesrat in looking to the constitutional rights of their respective governments betrayed a visibly keener interest in protecting Land ministerial authority within the range of a given policy than in helping to re-shape that policy. On the *Personal-gutachterausschuss-gesetz* the Bundesrat's attention was addressed to legal and procedural aspects. Thus a tendency toward bureaucratization, in the sense of making judgments according to "internal criteria of correctness" and in the sense of leaning toward a "routinization of duties," was seen operating in every phase of Bundesrat actions. It would be difficult to determine in any case whether the pressures of *Beamtentum* could be accounted for more by the administrative urge to have a clear delineation of jurisdictional lines favorable to the administering party, or by the peculiar nature of German federalism. The difference is probably academic.

42. On this point Dr. Zimmer said, "Das eröffnet Möglichkeiten, die sich sehr unliebsam auswirken können. Sie hätte es lieber gesehen, wenn ein echter kleiner Ausschuss gebildet worden wäre, etwa von 10 Mitgliedern." *Ibid.*, p. 229.

To a great extent the nature of German federalism determines the executive-administrative type of representation of the Länder in the Federal Parliament, and hence their preoccupation with administrative matters. Furthermore it is seldom disputed that the Land *Beamten* through their expert knowledge are in the best position to pass judgment on administration of federal laws.[43] To eliminate this supervisory function would be to impair seriously the functional competence of the West German Länder. One writer speaks of the execution of federal law by Land governments as no mere mechanical subordinate process, but "the main field for the formation and demonstration of the political character of each Land."[44] If the present disposition of the Bundesrat encourages a tendency to exalt administrative problems at the expense of a broader concern with policy goals and responsibilities, it more or less guarantees at the same time that the federal bureaucracy will be held in check by counterpressures from the Land bureaucracies. Still the simple demonstration that a major functional role of the Bundesrat is a bureaucratic one is not in itself particularly rewarding. Some of the implications of this finding demand further consideration.

43. In conversations with the author, Land civil servants attached to the Bundesrat committees also tended to believe that federal legislation would be ineffective if the views of local ministerial administrators were not accorded close attention in most matters.

44. Peter Merkl, "Executive-Legislative Federalism in West Germany," *American Political Science Review*, LIII (December, 1959), 740.

CHAPTER VII

Conservatism

The literature of western legislative chambers has traditionally accepted the idea that second chambers as "upper houses" are promoted as conservative impediments to the popular will, or in rapidly industrializing states as blocks to the dominant power in the Constitution, and sometimes even as contrivances to protect the entrenched privileges of a particular class.[1] The common value of these ascribed characterizations is conservatism. The third hypothesis of this study states that the Bundesrat is an instrumentality through which conservative interests not effectively represented in the Bundestag seek modification of legislative bills favorable to them.

In this case the term "conservative interests" is not intended to mean a conspiratorial alignment of forces within the Bundesrat to combat the menace of liberalism. Rather, the term is used in a non-categorical way to mean a disinclination to accept departures from the status quo and an inclination to be defensive of existing arrangements, especially as related to political and social order and administrative routine. The idea of the Bundesrat as

1. See, for example, Walter Bagehot, *The English Constitution* (rev. ed.; New York, 1890), chap. 5; and John Stuart Mill, *Considerations on Representative Government* (New York, 1875), chap. 13. See also H. B. Lees-Smith, *Second Chambers in Theory and Practice* (London, 1923), chap. 2; J. A. R. Marriott, *Second Chambers: an Inductive Study in Political Science*, (rev. ed.; Oxford, 1927), pp. 238-89; and *The Federalist*, LXII-LXIII.

"conservative" in this sense springs from its heavy orientation to administrative problems, an orientation which could easily cause a pattern of hostility to new or liberal attitudes on controversial policy questions. In any case conservative values in the Bundesrat, should they exist, must be a thing apart from the extent to which political parties determine the voting record and from the federal character of that chamber. Whereas there might be some justification for speaking of particularism in Germany as being traditionally conservative, anti-republican, and anti-democratic, events since 1945 have made those characterizations obsolete. Nor would it make much sense to ascribe conservative attitudes to the Bundesrat as a permanent institution of the Federal Republic because it is temporarily controlled on crucial bills by a conservative political party.

The basis for a conservative attitude toward legislative bills would rest upon the bureaucratic leanings of the Bundesrat. The type of position taken on the bills examined in the preceding chapter suggests that a conservative emphasis in federal legislation in the Bundesrat is contingent upon the dominance of administrative elements. This idea might be called bureaucratic conservatism.[2] The "bureaucratic conservative" of course is a stereotype of an administrator and is useful only for pointing up or isolating certain identifiable properties that are characteristic of the type. As such it may not be generally appropriate for studying the social biases of persons acting in a strict administrative capacity, but the model is useful within reason and appears to bear directly

2. The term is used by Peter Blau, *Bureaucracy in Modern Society* (New York, 1956), pp. 96-100; and by Karl Mannheim, *Ideology and Utopia* (New York, 1936), pp. 118-222; see also Hans Gerth and C. Wright Mills, *From Max Weber: Essays in Sociology* (New York, 1958), pp. 228-35. Although Weber did not use this specific appellation, the idea is implicit in his discussion of "The Power Position of Bureaucracy."

upon the Bundesrat. Despite the believed similarity between the second and third hypotheses, an entirely different set of legislative histories is here introduced to test the factor of conservatism—the codetermination *(Mitbestimmung)* laws in the industrial relations field. The codetermination issue was one on which all major social groups in western Germany have had rather clear opinions, and the overall subject presumably offers a good framework for conservative and liberal attitudes.

A primary characteristic of bureaucratic thought is an inclination to convert real political problems into problems of administration. Because of the "socially-limited horizon of the functionary," he often fails to see that every rationalized set of orders and regulations is only one of many possible forms in which reconciliation is forged among conflicting irrational forces.[3] It is a peculiarity of this conservative mentality that it conceives of spontaneous political energies as unsystematic temporary disturbances which are no more than mischievous extensions of the original system and must be incorporated into "routine matters of state." Roughly this same idea is described by Peter Blau and R. K. Merton as the "ritualistic displacement of goals."[4] According to this idea, "Adherence to the rules, originally conceived as a means, becomes transformed into an end-in-itself; there occurs the familiar process of displacement of goals whereby an instrumental value becomes a terminal value." It follows that an administrator's tendency toward goal-displacement makes him conservative in the given sense, that he identifies with the existing order and is typically unsympathetic with proposals for change.

None of the above can be taken to mean that regular

3. Mannheim, *Ideology and Utopia*, p. 118.
4. Robert K. Merton, *Social Theory and Social Structure*, (rev. ed.; Glencoe, Ill., 1957), p. 155; and Blau, *Bureaucracy in Modern Society*, pp. 86-91.

members of the Bundesrat are "ritualists." Unlike the ritualistic bureaucrat, if in fact such a person exists outside the sphere of model-builders, Bundesrat members are men with policy-making responsibilities in their own right at the Land Level. Awareness of this responsibility is expressed at every turn. To this extent they are politicians, whose membership in the Bundesrat attests to their effectiveness in that role, and the ritualistic model of bureaucratic thought and action cannot be altogether useful in generalizing about the overall picture. Still the point has been made that members of the Bundesrat fulfill a bureaucratic role also, thereby justifying the contention that the Bundesrat articulates the point of view of professional bureaucrats specifically and of a bureaucratic orientation generally. The point should be that the influence of the Bundesrat on federal legislation, while not necessarily ritualistic, is nonetheless conservative by virtue of its formidable administrative obligation. This would be so because every Bundesrat member, in addition to his formal parliamentary role, must also look for likely inconveniences of execution that would have to be worked out by the administrative substructure of his own Land. The presumption is that this necessity to some extent sets into motion the process of goal displacement.

The issue of codetermination has been one of the most important of postwar Germany. There was a great deal of bitterness over the question between the major trade union federation, the *Deutscher Gewerkschaftsbund* (DGB) on the one hand and leaders of industry on the other, especially the *Bundesverband der Deutschen Industrie* (BDI).[5] As a result the attitudes of the major

5. A discussion of labor unions and employer associations as pressure groups can be found in Theodor Eschenburg, *Die Herrschaft der Verbände* (Stuttgart, 1955); and Rupert Breitling, *Die Verbände in der Bundesrepublik: Ihre Arten und ihre politische Wirkungsweise* (Meisenheim a/G, 1955); and Ronald Bunn, "Codetermination and

political parties on the whole controversy were reasonably distinct. One might expect this issue to yield a reasonable basis for a conservative-liberal split. Based on this expectation the following scheme is devised: hostility to codetermination legislation, to the extent that it actually alters existing economic or political relationships, is conservative. It would follow that the intensity of feeling among conservatives in this sense must depend upon the magnitude of the change being introduced. That essentially is the idea to be applied, and hopefully the position of "liberals" is in no way compromised.

The term "codetermination" refers to participation by the workers in the making of decisions and policies affecting German industry. Although by no means a concept novel to German experience,[6] codetermination was embodied in concrete form only after World War II, and after considerable groping in the dark. In 1949 the DGB gave notice that it wanted henceforth to be treated as a full partner in all economic affairs, and labor codetermination was therefore championed by it in a sustained effort to effect a redistribution of power in postwar Germany.[7] The connection between codetermination and conservatism rests on one or two assumptions. Conservatives were opposed to the advance of codeter-

the Federation of German Employers' Association," *Midwest Journal of Political Science*, II (August, 1958), 278-98.

6. The beginnings of codetermination can be traced to the Works Council Law of 1920, which extended to workers at the plant level a degree of participation in personnel affairs. *Cf.* Goetz Briefs, *Zwischen Kapitalismus und Syndicalismus—Die Gewerkschaften am Scheideweg* (München, 1952).

7. The DGB is more accurately described as a working class movement than a trade union in the British or American sense. Since its inception in 1949 it has been less interested in getting more wages today than in getting more power tomorrow. Because codetermination is a step in this direction, it is aptly termed "joint economic pluralism" by Clark Kerr in "The Trade Union Movement and the Redistribution of Power in Postwar Germany," *Quarterly Journal of Economics*, LXVIII (November, 1954), 552-64.

mination because this new practice threatened to bring a substantial alteration of the prewar power structure. It does not necessarily follow that defenders of codetermination were liberals, however; for the traditional ideologue of the liberal school in Germany is an implacable foe of the trade unions. But because socialist-oriented elements and groups sympathetic to the working class have pre-empted the role of opposition to the bourgeois parties, their opposition is anti-conservative. Whether or not this makes a socialist liberal is beside the point.[8]

Codetermination was begun by the British in the Ruhr district among the twenty-four recognized steel concerns. In 1951 the Federal Parliament continued the codetermination system and extended it to cover the coal mines. This was the *Mitbestimmungsgesetz* passed by the Bundestag on April 10, 1951. For several reasons, the most important being Allied interest, some form of codetermination at least in the primary industries (iron, steel and coal) was acceptable to the major political forces.[9] So the Special Codetermination Law (for iron, steel and coal) easily passed the Bundestag, supported solidly by the SPD and most of the CDU and the small Center Party. Other

8. Even with the development of party life in Western Germany into a virtual two-party system it is not possible to identify a conservative-liberal breakdown such as tends to characterize British and American party differences. This is accounted for by the confused liberal heritage carried by the Free Democratic Party, and by the fact that the Social Democratic Party, until recently at least, has always espoused some variation of the Marxist theme. See Friedrich C. Sell, *Die Tragödie des deutschen Liberalismus* (Stuttgart, 1953).

9. It is worth noting, however, that Chancellor Adenauer was only brought around to a compromise satisfactory to the DGB after the outbreak of strikes in December, 1950, and January, 1951, by the Metal Workers Union and the Mine Workers Union. Cf. Herbert Spiro, *The Politics of Codetermination* (Cambridge, 1958), pp. 37-41; and Jack Dowell, *The Legislative Process in the West German Bundestag: The Codetermination Law of May, 1951* (Ph.D. Thesis, Stanford University, 1958).

than the organized resistance of the FDP and DP, there was only scattered opposition. Passage of this law resulted in retention of the arrangements which had prevailed in the steel industry since its reorganization and introduction of the same requirements for mining corporations. It gave the unions most of what they had originally demanded. It might also be considered as something of a meeting ground between liberalism and social control, between private enterprise and socialism.

Essentially this law established an eleven-member supervisory council *(Aufsichtsrat)*, five members selected by labor, five by stockholders, and "one additional man."[10] It provided also for a labor director (labor manager) to be nominated by labor as one of three members of the managing board *(Vorstand)*. When this measure went to the Bundesrat in first passage as a Government bill on January 30, 1951, the position of all party Fractions had been made quite clear. Following Adenauer's announcement of his support for the idea in early January, there was little likelihood of its failure in the Bundestag. That was the situation when the bill was first brought up in the Bundesrat in its 48th meeting on February 2, 1951.

The codetermination bill was introduced without discussion in detail. Chairman Hans Ehard (Bavaria) explained that the bill had not been put on the calendar by the Presidium when first received because he had gotten notice from the Executive Council of the DGB that it sought to have some changes made in the Government draft. Having received this information Ehard wrote

10. The five labor members of the *Aufsichtsrat* were to be selected as follows: two from the works councils, two from the unions (one from the national union and one from the federation), and "one other member" from public life who is sympathetic to labor. The "eleventh man" was to be chosen jointly by the other ten. (Bundestag *Drucksache* 2117: *Zusammenstellung des Entwurfs eines Gesetzes über die Mitbestimmung der Arbeitnehmer in Unternehmen des Bergbaus sowie der Eisen und Stahl erzeugenden Industrie*, April 4, 1951.)

the Chancellor asking for clarification and affirming that the Bundesrat would act promptly on the matter once it had been clarified. In the meantime Ehard had spoken with the Federal Minister of Labor, Anton Storch, who informed him briskly that the Federal Government had worked out this draft only after long consultations with all interested parties, and that "the Federal Government does not want this law changed at least until it reaches the Bundestag."[11] The *Frankfurter Rundschau* explained the Labor Minister's curt reply to the Bundesrat President as owing to the fact that it was Minister Storch, in combination with Cabinet Ministers of the Free Democratic and German Parties, who had juggled some of the provisions of the Government's bill to the distinct disadvantage of the DGB.[12]

Before Ehard addressed the plenum, Herr Alfred Kubel (SPD, Lower Saxony) proposed that the Bundesrat avoid any action which might delay passage of this measure through the Bundestag. In order to save time Kubel also proposed that a special *kombinierter Ausschuss* be formed of the Economics Committee, the Labor and Social Affairs Committee, and the Judiciary Committee. This way the interested committees could concentrate their efforts, and any suggested changes could be despatched promptly to the Federal Government and to the Bundestag. Because there was some mystery connected with certain portions of the Government bill, especially in view of the DGB's renewed hostility to it, President Ehard quoted from his earlier conversation with Labor Minister Storch, whose impatience with the DBG was no secret:[13]

The equality of both social partners was at least doubtful [at the last negotiation conference]. On the one side only

11. Bundesrat *Sitzungsberichte, 48. Sitz.*, February 2, 1951, p. 76.
12. *Frankfurter Rundschau*, February 3, 1951.
13. Bundesrat *Sitzungsberichte, 48. Sitz.*, February 2, 1951, p. 77.

the labor unions were represented, while on the other were, not the employers or employer associations, but simply persons having a special connection with the Ruhr industries who were invited especially by the Chancellor.

From the chair Ehard proposed adopting the position that "the Bundesrat raises no objections to the basic principles of the existing draft." Ehard persisted after an objection from Dr. Spiecker (Northrhine-Westphalia) that the Bundesrat could do no more than take cognizance of the Government draft before hearing the results of committee examination. The Bundesrat adopted Ehard's view, and the decision was made to forward the Bundesrat's ideas for changes (if any) directly to the Bundestag.

When the plenum met again to consider the *Mitbestimmungsgesetz* the Coordination Committee had held two meetings, both of them including representatives of the DGB and representatives of the steel, iron and coal industries. Herr Kubel, as *Berichterstatter* for the special committee, cheerfully reported that all substantial disagreements had been settled within the committee. At his committee's request the two contesting parties had met separately and, on February 7, reported back to the special Bundesrat committee the results of their talks. Since the points of real difference were so few, Kubel confined his discussion to the committee's recommendations on two issues covering Sections 9 and 13.

The DGB wanted to strike the second sentence in Section 9, dealing with appointments to the managing board by the supervisory council. This provision conditioned the power of the supervisory council to name members of the managing board in these words:[14] "In cases wherein the supervisory council . . . is not chosen by

14. Bundestag *Drucksache 1858,* January 30, 1951: *Entwurf eines Gesetzes über die Mitbestimmung der Arbeitnehmer in Unternehmen des Bergbaus sowie der Eisen und Stahl erzeugenden Industrie.*

the assembly of stock holders, the appointment and removal of members of the managing board require the consent of the stock holders."

The contention of the DGB was that this provision would imperil the principle of parity representation on the supervisory councils and permit outside elements indirectly to control appointments to the managing boards. The employment interest felt on the other hand that the DGB's demands would mean complete elimination of the influence of free capital. According to Kubel, the experts and legal assistance for the special committee agreed that the legal forms of the iron, steel, and coal-producing industries were such that the provision in question would be applicable only in a small number of cases. The committee therefore recommended keeping to the Government's draft and leave the sentence intact.

Probably the most discussed provision in the Government's draft was Section 13, and it was here that the Bundesrat was most receptive to the wishes of the DGB. Section 13 stipulated: "This law is valid for concerns which employ more than 1,000 workers or have a total capitalization of more than 1,000,000 DM." This section was explained by Labor Minister Storch mainly on technical grounds, with emphasis on the desirability of a fixed limitation. Storch also made it clear that whether the dividing line should be 300, as urged by the DGB, or 1,000, as provided in the existing draft, would probably have only trifling importance. In their earlier representations and during the January-February negotiations with the Federal Government, DGB leaders had placed especial importance on the 300-worker dividing line. Otherwise, they were afraid German industrial leaders would simply shift their manpower around among plant sites to avoid the law's applicability.

On the basis of these considerations the Bundesrat

committee "came around to the recommendation of fixing a definite number on the basis of the Labor Ministry's suggestion; but not at 1,000. Rather we have put the figure at 300 as proposed by the DGB, whose proposal encountered no objections from the employers' representatives."[15] These two recommendations by the Bundesrat committee, neither of which was unfavorable to the labor unions and one of which was distinctly favorable, were adopted by the plenum without debate and sent to the Bundestag. No further objection was raised, and the issue did not come up again until second passage on the law on April 19, 1951.

On that date the codetermination bill was reported out of the Bundesrat Committee for Labor and Social Affairs. It had passed the Bundestag with the almost unanimous support of the SPD and with most of the CDU deputies, but without the change recommended by the Bundesrat in February. The Labor Committee regretted that the suggestion to change the 1,000-workers limitation to 300 was not incorporated into the draft, a course that would probably have driven away marginal CDU support, but the Committee recommended that the plenum forego recourse to the *Vermittlungsausschuss*. The Bundesrat decision in second passage was unanimous and took place without discussion. This marked the end of the first phase of the codetermination movement.

While the *Mitbestimmungsgesetz* was being put into operation, the DGB carried into the Bundestag the fight for its extension to other areas of industry. The situation with industries other than iron and steel, however, was quite different. There was no Allied pressure for continuation of occupation policy, and there was no counterpart to the already existing (in 1951) administrative machinery that had been established to deal with iron and steel.

15. Bundesrat *Sitzungsberichte, 49. Sitz.,* February 9, 1951. p. 86.

The outcome of party conflict in 1952 differed radically from that in 1951. For one thing the attitude of the CDU toward the demands of labor for a general codetermination bill became increasingly less friendly. The growing coolness can be partially explained by a papal message the preceding year warning of the collectivistic danger that could come from a codetermination law of the type demanded by the DGB. Even trade union deputies in the CDU were aggravated when the SPD took over the DGB's proposed draft for such a law and introduced it unchanged into the Bundestag. This plan would have made the important provisions of the *Mitbestimmungsgesetz* applicable to the rest of German industry, extending parity on the supervisory councils to labor and offering labor a director on the managing boards.

The General Codetermination Law that passed the Bundestag on July 19, 1952, represented a significant defeat for the DGB and was quite different from the Socialist bill. The new measure fell far short of the expectations of the DGB, and in fact it fitted in more with employer strategy than with union strategy. The 1952 law is considered by some to be even less desirable for labor than the 1920 law.[16] The main parts of the new law dealt with the operation and make-up of the works councils. The SPD and DGB had wanted to give the unions the power to make nominations to the works council, whereas the law left this function entirely with the workers at the plant level. Similarly the SPD draft would have enabled the union to convene a meeting of the works council and would have excluded employers from the quarterly meetings of the employees. Both were rejected. With regard to labor's representation on the

16. Kerr, "The Trade Union Movement and the Redistribution of Power in Postwar Germany"; and Frieda Wunderlich, "Codetermination in German Industry," *Social Research* (April, 1953), pp. 77-79.

supervisory councils, the SPD's demand for full parity was replaced by authorization for one-third representation. And whereas organized labor—and the SPD—had wanted these persons elected by the union-dominated works councils, the Government's draft required their election by the employees at large and ruled out union nominations. Finally, the established minimum of employees to make the provisions of this law applicable was set at 500, while the SPD and DGB had demanded a 300-employee minimum. The fact that union labor was not guaranteed an influence on the supervisory councils made them fearful of company-mindedness among the workers, or even collusion between works councils and management for mutual aggrandizement at the expense of social reforms.[17]

When this bill reached the Bundesrat it was given prompt attention by the Labor Committee and reported out on July 30, 1952.[18] Bundesrat action in this case has been discussed in another connection, with the conclusion that voting in the Bundesrat was determined by the party commitments of each Land government. The fact that the Bundesrat Labor Committee recommended calling the *Vermittlungsausschuss* to revive most of the lost claims of the DGB has no clear positive or negative correlation with bureaucratic conservatism. That plenary voting on the committee recommendation to call the *Vermittlungsausschuss*, and then the vote to concur with the measure as passed by the Bundestag paralleled the party make-up is convincing evidence that partisan considerations were dominant.[19]

17. For a description of possible courses of action open to the works councils that were fearfully anticipated by the DGB, see Wunderlich, "Codetermination in German Industry," pp. 84-87.
18. Bundesrat *Drucksache 311/52: Entwurf eines Betriebsverfassungsgesetzes*, July 21, 1952.
19. The Labor Committee's proposal to call the *Vermittlungsaus-*

Because of later developments one of these committee recommendations was particularly important. It had been the SPD-DGB plan to make general codetermination applicable to all sectors of the economy, public as well as private. This would affect approximately 2,000,000 workers and officials in the government public services, public enterprises and railroads. The Bundesrat Labor Committee wanted to have this plan put into the draft and eliminate the difference between public and private as far as codetermination was concerned, but this view ran counter to the intentions of the Adenauer Government. In fact the Bundesrat had already considered the Government's initial draft of the Personnel Representation Law the previous March, establishing codetermination for the public services separately from the rest of the economy. Despite the Government's plan, Dr. Oeschsle pointed out in the 90th meeting that the most important proposal of his committee for change was to include the overall public service into the General Codetermination Law.

The decisive factor in the Labor Committee's request was the desire "to avoid unnecessary overlapping between the General Codetermination Law and the forthcoming Personnel Representation Law." But like all the other important suggestions made by the Labor Committee, this one received less than a majority of plenary votes. The Personnel Representation Law,[20] which ultimately established codetermination for 900,000 civil service employees and 1,300,000 workers employed by Land governments and public enterprises, required three years

schuss won only the 15 votes of the socialist Länder, and the only opposing votes on the motion to concur with the bill were those same 15. (Bundesrat *Sitzungsberichte, 90. Sitz.*, July 30, 1952, pp. 355-56.)

20. Bundesrat *Drucksache 100/52: Entwurf eines Gesetzes über die Personalvertretungen in den öffentlichen Verwaltungen und Betrieben (Personalvertretungsgesetz)*, March 10, 1952.

in the passing. The main obstacle to its early passage was strong union opposition. It was described by a leader of the DGB as "antilabor," and both SPD and DGB newspapers criticized the new law as another manifestation of the general trend toward a *Restauration* of obsolete and undemocratic social forms.

The DGB was not just ideologically opposed to the bill. It was at least as apprehensive about its own organizational strength. This law gave most of the power over "joint management through the personnel councils" to the highest class of civil service employees—the *Beamten.*[21] The DGB has always been least strongly organized in this class of the civil service, which has its own organization in the *Deutscher Beamtenbund* (DBB). Because the traditional class consciousness of the German official structure is particularly strong among civil service officials of the highest rank, the DGB felt that this law strengthened the organizing appeal of rival unions (i.e., the DBB and the *Deutscher Angestellten Gewerckschaft,* or DAG). So the DGB was unconditionally opposed to a separate codetermination law for government workers and to different court jurisdictions (i.e., referral of disputes involving the personnel councils' composition and conduct to the established administrative court system rather than to the quasi-legal Labor Court as under the first two codetermination laws).

Because of the long and irregular history of the Personnel Representation Law and the fact that it applied

21. U. S. Bureau of Labor Statistics, "Codetermination for Government Workers in West Germany," *Monthly Labor Review,* LXXVII (December, 1955), 1470-71. The personnel councils are comparable to the works councils in private industry. The conflicting interests between the DGB and the more conservative DBB are described briefly by Wolfgang Hirsch-Weber in "Some Remarks on Interest Groups in the Federal Republic of Germany," in Henry Ehrmann (ed.), *Interest Groups on Four Continents* (Pittsburgh, 1958), pp. 98-100.

codetermination to a field in which the Bundesrat had a special interest—bureaucracy—Bundesrat action on this measure is particularly relevant. The measure went to the Bundesrat for first passage in early March, 1952. On March 28 the Bundesrat forwarded its *Stellungnahme* to the Federal Government. Dr. Zimmer (Rhineland-Palatinate) reported to the plenum for the three committees that had acted on the bill—Labor and Social Affairs, Interior, and Judiciary. Although the latter two committees did not agree, the contention of the Labor Committee was that the Federal Government should be asked to shelve the bill and that there was no reason why this bill should be given preference over the General Codetermination Law, which was still being debated in the Bundestag.[22]

The Socialist Länder supported this view. Herr Neuenkirch (Hamburg) and Herr Troeger (Hesse) both felt that an easier approach would be to regulate private and public activities in the same law. Then clear distinctions could be made in cases involving the public service in which a deviation from the General Codetermination Law would be necessary. Accordingly the bill should be put aside in order to avoid separate and possibly conflicting developments. The Bundesrat vote on the Labor Committee's proposal to ask the Federal Government to put off the law so the General Codetermination Law could be handled "as a single law" had the following results:

Berlin	Abstained
Baden	No
Bavaria	No
Bremen	Yes
Hamburg	Yes
Hesse	Yes
Lower Saxony	Yes

22. Bundesrat *Sitzungsberichte, 81. Sitz.,* March 28, 1952, p. 140.

Northrhine-Westphalia	No
Rhineland-Palatinate	No
Schleswig-Holstein	No
Württemberg-Baden	Yes
Württemberg-Hohenzollern	No

The proposal won only the 15 votes of the Socialist Länder plus the 4 votes of Württemberg-Baden, and hence it failed.

The Bundesrat had now established that a different codetermination law was needed for the public service. In this same meeting a great deal of discussion immediately followed about the terms of the public Personnel Representation Law. It was generally agreed in the Bundesrat that this law, treated as a separate set of regulations, could lead to complications with the anticipated General Codetermination Law. A motion by Minister-President Heinrich Lübke of Schleswig-Holstein was adopted to recommend incorporating the important procedural and material specifications of the measure into a "framework-law" *(Rahmengesetz)* for variable Land administration. In this way reservations could be made by each Land for special regulation in the "cultural areas," especially the schools, but the "framework-law" would have a reasonably standard treatment throughout the Federal Republic in the interests of continuity of codetermination policy in public administration. Another part of Lübke's motion concerned the separation of personnel representatives into groups recognizing the traditional classes of the public service, an idea particularly abhorrent to the DGB and to the Socialists. In this regard Herr Lübke said:[23]

The clear execution of the division of public personnel representatives according to the three groups of officials *(Beamten)*, salaried employees *(Angestellten)*, and wage-earners *(Arbeiter)*, as well as group participation by personnel

23. *Ibid.*, p. 141.

representatives in matters which affect only group relations, has distinct advantages and should remain as it is. Since the *Beamten* exercise functions of soverign importance *(hoheitliche Funktionen)*, participation by the remaining groups in their personal affairs violates the principle of a healthy state structure *(gesunden Staatsaufbaues)*. The responsibility for separate treatment of these things cannot be shifted to members of the personnel representation group. Rather they must be provided in this law.

Lübke's point, which was incorporated by the Bundesrat into its *Stellungnahme* and sent to the Federal Government, obviously rested on one or more assumptions about the administrative requirements of state-form stability and about structural desiderata in the public service.

As it turned out this bill was not acted on by the Bundestag during the first electoral period. So the "new" Federal Government delivered the bill to the Bundestag again in February, 1954, this time after having incorporated most of the Bundesrat's ideas of two years earlier. First reading of the bill took place the following month in the Bundestag. After many months of work a special sub-committee changed the Government draft considerably, returning it for second reading on March 17, 1955. Third reading followed in June, and it finally went to the Bundesrat for second passage on June 24, 1955.

The Bundesrat Interior Committee report, which was to recommend calling the *Vermittlungsausschuss*, was the occasion for a rather long and unsympathetic description of the possible consequences of this bill. Zimmer emphasized the role of the new personnel councils as participants in decisions that involved introduction of new working methods or other basic changes affecting the service bureaus *(Dienstellen)*. In fact the right of participation in these respects granted the personnel councils was radically weaker than what the DGB had requested. The same was true with personnel and social questions. At the meeting of the Bundesrat Interior Committee from which these recommendations came only the reporting member, Dr. Zimmer, (Rhineland-Palatinate) was a regular member of the Bundesrat. The other Länder were represented on this committee meeting by civil servants. The legal argumentation of Dr. Zimmer is not easily put into any framework relevant to the idea of Bundesrat conservatism, but the following data derived from Bundesrat discussion of the new bill are indicative on that score.

The greatest cause for concern was that things heretofore understood as belonging to the area of state-management were now being turned over to so many discrete parts of the administrative sub-structure acting as free agents. The Committee believed this would disturb the clarity of ministerial responsibility and ultimately result in weakening the hand of Parliament. Zimmer of course was only raising these points as questions which might have to be faced later. Furthermore, the committee wanted to express its concern that this bill might give critical administrative influence to "outside" social organizations—the trade unions and employers associations. All these new developments Zimmer interpreted as potentially subversive of the traditional and venerated *Rechtsstaat*. He said in this connection:[24]

The question is raised to what extent the parliamentary-democratic state, which according to all Land Constitutions and the Basic Law is a *Rechtsstaat,* can hand over the organization and functions of its service bureaus to the corporate influences of fragmented groups seeking their own advantage, as is provided in this draft. It must not be overlooked that on the basis of this draft all acts of administration in the field of personnel policy can and will be challenged before the administrative courts. Therefore we must assume

24. Bundesrat *Sitzungsberichte, 143. Sitz.,* June 24, 1955, p. 163.

that in the future all such acts will be challenged as come under the codetermination of the personnel councils. . . . It seems to me this viewpoint up until now has not been given the attention it deserves.

For Dr. Zimmer, as for most of the members of the Bundesrat, the bare text of the Government's draft left to conjecture the dynamic possibilities for redirecting constitutional development of the republic. He asked the State Secretary in the Federal Interior Ministry what would be the likelihood of the personnel councils' forming something of a "Congress" competent to pass resolutions that would be binding on the branches of the Federal Government. And furthermore, would such a development result in a weakening or strengthening of the Executive as the second branch of government? The critical attitude of the Bundesrat Interior Affairs Committee rested on its feeling that this draft was "a very daring law," and one which made a number of questionable assumptions "about administrative operations in a democratic state." The opinion of the majority, which voted to demand a meeting of the *Vermittlungsausschuss*, was "that a further postponement of a few weeks must be taken into the bargain in view of its deliberation for several years."

Except for the division of the voting, which took consistently the same party lines that existed in the Bundestag, there was only one general dissent. The Interior Minister for Land Hesse expressed the dissatisfaction of his government with the existing draft, but the four Hessian votes were not cast to call the *Vermittlungsausschuss*. Hesse's main objection to the bill was "its creation of graded representations," or of separate representatives for officials, salary-earners and workers. The specific complaint was that this would inevitably lead to a complication of the procedure and to a delay in the desired developments. Hesse's dissent on the *Vermitt-*

lungsausschuss vote was based on the fear that this would only tempt the dangers of further complicating the measure.

In all some twenty-two specific changes were recommended by the Interior Committee as a basis for a meeting of the Joint Mediation Committee, of which sixteen were adopted by the Bundesrat. Most of these had to do with technical changes and rearrangements, but a few dealt rather more directly with such terms of the bill as the powers of the personnel councils and the private rights of employees in the public service. Two of these stand out as more important than the rest. One of the provisions of the *Personalvertretungsgesetz* was that in the event of a failure to reach agreement between the highest service officials and the appropriate employee representatives in a matter of codetermination, the issue must be settled by a special "agreements office."[25] The Committee asked that this be changed and suggested that no "agreements office" be created, explaining:

> The present form of this Article departs from that prepared by the Federal Government and leads to undermining the parliamentary responsibility of the Minister. In connection with the personnel council's right of initiative in such cases of codetermination issues, the possibility is created of carrying through personnel decisions against the wishes of the bureau chief.

The other change proposal concerned the personnel council's power of codetermination in the personal affairs of *Beamten*. The bill discharged from the Bundestag provided that the personnel councils would participate in the personal affairs of *Beamten* when they concerned (among other things) (1) recruitment, suspension and promotion; or (2) transfer to another

25. Bundesrat *Drucksache 85/55: Entwurf eines Gesetzes über die Personal vertretungen in den öffentlichen Verwaltungen und Betrieben (Personalvertretungsgesetz)*, June 10, 1955.

service bureau. The Interior Committee recommended abolishing the first sentence and changing the second sentence to read: "Transfer to another service bureau when it is proposed by the *Beamte* himself." The reason given for making these two alterations was that "The far-reaching participation of personnel representatives in the personal affairs of *Beamten* runs counter to traditional *(hergebrachten)* principles of the rights of the public service."

A show of hands brought a minority of seventeen votes against calling the *Vermittlungsausschuss*, all from Länder with strong-to-very strong commitments to the Bonn coalition parties. Since in Bundesrat procedure a formal recommendation of the appropriate committee is considered accepted unless a contrary proposal is carried by majority vote, it was not necessary for a clear majority of the plenum to vote for the committee's proposal. Interestingly the vote within the Interior Committee was different, with only Northrhine-Westphalia casting its vote against the proposal to demand a meeting of the *Vermittlungsausschuss*. The discrepancy in Länder attitudes here can be explained by the relatively autonomous position of the Land governments in the committees as administrative agents, in contrast with the tendency of the plenum to vote according to party considerations.[26]

When the Personnel Representation Law returned to the Bundesrat from the Joint Mediation Committee, only Schleswig-Holstein voted against it while Rhineland-Palatinate abstained. Actually the changes made in the *Vermittlungsausschuss* were distinctly sympathetic to the Bundesrat's demands. In the few cases when the Bundesrat's viewpoint was not adopted the decision of the

26. Although the great majority of decisions made in committees are approved and adopted by the plenary Bundesrat, some discrepancy between the committee and plenum is common on controversial bills.

Joint Committee was to strike a middle course between the desires of both houses. The compromise version passed the Bundesrat with virtually no discussion. Nor was there any explanation of divergent points of view. The lone dissenting votes of Schleswig-Holstein can be traced to the meeting of the preceding month and to the committee deliberations. The representative of Land Schleswig-Holstein, which was always the strongest supporter of CDU programs on the Bundesrat, opposed the principles underlying the bill and pointed to the dangers of a "double standard in the field of Personnel management." Schleswig-Holstein further agreed with the observations of the SPD Interior Minister of Hesse (!) when he said, in reference to permitting representatives from the trade unions and employer associations to appear before the personnel councils: [27]

In the interest of clarity of responsibility [the government of Hesse] considers the insertion of foreign elements into the administrative organization to be an impossible situation. We are specifically against building up dangers to the confident and healthy relationship between the service bureaus and service employees in the fields of social and personnel matters. This foreign intrusion into personnel processing and social control of employees leads to irresponsible control of responsible offices, which is not constitutional. But most important, it is particularly suited to encroach upon the parliamentary responsibility of the Minister on an important point. In the opinion of my government, such a development can only impair the legal balance of our *Rechtsstaat*.

27. Bundesrat *Sitzungsberichte, 143. Sitz.*, June 24, 1955, p. 165. Although by 1955 the convergence of Land and Federal government attitudes had become more or less complete on important issues, results in the Bundesrat often crossed party lines, especially when a particular area of Land concern such as the bureaucracy was concerned. Roughly the same thing occurred, for example, with the disputed *Rundfunkgesetz* of 1960. See Gerhard Braunthal, "Federalism and the Party System in Germany: the Broadcasting Controversy," (Paper delivered for the American Political Science Association Convention, September, 1961), pp. 9-10.

The evidence is slender to support the idea of a conservative Bundesrat based simply on the merits of the *Personalvertretungsgesetz*, although it points in that direction. It is not difficult, for example, to detect the Bundesrat's concern for traditional prerogatives of civil servants, especially the *Beamten*. Also the Federal Chamber was unfriendly to the introduction of new techniques into public administration, such as codetermination through the personnel councils, when the new techniques might be disruptive of administrative smoothness and responsibility. At least on this phase of codetermination the Bundesrat indicates a conservative bias by being defensive of existing arrangements, especially as related to political and social order and administrative routine.

One further law in the codetermination field is relevant. While the DGB was denouncing the General Codetermination Law of 1952 as a serious affront to organized labor and seeking throughout 1953 to "elect a better Bundestag," new troubles began to develop on the older codetermination front. The decartelization laws of British Military Government had expired, and re-cartelization of German heavy industry was proceeding at full speed. This meant that holding companies were being formed in the Ruhr by corporations not primarily engaged in the production of coal, iron and steel. Things worked smoothly until late in 1953 because these corporations, wanting to avoid unfavorable publicity, signed informal agreements with the unions temporarily validating the terms of the *Mitbestimmungsgesetz*. But in December, 1953, a federal court ruled "that the holding companies were not governed by the special codetermination law, but came under the provisions of the . . . General Codetermination Law."[28]

28. Spiro, *The Politics of Codetermination*, p. 78.

This decision necessitated new federal legislation to settle the controversy about the holding companies. The main questions to be answered were: when is a holding company sufficiently involved in iron, steel, and coal to make special codetermination applicable? And is there to be a labor director on the managing boards of these corporations? The second question developed as a crucial one because the most important decisions affecting a plant were made at the highest (managing board) level, not by the supervisory council of the plant.[29] Several bills were introduced in the scramble to fit holding companies into the overall codetermination structure. It was not until June 29, 1956, that the matter was finally closed by a compromise which, like the 1951 law, was passed by a Bundestag coalition of CDU and SPD votes. The new law grew out of a bill introduced by the Federal Government fully two years earlier, which had been introduced into the Bundesrat for first passage as a supplement to the *Mitbestimmungsgesetz* in October, 1954. The Bundesrat discussed it that same month.

The basic idea of the Government measure was to distinguish between holding companies which were primarily engaged in producing a basic commodity (coal, iron or steel) and therefore held to the *Mitbestimmungsgesetz*, and those which were not so engaged, for which the *Betriebsverfassungsgesetz* was applicable. Those holding companies which did not themselves come under the *Mitbestimmungsgesetz* but which control industrial

29. Socialist Deputy Dr. Deist said in the Bundestag that the essence of codetermination in the Ruhr hinged upon the role of the labor director on the managing board. "The controlling arrangements are fully removed from the influence of small functionaries. All major decisions affecting the great industries of the Ruhr are made, not at the level of the supervisory council, but at the top of the pyramid. Without a labor representative on the managing board, authoritarian economic strength would destroy the delicate democratic controls we have been working toward." (Bundestag *Verhandlungen, 148. Sitz., [Steno-graphische Berichte Band 30*, Bonn, 1956], 7866-67).

undertakings that do, were to be held accountable to special provisions in the new draft. These provisions represented a synthesis of the essential ideas of both the 1951 and 1952 laws in regard to the composition of the supervisory councils and managing boards. The Bundesrat Labor committee reporter told the plenary meeting that the committee had unanimously agreed to discourage efforts to append any but the most necessary changes. The Labor Committee thus recommended a *Stellungnahme* in which the Bundesrat would request two changes but would have no other objections to the bill.

First, the Labor Committee wanted the Federal Government to abandon its modification of the composition of the supervisory councils. In the Government draft there would be fifteen members, seven from the stockholders, seven from the workers, and the last as an impartial member corresponding to the "eleventh man" in the original law.[30] Second, the committee wanted to eliminate the complicated process by which employee representatives were chosen as members of the supervisory councils. Instead of an indirect election involving electors, who in turn were to be selected by the plant workers at large, the committee's suggestion was to leave this task with the works councils. Here the idea was that "with most concerns the great majority of the working crew will not be able to evaluate individual candidates. The necessary care in the selection of worker representatives . . . seems more secure with the works councils."[31] The Labor Committee did not, however, suggest that the Federal Government alter its plan in order to include a labor director on the managing board. Still the com-

30. Bundesrat *Sitzungsberichte, 130. Sitz.*, October 29, 1954, p. 289.
31. *Ibid.*, p. 290. This was a major claim of the unions. The DGB had consistently demanded that labor representatives on the supervisory councils be chosen by the works councils, which were usually controlled by the unions.

mittee felt that a member of the managing board, however named, should be chosen by the supervisory council and should be someone enjoying the confidence of the workers. The Bundesrat plenum adopted both recommendations of the Labor Committee, as well as the reporter's remark about the managing board. These were forwarded to the office of the Chancellor, and the Bundesrat was not to see this bill again for almost two years.

The Bundesrat again received the holding companies amendment which had been considerably modified in the Bundestag, on June 29, 1956. This time the measure consisted of a delicately balanced series of compromises that had been a long time in the making. Because of that fact, Karl Siemsen (Northrhine-Westphalia) recommended to the plenum on the Labor Committee's behalf that it not call the *Vermittlungsausschuss* or raise objections to the bill, despite a valid basis for some disagreement with it.[32] The most important point Siemsen raised, about which there had been some doubt in the Bundestag, concerned the office of the labor director on the managing board. Whereas the Bundesrat had sought a compromise on this issue by limiting the labor director's functions, the Bundestag found a compromise through the procedures by which he was appointed.

To some extent the new law contained the provisions of the *Mitbestimmungsgesetz* for the labor director in that no member could be appointed to the managing board against the wishes of a majority of the supervisory council's labor representatives. From this the Bundesrat Labor Committee concluded that a labor director existed for practical purposes, since this person would have to have a "good understanding with the workers' side." The gist of the committee report was moderate overall approval, although there were one or two points made in

32. Bundesrat *Sitzungsberichte, 161. Sitz.,* July 29, 1956, p. 239.

first passage that were ignored by the Bundestag. Siemsen did not specify the details of the committee's dissatisfaction, except to observe that "at one or two points the workers' interests appear not to have been properly taken into account in this compromise bill."[33]

CONCLUSIONS

That the codetermination law for holding companies passed the Bundesrat with only two dissenting Länder and received in the process little unfavorable discussion can hardly be adduced to support the conservative idea of this chapter. In fact most of the above evidence points generally to a negative finding relative to the Bundesrat as a "conservative" agency. The Bundesrat with only one exception proved at least as sympathetic as the Bundestag to the introduction of new techniques of economic control through worker codetermination. The one exception is the Personnel Representation Law, on which Bundesrat action was considerably more in line with an anticipated "typical conservative" response. The statements of Lübke and Zimmer on this phase of the broader issue represented not only the views of the Interior Affairs Committee, but of the Bundesrat plenum as well. The Bundesrat was distinctly unenthusiastic about a law that authorized meddling in the legal processes of public administration by agents acting outside the routinized inhibitions of office. If, in fact, party lines had not been so strongly drawn on the whole codetermination complex, the Bundesrat would probably have been more articulate in its disapproval. That possibility is given credence by the fact that Land votes in the Bundesrat were heavily influenced by party positions in the Bundestag. There was, for example, an impressive coincidence of expression between the Socialist *Parteifraktion* in the Bundestag and

33. *Ibid.*

SPD-controlled Länder in the Bundesrat. Similarly the votes of CDU Länder were sensitive to the wishes of the Federal Government.

The somewhat ambiguous and inconsistent attitude of the Bundesrat on all aspects of the codetermination issue, for public as well as for private affairs, can be only partially accounted for by the tendency of the Federal Chamber to act according to party strengths and policies. The key idea of conservatism involves the process of change. A conservative bias would incline one against anything that could not be handily accommodated into the existing order and therefore against changes which, although intrinsically desirable, threatened established canons of administrative management and responsibility. Although industrial codetermination was looked on by most interested persons as effecting a genuine redistribution of power in the West German economy, nothing in worker representation would necessarily disturb the status quo from an administrator's point of view. Bundesrat members could express views that might seriously alter power relations among economic classes, but which would have no palpable effect on the maintenance of order in the administrative hierarchy.

The same would not be quite true of the codetermination law for personnel in the public bureaucracy. Here the Bundesrat, with an established and legitimate concern for administrative affairs, revealed its greatest measure of resistance. The language of the committee reports and the whole tone of plenary discussions showed a distaste for the overall purpose of this law. The Bundesrat was reluctant to accept a system in which traditional principles of command and responsibility were reduced to informal agreements arrived at by open bargaining, especially when bargaining agents were likely to be totally external to the official administrative structure.

From the instances of the codetermination laws the Bundesrat can be seen as a conservative force only in a carefully defined sense. Contrary to much stereotypic thought about the bureaucratic conservative, members of the Bundesrat showed a high degree of flexibility with respect to some major policy changes and were definitely amenable to important alterations in the economic status quo favorable to organized labor. Even apart from the factor of party considerations, which must be adjudged of primary importance on these laws, the Bundesrat was often more friendly to the DGB in its specific demands than the Bundestag. This friendliness came from the civil service-staffed and service-dominated committees at least as much as from the plenum, where party divisions were more clear.

The very important possibility does exist that the difference in the codetermination episode between "bureaucratic conservatism" and "bureaucratic flexibility" is a function of propinquity. Changes made outside the professional ambit of these politician-administrators (i.e., in private industry) would not necessarily be understood by them as a strategic change. This being so they could accept radical revisions without regrets, depending on alignment of the political parties. On the other hand, with the introduction of changes that strike these same people as bringing about a major shift in the traditional legal-administrative order, they would no doubt react differently. That was true in the laws dealing with codetermination. To the extent that decisions of the Bundesrat are prompted by concern for administrative developments, then the "upper house" in the Federal Republic can fairly be described as conservative, and as representing conservative interests that do not find adequate expression in the Bundestag.

CHAPTER VIII

Conclusions

Any research effort dealing with a political institution and proceeding from the case-study technique carries with it certain inherent limitations. This study of the German Bundesrat is consciously limited in these respects and no doubt unconsciously limited in many more. Description of the habits, pressures, and institutional desiderata affecting Bundesrat action and then examination of that chamber's most distinctive characteristics have been based on a limited number of legislative histories. Complete substantiation or rejection of the major hypotheses would obviously require application of the same research design to a larger number of bills. In the absence of a broader research inventory conclusions about the Bundesrat's legislative role in western Germany must remain tentative.

Still the data presented in the above chapters permit some generalizations. First of all, the Bundesrat has been demonstrated to be a truly federal organ in that it does represent and protect the interests of the separate German Land governments. This overall purpose is often characteristic of federal Second Chambers, but this characteristic explains only a part of the attitudes and practices of the Bundesrat. Could it be true that the interests of the separate German Land governments are determined by national forces, such as party oligarchies, rather than by forces peculiar to several specific Land governments? The answer of course is yes, but only in cases where national party domination forestalls even a margin of latitude among political leaders at the Land level. The refugee legislation indicated, for example, that the Bundesrat can be used by Land governments to promote their own particular interests, national party attitudes notwithstanding. In the refugee case the dominant concern was the financial solvency of the Land governments and the standard of living of their respective citizens.

The evidence in Chapter V is enough to justify description of the Bundesrat as a vehicle for the Land governments to protect themselves in federal legislation, although admittedly the description must be superimposed on an inner layer of national power politics. There is little indication anywhere that the commitment of Bundesrat members to a federal consciousness gives priority to independence of action by the Land governments if that independence conflicts with national party controls. Rather the reverse is true. Independence of action among the Land governments via their representatives in the Bundesrat is safe only when no strong motivation exists for party conformity at all levels. The "dovetailing of purposes" between Bund and Land since 1950 means that the sphere of action within which Land leaders might exercise their political autonomy has been considerably curtailed.

The necessary result in the Bundesrat is a paradox of roles. By being an instrument to give the Land governments an appreciable influence in federal legislation, the Bundesrat has encouraged development of a high degree of national party conformity. The more important the Bundesrat became in legislation, the less could national party leaders afford to let the Land governments go their own diverse ways. Taken together with the natural

Land bias of members of the Bundesrat, the elements of party direction make that chamber something of a staging area for conflicting currents in German politics. If Hans Ehard's observation is valid, that freedom in Germany is contingent upon some successful variation of the federal theme,[1] then probably no less true is Theodor Eschenburg's opinion that permeation of the national party spirit through the Bundesrat gives the federal chamber a vitality and meaning it otherwise would not have.[2] Should a showdown occur between centralism and demands for a federal order, a rather remote possibility under present circumstances, organized Land resistance to oligarchical party controls from the center would probably disappear. Short of this one may expect the Bundesrat to continue to press the case in legislation for Land interests as these are understood by the Land governments themselves.

Probably no less of a paradox than this is the confusion of aims seeking appropriate Bundesrat action among the members of that house. In Chapter VI the factor of bureaucracy, with both latent and manifest functions, was found to be an important indicator of Bundesrat action. Discussions in first passage made it clear that the Bundesrat approaches bills to the Federal Government with a "manifest bureaucratic orientation." The Bundesrat in its representations to the Federal Government tended openly to accept the views of professional members of the Land bureaucracies who were attached to the committees, but who were not themselves regular members of the house. Regular members on the other hand, being Land politicians responsible for their acts to partisan legislative bodies, are necessarily prompted by motives of a different, non-bureaucratic sort. Reports of the meetings repeatedly

1. Hans Ehard, *Freiheit und Föderalismus* (München, 1948).
2. Theodor Eschenburg, *Staat und Gesellschaft in Deutschland*, (rev. ed.; Stuttgart, 1957), pp. 615ff.

illustrated that a Land's delegation to the Bundesrat are always sensitive to their own political necessities. Despite this fact even the debates in second passage, when the career civil servants have no inside track to legislative bills, demonstrated more or less crudely that Bundesrat discussions and decisions lean to the administrator's "point of view." By this "point of view" is meant simply an inclination to reduce the debates over serious policy issues to a sober discussion of and concern with the more settled and routinized phases of legislative and administrative problems. In this sense the Bundesrat reveals a latent bureaucracy factor growing, paradoxically, out of its obvious policy responsibilities.

That career bureaucrats and a bureaucratic attitude are dominant in the Bundesrat is not easily related to the goals of democracy in the Federal Republic, or even to the specific policy aims of the Adenauer regime in its first thirteen years. Relating ends to means must depend on exactly what one wishes to appraise. Arnold Brecht in speaking of the German civil service and their political attitudes came to the following estimate:[3]

If it is the percentage of those that entertain authoritarian patterns of thought, the estimate would have been higher for German officials than for the German people at large (where it could not be quite low either), and so would, consequently, the estimate of those whose basic inclinations prefer a form of government slightly to the right of democracy.... If it is desired, however, to know the percentage of those officials whose tendencies go so far as to make them wish to see abolished the rule of law *(Rechtsstaat)* and the bill of rights, the estimate would have to be very low; for the German civil service has a *Rechtsstaat* tradition reaching far back into the monarchic period.

3. Arnold Brecht, "Personnel Management," in Edward H. Litchfield (ed.), *Governing Postwar Germany* (Ithaca, N. Y., 1953), p. 271.

From an entirely different point of view here is a foundation for study in administrative behavior and values at the juncture of legislative policy-formulation. Apart from the implications of Brecht's statement and the above findings for democratic-authoritarian theory, the infusion of administrative values into the Bundesrat suggests its importance as a potential check on the operations of bureaucracy. This importance of course presumes that a pre-disposition is felt to do the checking. Being composed of political elements (the ministers) and purely administrative elements (the high administrative officials on the delegation staffs), the Bundesrat is in a unique position to bridge the gap which twentieth century critics believe exists between accredited policy-makers and those who actually make policy by administration. From this possibility several others come to the fore at once. The idea deserves notice that the Bundesrat, by the unquestionably high competence of its members and their business-like scrutiny of legislative complexities, has accepted a major responsibility for that part of parliamentary management that has been surrendered wholesale in this century to the on-the-spot control of executive agencies. No systematic effort has been made to measure the conscious involvement of Bundesrat members in this responsibility, but the idea persists to give that institution even greater potential importance.

At least one further idea arises from the factor of bureaucracy. That is the element of conservatism. The notion of the Bundesrat as a conservative force in German politics is certainly no paradox, falling into line with traditional western folklore about Second Chambers as only another example of the many barricades erected by conservative interests in defense of the existing order. The idea develops naturally from the tendency of Land governments to rely heavily in the Bundesrat on the recommendations of professional administrators. Add to this a rational concern for enforcement aspects of legislation that would cause regular Bundesrat members to be apprehensive about major policy shifts, especially those that might disrupt administrative smoothness and continuity. This would create an urge to avoid the uncertainties of broad policy decisions by interpreting new policy questions in terms of their adaptation to existing ones.

One cannot assume that identification of the federative legislative house as less "policy-oriented" than "bureaucracy-oriented" automatically leads that body into doctrinal conservatism. The idea is rather that the Bundesrat is encouraged to play a conservative role in legislative policy-formulation by virtue of its institutionalized expertise and skills and its preoccupation with meeting existing administrative standards. This in itself would be conservative. The fact that the conservative-bias idea is only partially supported by evidence in the codetermination laws leaves the matter inconclusive. In all likelihood the codetermination issue did not countenance the type of change that would excite the antagonism of a bureaucratic conservative. In the absence of the type of change that would, the Bundesrat is quite willing within the limits of party control to go along with major alterations in the economic class structure favorable to the industrial worker class.

Of the bills examined in this connection the one outstanding exception is important. When the practices of employee codetermination in industry were to be extended into public administration and public enterprises, the Bundesrat's reaction was distinctly unfavorable. Whereas with industrial codetermination the Bundesrat collectively had been more permissive than the Federal Government with the labor unions' demands, with codetermination in the public services it was much less so. A particularly odious innovation was the idea that administrative decisions made in hundreds of administrative agencies and departments should have to take account of the results of informal bargaining between employer and employees, probably even introducing nonofficial elements into the bargaining process. Furthermore, the Bundesrat insisted that the highest-ranking civil service officials *(Beamten)* should continue to enjoy a privileged status distinct from the other classes of civil servants. Even in codetermination these caste lines traditionally characteristic of German public administration had to be safeguarded in the interests of internal stability.

Arnold Brecht observed of German politics that the inherent danger to democracy is in bureaucratization. He further said:[4]

There is danger of sympathy, not with totalitarian principles, but tendencies toward bureaucratic authority and bureaucratic privilege. There is a common innate lack of understanding, not so much for the ideals of liberty as for the practices of equality and of the democratic processes.

It is quite possible to detect in the functioning of the Bundesrat a tension and a not quite perfect balance between Friedrich Meinecke's *homo sapiens* and *homo faber*. The awesome importance ascribed by Professor Meinecke to a harmonious relationship between the rational and the irrational forces of life gives added meaning to any instrument of political control where these forces meet.[5] Any suggestion, however, that a bureaucratized Bundesrat constitutes a serious menace to democratic processes in western Germany must consider that the fortunes of

4. *Ibid.*, p. 270.
5. Friedrich Meinecke, *The German Catastrophe* (Cambridge, 1950), pp. 34-39.

constitutional-federal government in the Federal Republic are inextricably bound up with the fortunes of the several Land governments. To the extent that the Bundesrat is functionally related to federalism in Germany and to the genuine representation of Land interests at the federal level, it finds easy defenses in the literature of classical democratic thought. A similar defense can be made for the Bundesrat as a partisan instrumentality in West German power politics, a factor that tends to stimulate Bundesrat members out of the area of consensus and into that of conflict.

These considerations justify a basis for cautious optimism about the role of the contemporary Bundesrat in West German democratic development, or at least in failing to obstruct that development. The same might even be said of the Bundesrat in its strictly technical or expert capacity. The urge of the Bundesrat to "improve" legislation by offering expert advice and constraints, a feature which has always been characteristic of the German "upper house," leads the Bundesrat into attitudes which, if not anti-democratic, are at least non-democratic. But traditional defenders of democratic values have also shown high regard for specialized institutions that bring order and certainty to political affairs, particularly when these institutions operate within a framework whose outer limits are fixed through democratic processes. If the actual and potential vitality of democratic values is strong in western Germany, there is little likelihood that the Bundesrat can become an effective block to ultimate expression of the popular will. If the strength of the Federal Republic's commitment to democracy is only marginal, then the Bundesrat can become co-arbiter of a system in which political values are simply imposed on an obedient population.

Bibliography

DOCUMENTS

WESTERN GERMANY

Bundesministerium für Angelegenheiten der Vertriebenen. *Some Facts about Expellees in Germany.* Bonn, 1952.

——. *Vertriebene, Flüchtlinge, Kriegsgefangene, Heimatslose Ausländer, 1949-1952.* Bonn, 1953.

——. *Care and Help for the Expellees, Refugees, War Victims, and Evacuees.* Mellrichstadt, 1956.

——. *Der Betreuung der Vertriebenen.* Mellrichstadt, 1959.

Bundesministerium für Innern. *Gemeinsames Ministerialgesetzblatt.* Bonn, 1951-1956.

——. *Handbuch für die Bundesrepublik Deutschland.* Köln, 1953.

Bundesministerium der Justiz. *Bundesgesetzblatt.* Parts I and II. Bonn, 1951-1957.

Bundesrat. Drucksache 1041/50: *Entwurf eines Gezetzes über Sofortnahmen zur Sicherung der Unterbringung der unter Artikel 131 des Grundgesetzes fallenden Personen.* December 22, 1950.

——. Drucksache 90/51: *Entwurf eines Gesetzes über die Mitbestimmung der Arbeitnehmer in Unternehmen des Bergbaus sowie der Eisen und Stahl erzeugenden Industrie.* January 30, 1951.

——. Drucksache 236/51: *Entwurf eines Gesetzes zur umsiedlung von Heimatvertriebenen aus den Ländern Bayern, Niedersachsen und Schleswig-Holstein.* March 9, 1951.

——. Drucksache 236/1/51: *Antrag des Landes Nordrhein-Westfalen zum entwurf eines Gesetzes zur Umsiedlung von*

Heimatvertriebenen aus den Ländern Bayern, Niedersachsen und Schleswig-Holstein. March 14, 1951.

——. Drucksache 236/2/51: *Erklärung und Antrag des Landes Württemberg-Baden zum Entwurf eines Gesetzes zur Umsiedlung von Heimatvertriebenen aus den Ländern Bayern, Niedersachsen und Schleswig-Holstein.* March 15, 1951.

——. Drucksache 330/51: *Entwurf eines Gesetzes über die Mitbestimmung der Arbeitnehmer in Unternehmen des Bergbaus sowie der Eisen und Stahl erzeugenden Industrie.* April 11, 1951.

——. Drucksache 340/51: *Entwurf eines Gesetzes zur Regelung der Rechtsverhältnisse der unter Artikel 131 des Grundgesetzes fallenden Personen.* April 13, 1951.

——. Drucksache 562/51: *Entwurf eines Bundesbeamtengesetzes.* September 6, 1951.

——. Drucksache 630/51: *Entwurf eines Gesetzes über die Angelegenheiten der Vertriebenen und Flüchtlinge (Bundesvertriebenengesetz).* October 12, 1951.

——. Drucksache 123/52: *Entwurf eines Gesetzes zur Änderung und Ergänzung des Gesetzes zur Umsiedlung von Heimatvertriebenen aus den Ländern Bayern, Niedersachsen und Schleswig-Holstein.* March 28, 1952.

——. Drucksache 311/52: *Entwurf eines Betriebsverfassungsgesetz.* July 19, 1952.

——. Drucksache 361/52: *Entwurf einer Verordnung zur Durchführung der Umsiedlung von Heimatvertriebenen aus den Ländern Bayern, Niedersachsen und Schleswig-Holstein.* September 10, 1952.

——. Drucksache 382/52: *Entwurf eines Gesetzes über die Förderung des Wohnungsbaus für Umsiedler in den Aufnahmeländer und des Wohnungsbaus für Sowjetzonenflüchtlinge in Berlin.* September 20, 1952.

——. Drucksache 241/53: *Entwurf eines Bundesbeamtengesetzes.* June 10, 1953.

——. Drucksache 24/54: *Entwurf ersten Durchführungsverordnung zu Abs. 4 des Gesetzes über die Entschädigung ehemaliger deutscher Kriegsgefangener vom 30. Januar 1954.* February 2, 1954.

——. Drucksache 25/54: *Entwurf eines Gesetzes über die Personalvertretungen in den öffentlichen Verwaltungen und Betrieben (Personalvertretungsgesetz).* February 20, 1954.

——. Drucksache 25/2/54: *Antrag des Landes Schleswig-Holstein zum Entwurf eines Gesetzes über die Personalvertretungen in den öffentlichen Verwaltung und Betrieben (Personalvertretungsgesetz).* February 17, 1954.

——. Drucksache 321/54: *Entwurf eines Gesetzes zur Ergänzung des Gesetzes über die Mitbestimmung der Arbeitnehmer in den Aufsichtsräten und Vorständen der Unternehmen des Bergbaus und der Eisen und der Stahl erzeugenden Industrie.* October 29, 1954.

——. Drucksache 85/55: *Entwurf eines Gesetzes über die Personalvertretungen in den öffentlichen Verwaltungen und Betrieben (Personalvertretungsgesetz).* June 10, 1955.

——. Drucksache 85/1/55: *Der federführende Ausschuss für Innere Angelegenheiten (In) und der Rechtsausschuss (R) betr.: Entwurf eines Gesetzes über die Personalvertretungen in den öffentlichen Verwaltungen und Betrieben (Personalvertretungsgesetz).* June 18, 1955.

——. Drucksache 85/2/55: *Antrag des Landes Rheinland-Pfalz zum Entwurf eines Gesetzes über die Personalvertretunge in den öffentlichen Verwaltung und Betrieben (Personalvertretungsgesetz).* June 22, 1955.

——. Drucksache 85/3/55: *Antrag des Landes Bayern zum Entwurf eines Gesetzes über die Personalvertretungen in den öffentlichen Verwaltung und Betrieben (Personalvertretungsgesetz).* June 22, 1955.

——. Drucksache 85/4/55: *Antrag des Landes Schleswig-Holstein zum Entwurf eines Gesetzes über die Personalvertretungen in den öffentlichen Verwaltung und Betrieben (Personalvertretungsgesetz).* June 22, 1955.

——. Drucksache 172/55: *Entwurf eines Gesetzes über die vorläufige Rechtsstellung der Freiwilligen in den Streitkräften (Freiwilligengesetz).* May 28, 1955.

——. Drucksache 177/55: *Entwurf eines Gesetzes über den Einfluss von Eignungsübungen der Streitkräfte auf Vertragsverhältnisse der Arbeitnehmer und Handelsvertreter sowie auf Beamtenverhältnisse (Eignungsübungsgesetz).* June 3, 1955.

——. Drucksache 177/1/55: *Der federführende Ausschuss für Fragen der europäischen Sicherheit betr.: Entwurf eines*

Gesetzes über den Einfluss von Eignungsübungen der Streitkräfte auf Vertragsverhältnisse der Arbeitnehmer und Handelsvertreter sowie auf Beamtenverhältnisse (Eignungsübungsgesetz). June 23, 1955.

————. Drucksache 211/55: *Entwurf eines Gesetzes über die Rechtsstellung der Soldaten (Soldatengesetz).* July 1, 1955.

————. Drucksache 267/55: *Entwurf eines Gesetzes über den Personalgutachterausschuss für die Streitkräfte (Personalgutachterausschussgesetz).* July 15, 1955.

————. Drucksache 222/56: *Entwurf eines Gesetzes zur Ergänzung des Gesetzes über die Mitbestimmung der Arbeitnehmer in den Aufsichtsräten und Vorständen der Unternehmen des Bergbaus und der Eisen und Stahl erzeugenden Industrie.* June 15, 1956.

————. *Handbuch des Bundesrates.* Darmstadt: Neue Darmstädter Verlagsanstalt, 1958.

————. *Sitzungsberichte (Verhandlungen des Bundesrates, Stenographische Berichte).* Bonn, 1950-1959.

————. *Statistik: aus der Arbeit des Bundesrates.* Bonn, 1958.

————. *10 Jahre Bundesrat.* Bonn, 1959.

Bundestag. Drucksache 1858 (1. Wahlperiode): *Entwurf eines Gesetzes über die Mitbestimmung der Arbeitnehmer in Unternehmen des Bergbaus sowie der Eisen und Stahl erzeugenden Industrie.* January 30, 1951.

————. Drucksache 2846 (1. Wahlperiode): *Entwurf eines Bundesbeamtengesetz.* November 19, 1951.

————. Drucksache 2872 (1. Wahlperiode): *Entwurf eines Gesetzes über die Angelegenheiten der Vertriebenen und Flüchtlinge (Bundesvertriebenengestz).* November 26, 1951.

————. Drucksache 3272 (1. Wahlperiode): *Entwurf eines Gesetzes zur Änderung und Ergänzung des Gesetzes zur Umsiedlung von Heimatvertriebenen aus den Ländern Bayern, Niedersachsen und Schleswig-Holstein.* April 2, 1952.

————. Drucksache 160 (2. Wahlperiode): *Entwurf eines Gesetzes über die Personalvertretungen in den öffentlichen Verwaltungen und Betrieben (Personalvertretungsgesetz).* March 4, 1954.

————. Drucksache 842 (2. Wahlperiode): *Entwurf eines Gesetzes über die Personalvertretungen in den öffentlichen*

Verwaltungen und Betrieben (Personalvertretungsgesetz). September 24, 1954.

———. Drucksache 842 (2. Wahlperiode): *Entwurf eines Gesetzes zur Änderung des Gesetzes über die Mitbestimmung der Arbeitnehmer in den Aufsichtsräten und Vorständen der Unternehmen des Bergbaus und der Eisen und Stahl erzeugenden Industrie.* n.d.

———. Drucksache 986 (2. Wahlperiode): *Entwurf eines Gesetze zur Ergänzung des Gesetzes über die Mitbestimmung der Arbeitnehmer in den Aufsichtsräten und Vorständen der Unternehmen des Bergbaus und der Eisen und Stahl erzeugenden Industrie.* November 15, 1954.

———. Drucksache 2387 (2. Wahlperiode): *Schriftlicher Bericht des Ausschuss für Arbeit (27. Ausschuss) über den Entwurf eines Gesetzes zur Ergänzung des Gesetzes über die Mitbestimmung der Arbeitnehmer in den Aufsichtsräten und Vorständen der Unternehmen des Bergbaus und der Eisen und Stahl erzeugenden Industrie.* n.d.

———. *Verhandlungen (Stenographische Berichte).* Bonn, 1950-1958.

Büro der Ministerpräsidenten des amerikanischen, britischen und französischen Besatzungsgebietes. Dokumente betreffend die Begründung einer neuen staatlichen Ordnung in der amerikanischen, britischen und französischen Besatzungsgebietes. Wiesbaden, 1948.

Parlamentarischer Rat. Stenographischer Bericht: Verhandlungen des Plenums. Bonn: Bonner Universitäts-Buchdruckerei, 1949.

Presse-und Informationsamt der Bundesregierung. Bulletin (biweekly), 1951-1958.

———. *Mitteilungen an die Presse* (daily). Bonn, 1954-1958.

———. *Sechs Jahre danach: vom Chaos zum Staat.* Wiesbaden, 1951.

United States

Bureau of Labor Statistics. "Codetermination for Government Workers in West Germany," *Monthly Labor Review,* LXXVIII (December, 1955), 1470-71.

———. "Codetermination in Western Germany," *Monthly Labor Review,* LXXIII (December, 1951), 649-56.

Department of State. *Germany 1947-1949, the Story in Documents* (Publication 3556, European and British Commonwealth Series 9). Washington: Government Printing Office, 1950.

Office of the High Commissioner for Germany. *Allied High Commission Relations with the West German Government, 1949-1951* (by Elmer Plischke). Bad Godesberg-Mehlem, 1952.

———. *State and Local Government in West Germany* (Historical Division Monograph by J. F. J. Gillen). Bad Godesberg-Mehlem, 1953.

———. *The West German Federal Government* (Historical Division Monograph by Elmer Plischke). Bad Godesberg-Mehlem, 1952.

———. *Works Councils in Germany* (Labor Affairs Office Monograph by Paul Fisher). Bad Godesberg-Mehlem, 1951.

BOOKS

Allemann, Fritz René. *Bonn Ist nicht Weimar*. Köln: Kiepenheuer and Witsch, 1956.

Almond, Gabriel. *The Struggle for Democracy in Germany*. Chapel Hill: The University of North Carolina Press, 1949.

Anschütz, Gerhard. *Die Verfassung des deutschen Reichs*. 12th ed. Berlin: Georg Stilke, 1930.

Bagehot, Walter. *The English Constitution*. Rev. ed. New York: Appleton, 1890.

Bailey, Sydney D. (ed.). *The House of Lords: A Symposium*. New York: Praeger, 1954.

Bergsträsser, Ludwig. *Geschichte der politischen Parteien in Deutschland*. München: Isar Verlag, 1955.

Blachly, Frederick and Oatman, Miriam. *The Government and Administration of Germany*. Baltimore: The Johns Hopkins Press, 1928.

Blau, Peter. *Bureaucracy in Modern Society*. New York: Random House, 1956.

Blumenthal, Werner. *Codetermination in the German Steel Industry*. Princeton: Princeton University Department of Economics and Sociology, 1956.

von Borch, Herbert. *Obrigkeit und Widerstand: Zur politischer*

Soziologie des Beamtentums. Tübingen: J. C. B. Mohr, 1954.

Bouman, Pieter J. et al. *The Refugee Problem in Western Germany.* The Hague: Martinus Nijhoff, 1950.

Bowie, Robert R. and Friedrich, Carl J. *Studies in Federalism.* Boston: Little, Brown, 1954.

Bracher, Karl Dietrich. *Die Auflösung der Weimarer Republik: Eine Studie zum Problem des Machtverfalls in der Demokratie.* Stuttgart: Ring Verlag, 1955.

Brecht, Arnold. *Federalism and Regionalism in Germany: The Division of Prussia.* New York: Oxford University Press, 1945.

Breitling, Rupert. *Die Verbände in der Bundesrepublik: Ihre Arten und ihre politische Wirkungsweise (Parteien, Fraktionen, Regierungen, Bd. 6).* Meisenheim a/G: Anton Hain, 1955.

Briefs, Goetz. *Zwischen Kapitalismus und Syndicalismus—Die Gewerckschaften am Scheideweg.* München: Leo Lehnen Verlag, 1952.

Cantril, Hadley. *The Psychology of Social Movements.* New York: John Wiley, 1941.

Clay, Lucius D. *Decision in Germany.* Garden City, N. Y.: Doubleday, 1950.

Craig, Gordon A. *NATO and the New German Army* (Memorandum Number Eight). Princeton University Center of International Studies, October 24, 1955.

Dennewitz, Bobo et al. *Kommentar zum Bonner Grundgesetz.* Hamburg: Hansischer Gildenverlag, Joachim Heitman, 1950.

Dechamps, Bruno. *Macht und Arbeit der Ausschüsse: Der Wandel der Parlamentarischen Willensbildung.* Meisenheim a/M: Glan: Westkultur Verlag, Anton Hain, 1954.

Ehard, Hans. *Freiheit und Föderalismus.* München: Richard Pflaum, 1948.

Eschenburg, Theodor. *Der Beamte in Partei und Parlament.* Frankfurt a/M: Metzner, 1952.

——. *Die Herrschaft der Verbände?* Stuttgart: Deutsche Verlags-Anstalt, 1955.

——. *Staat und Gesellschaft in Deutschland.* 2nd. ed. Stuttgart: Schwab, 1957.

Finer, Herman. *Theory and Practice of Modern Government.* Rev. ed. New York: Henry Holt, 1949.

Friedman, Wolfgang. *The Allied Military Government of Germany.* London: Stephens, 1947.

Fromm, Erich. *Man For Himself: an Inquiry into the Psychology of Ethics.* New York: Rinehart, 1947.

Gerth, Hans and Mills, C. Wright. *From Max Weber: Essays in Sociology.* New York: Oxford University Press, 1958.

Golay, John Ford. *The Founding of the Federal Republic of Germany.* Chicago: University of Chicago Press, 1958.

Grosser, Alfred. *Die Bonner Demokratie.* Düsseldorf: K. Rauch, 1960.

―――. *The Colossus Again:Western Germany From Defeat to Rearmament.* London: Allen and Unwin, 1955.

Gurland, A. R. L. *Political Science in Western Germany: Thoughts and Writings, 1950-1952.* Washington: Library of Congress, 1952.

Habel, Walter. *Wer Ist Wer.* Berlin: arani-Verlags, 1955.

Hallowell, John. *The Decline of Liberalism as an Ideology: With Particular Reference to German Politico-Legal Thought.* Berkeley: University of California Press, 1943.

von der Heydte, F. A. and Sacherl, Karl. *Soziologie der deutschen Parteien.* München: Isar, 1955.

Hiscocks, Richard. *Democracy in Western Germany.* London: Oxford University Press, 1957.

Horne, Alistair. *Return to Power.* New York: Praeger, 1956.

Kaiser, Joseph H. *Die Repräsentation organisierten Interessen.* Berlin: Duncker & Humblot, 1956.

King-Hall, Stephen and Ullman, Richard. *German Parliaments: a Study of the Development of Representative Institutions in Germany.* London: Hansard Society, 1954.

Kliemann, Horst and Taylor, Stephen S. (ed.) *Who's Who in Germany.* München: Intercontinental Book and Publishing Co., 1960.

Knight, Maxwell. *The German Executive, 1890-1933* (Hoover Institute Studies, Series B, Elites, Number 4). Palo Alto: Stanford University Press, 1952.

Koehler, A. and Jansen, K. *Die Bundesrepublik 1957/1958 (Vereinigt mit Handbuch für die Bundesrepublik Deutschland).* Berlin: Carl Heymanns Verlag, 1959.

Kraus, Herbert. *Die Auswärtige Stellung der Bundesrepublik nach dem Bonner Grundgesetz.* Göttingen: "Muster-schmidt" Wissenschaftlicher Verlag, 1950.

———. *The Crisis of German Democracy: A Study of the Spirit of the Constitution of Weimar.* Princeton University Press, 1932.

Lees-Smith, H. B. *Second Chambers in Theory and Practice.* London: George Allen, 1923.

Lidderdale, D. W. S. *The Parliament of France.* London: The Hansard Society, 1951.

Lipset, Seymour M. *Political Man: The Social Bases of Politics.* Garden City, N. Y.: Doubleday, 1960.

Litchfield, Edward H. et al. *Governing Postwar Germany.* Ithaca: Cornell University Press, 1953.

Loewenstein, Karl. *Political Power and the Governmental Process.* Chicago: University of Chicago Press, 1957.

Mannheim, Karl. *Ideology and Utopia: An Introduction to the Sociology of Knowledge.* New York: Harcourt, Brace, 1936.

Markmann, Heinz. *Das Abstimmungsverhalten der Parteien-fraktionen in Deutschen Parlamenten (Parteien, Fraktionen, Regierungen, Bd. 5).* Meisenheim am Glan: Anton Hain, 1955.

Marriott, John A. R. *Second Chambers: An Inductive Study in Political Science.* Oxford: The Clarendon Press, 1927.

Matthews, Donard R. *United States Senators and Their World.* Chapel Hill: The University of North Carolina Press, 1960.

Mayer, J. P. *Max Weber and German Politics: A Study in Political Sociology.* London: Faber and Faber, 1943.

Meinecke, Friedrich. *The German Catastrophe.* Cambridge: Harvard University Press, 1950.

Merton, Robert K. *Social Theory and Social Structure.* rev. ed. Glencoe, Ill.: The Free Press, 1957.

———. *Reader in Bureaucracy.* Glencoe, Ill.: The Free Press, 1952.

Morgenthau, Hans J. (ed.). *Germany and the Future of Europe.* Chicago: University of Chicago Press, 1951.

Münchheimer, W. et al. *Die Bundesländer: Beiträge zur Neuglieder der Bundesrepublik.* Frankfurt a/M: Institüt zur Förderung öffentlicher Angelegenheiten, 1950.

Nawiasky, Hans. *Die Grundgedanken des Grundgesetzes für*

die Bundesrepublik Deutschland. Stuttgart: Kohlhammer, 1950.

Neumann, Franz. *Behemoth: The Structure and Practice of National Socialism*. London: Oxford University Press, 1942.

Neunreither, Karlheinz. *Der Bundesrat zwischen Politik und Verwaltung*. Heidelberg: Quelle & Meyer, 1959.

Noelle, Elisabeth and Neumann, Erich Peter. *Jahrbuch der Öffentlichen Meinung, 1957*. Allensbach a. Bodensee: Verlag für Demoskopie, 1957.

Nyman, Olle. *Der Westdeutsche Föderalismus: Studien zum Bonner Grundgesetz*. Stockholm: Almquist & Wiksell, 1960.

Oppenheimer, Heinrich. *The Constitution of the German Republic*. London: Stephens, 1923.

Parteien in der Bundesrepublik, Studien zur Entwicklung der deutschen Parteien bis zur Bundestagswahl 1953 (Schriften des Institüts für Politische Wissenschaft, Bd. 6). Stuttgart: Ring Verlag, 1955.

Pollock, James K. *German Democracy at Work: A Selective Study*. Ann Arbor: University of Michigan Press, 1955.

———. et al. *Germany Under Occupation: Illustrative Materials and Documents*. Ann Arbor: George Wahr, 1947.

Pritzkoleit, Kurt. *Die Neuen Herren: Die Mächtigen in Staat und Wirtschaft*. München: K. Desch, 1955.

Rosenberg, Hans. *Bureaucracy, Aristocracy and Autocracy*. Cambridge: Harvard University Press, 1958.

Roth, Goetz. *Fraktion und Regierungsbildung. Eine monographische Darstellung der Regierungsbildung in Niedersachsen im Jahre 1951*. Meisenheim am Glan: Westkultur-Verlag, Anton Hain, 1954.

Sänger, Fritz (ed.). *Die Volksvertretung: Handbuch des deutschen Bundestages*. Stuttgart: E. Klett, 1957.

Schäfer, Hans. *Der Bundesrat*. Köln: Heymann, 1955.

Schoppmeier, Karl Heinz. *Der Einfluss Preussens auf die Gesetzesgebung des Reiches*. Berlin: G. Stilke, 1929.

Schorske, Carle E. *German Social Democracy, 1905-1917: The Development of the Great Schism*. Cambridge: Harvard University Press, 1955.

Schramm, Friedrich Karl. *Das Bundeshaus: Aus der Arbeit des Bundestages und des Bundesrates*. Bonn: E. Beinheimer, 1958.

Sell, Friedrich C. *Die Tragödie des deutschen Liberalismus.* Stuttgart: Deutsche Verlags-Anstalt, 1953.

Selznick, Philip. *TVA and the Grass Roots.* Berkeley: University of California Press, 1949.

Simon, Herbert. *Administrative Behavior.* New York: Macmillan, 1951.

Speier, Hans (ed.). *German Rearmament and Atomic War: the Views of German Military and Political Leaders.* Evanston, Ill.: Row, Peterson, 1957.

———. *West German Leadership and Foreign Policy.* Evanston, Ill.: Row, Peterson, 1957.

Spiethoff, Bodo K. *Untersuchungen zum bayerischen Flüchtlingsproblem.* Berlin: Duncker & Humblot, 1955.

———. *Weimarer Verfassung und Bonner Grundgesetz.* Göt-
Spiro, Herbert J. *The Politics of German Codetermination.* Cambridge: Harvard University Press, 1958.

Sternberger, Dolf. *Lebende Verfassung: Studien über Koalition und Opposition (Parteien, Fraktionen, Regierungen, Bd. 1).* Meisenheim a/G Westkultur Verlag, Anton Hain, 1956.

Tönnies, Norbert. *Der Weg zu den Waffen: Die Geschichte der deutschen Wiederbewaffnung, 1949-1957.* Köln: Markus Verlag, 1957.

Trossman, Hans. *Der Zweite Bundestag, seine Vorgeschichte, sein Aufbau und sein Wirken.* Bonn: Bonner Universitäts-Buchdruckerei, 1954.

Wallenberg, Hans. *Report on Democratic Institutions in Germany.* New York: American Council on Germany, Inc., 1956.

Weber, Max. *The Theory of Social and Economic Organization* (transl. by Talcott Parsons). New York: Oxford University Press, 1947.

Weber, Werner. *Spannungen und Kräfte in westdeutschen Verfassungssystem.* Stuttgart: Vorwerck, 1958.

3/M *Weimarer Verfassung und Bonner Grundgesetz.* Göttingen: Verlag Karl-Friedrich Fleisher, 1959.

Wheare, K. C. *Federal Government.* New York: Oxford University Press, 1953.

Wildenmann, Rudolph. *Partei und Fraktion: Ein Beitrag zur Analyse der politischen Willensbildung und der Parteiensystems in der Bundesrepublik (Parteien, Fraktionen,*

Regierungen, Bd. 8). Meisenheim a/G: Westkultur Verlag, Anton Hain, 1954.

Zink, Harold. *The United States in Germany, 1944-1955.* Princeton: Van Nostrand, 1957.

ARTICLES

Almond, Gabriel. "The Political Attitudes of German Business," *World Politics,* VIII (January, 1956), 157-86.

Bukow, Willy. "Das Personalvertretungsgesetz, mit Beilage: Vergleichende Übersicht," *Das Mitbestimmungsgespräch,* I (July/August, 1955).

Bunn, Ronald. "Codetermination and the Federation of German Employers' Association," *Midwest Journal of Political Science,* II (August, 1958), 278-98.

Campion, Lord. "Second Chambers in Theory and Practice," in Sydney Bailey (ed.). *The House of Lords.* New York: Praeger, 1954, pp. 17-33.

Cole, Taylor. "The Democratization of the German Civil Service," *Journal of Politics,* XIV (February, 1952), 3-18.

Dahl, Robert A. "The Science of Public Administration: Three Problems," *Public Administration Review,* VII (Winter, 1947), 1-11.

Dehm, Walter. "Vermittlungsausschuss als Schlichter," *Das Parlament* (January 22, 1958), pp. 8-9.

———. "Stellung, Aufgaben und Bedeutung des Vermittlungsausschusses," *Neue Deutsche Beamtenzeitung,* I (January, 1960), 1-3.

Deneke, J. F. V. "Das Parlament als Kollecktiv," *Zeitschrift für gesamte Staatswissenschaft,* CIX (March, 1953), 503-31.

Ehard, Hans. "Aufgabe und Bewährung des deutschen Bundesrats," *Presseveröffentlichungen über den Bundesrat,* No. 126 (March 20, 1961), 29-37.

Fisher, Paul. "Labor Codetermination in Germany," *Social Research,* XVIII (November, 1951), 449-86.

Gouldner, Alvin W. "Metaphysical Pathos and the Theory of Bureaucracy," *American Political Science Review,* XXXXIX (June, 1955), 496-507.

von der Heide, Wolf. "Der Vermittlungsausschuss, Praxis und

Bewährung," *Die öffentlichen Verwaltung* (1953), pp. 129-36.

Heidenheimer, Arnold J. "Federalism and the Party System— the Case of West Germany," *American Political Science Review*, LII (September, 1958), 809-30.

——. "German Party Finance: the CDU," *American Political Science Review*, LI (June, 1957), 369-86.

Held, Kurt. "Der Autonome Verfassungsteil der Länder und das Bundesratsveto nach Art. 84 Abs. 1 GG," *Archiv des öffentlichen Rechts*, LXXIX (1953), 50-58.

Herz, John. "German Officialdom Revisited—Political Views and Attitudes of the West German Civil Service," *World Politics*, VII (October, 1954), 63-84.

Hirsch-Weber, Wolfgang. "Some Remarks on Interest Groups in the German Federal Republic," in Henry W. Ehrmann (ed.). *Interest Groups on Four Continents*. Pittsburgh: University of Pittsburgh Press, 1958, pp. 96-116.

Kerr, Clark. "The Trade Union Movement and the Redistribution of Power in Postwar Germany," *Quarterly Journal of Economics*, LXVIII (November, 1954), 535-64.

Koettgen, Arnold. "Der Einfluss des Bundes auf die deutschen Verwaltung," *Archiv des öffentlichen Rechts*, LXXX (1954), 68-82.

Kirchheimer, Otto. "The Composition of the German Bundestag, 1950," *Western Political Quarterly*, III (December, 1950), 590-601.

——. "The Political Scene in West Germany," *World Politics*, IX (April, 1957), 433-46.

Kratzer, Jakob. "Zustimmungsgesetze," *Archiv des öffentlichen Rechts*, LXXX (1954), 266-82.

Kutscher, Hans. "Verfassungsrechtliche Fragen aus der Arbeit des Bundesrates," *Die öffentlichen Verwaltung* (1952), pp. 717-19.

Lewis, Chester B. and King, Robert D. "The Southwest State," *Information Bulletin* (United States High Commissioner for Germany), February, 1952, pp. 3-7.

Loewenstein, Karl. "The Bonn Constitution and the European Defense Community Treaties, a Study in Judicial Frustration," *Yale Law Journal*, LXIV (May, 1955), 805-39.

Mason, John Brown. "Federalism—the Bonn Model," in Arnold J. Zurcher (ed.). *Constitutions and Constitutional Trends*

Since World War II. New York: New York University Press, 1955, pp. 134-54.

Marx, Fritz M. "The Bureaucratic State," *Review of Politics,* I (October, 1939), 457-72.

Mayntz, Renate. "Oligarchic Problems in a German Party District," in Dwaine Marvick (ed.). *Political Decision-Makers.* Glencoe, Ill.: The Free Press, 1961, pp. 138-193.

McClosky, Herbert. "Conservatism and Personality," *American Political Science Review,* LII (March, 1958), 27-45.

Merkl, Peter. "Executive-Legislative Federalism in West Germany," *American Political Science Review,* LIII (September, 1959), 732-44.

Meyer, Hans. "Zur Struktur der deutschen Sozialdemokratie," *Zeitschrift für Politik,* II (April, 1955), 348-60.

Moseley, Philip E. "The Occupation of Germany: New Light on How the Zones Were Drawn," *Foreign Affairs,* XXVIII (July, 1950), 580-605.

Parsons, Talcott. "Democracy and Social Structure in Pre-Nazi Germany," *Journal of Legal and Political Philosophy,* I (1942), 96-114.

Partsch, K. J. and Genzer, W. "Inkompatibilität der Mitgliedschaft in Bundestag und Bundesrat," *Archiv des öffentlichen Rechts,* LXXVI (1950), 186-204.

Pross, Harry. "West Germany: Unfinished Business," *Orbis,* II (Fall, 1958), 356-71.

Rohwer-Kahlman, Harry. "Verfassungsrechtsliche Schranken der Zustimmungsgesetze (Art. 84 Abs. 1 GG)," *Archiv des öffentlichen Rechts,* LXXIX (1953), 208-19.

Schneider, Hans. "Die Zustimmung des Bundesrates zu Gesetzen," *Deutsche Verwaltung* (October, 1953), 257-65.

Simon, Hans. "The Bonn Constitution and Its Government," in Hans Morgenthau (ed.). *Germany and the Future of Europe.* Chicago: University of Chicago Press, 1951, pp. 114-31.

Simon, Herbert. "Recent Advances in Organization Theory," in *Research Frontiers in Politics and Government* (Brookings Lectures, 1955). Washington: The Brookings Institution, 1955, pp. 23-45.

Wessel, Franz. "Der Vermittlungsausschuss nach Art. 77 des Grundgesetzes," *Archiv des öffentlichen Rechts,* LXXVII (1951), 283-92.

Wunderlich, Frieda. "Codetermination in German Industry," *Social Research,* XX (April, 1953), 75-91.

NEWSPAPERS

Frankfurter Allgemeine Zeitung (FAZ), 1952-1959.
Neue Zürcher Zeitung, 1953-1957.
The New York Times, 1949-1960.
The Times (London), 1949-1954.
Die Welt (Hamburg), 1954-1955.

UNPUBLISHED MATERIAL

Braunthal, Gerhard. "Federalism and the Party System in Germany: the Broadcasting Controversy." Paper presented at the American Political Science Association convention, St. Louis, September 6-9, 1961.

Dowell, Jack D. "The Legislative Process in the West German Bundestag: The Codetermination Law of May, 1951." Ph.D. thesis, Stanford University, 1958.

Jacob, Herbert. "The Quest for Responsiveness: German Field Administration, 1871-1959." Ph.D. thesis, Yale University, 1960.

Index

Index